Baegu: Social and Ecological Organization
in Malaita, Solomon Islands

UNIVERSITY OF ILLINOIS PRESS, URBANA, CHICAGO, LONDON

BAEGU

Social and Ecological Organization in Malaita, Solomon Islands

Harold M. Ross

ILLINOIS STUDIES IN ANTHROPOLOGY NO. 8

To the Malaitan people, and most especially to Micah Sedea Taloga of Walelangi, who worked the hardest to teach me something about the Baegu

Acknowledgments

Although an ethnographer works in isolated areas, and although he may at times feel agonizingly alone, there is always a supporting cast. To them in a very real sense belongs a large share of the credit for his work. My parents, Marion and Gerda Ross, through their love and understanding, and the U.S. Navy through its Halloway Scholarship Program, sent me to Harvard College, where I first began to study anthropology. The National Science Foundation subsidized my graduate education at Harvard University with a graduate fellowship, while the National Institute of Mental Health, U.S. Public Health Service, supported my research through fellowship MH-30,017 and research grant MH-12,647.

My advisor, Professor Douglas Oliver of Harvard and the University of Hawaii, led me through the difficult graduate student and dissertation years with tact and understanding. His advice and encouragement were invaluable. Some credit must go to the entire faculty of the Harvard Department of Anthropology during the periods 1954-58 and 1962-68, particularly to the late Clyde Kluckhohn, who was my undergraduate advisor.

Many Solomon Islanders, both Melanesians and expatriates, contributed. Richard Turpin, the District Commissioner of Malaita, his wife Peggy, and his administrative staff consistently treated me with the greatest hospitality and cooperation. Ian Morgan, the assistant superintendent of police for Malaita District, and Dr. Gordon Avery, the Malaita District medical officer, were particularly helpful. I especially thank Elizabeth Hunter of Honiara, Guadalcanal, and William and Janice Quan of Auki, Malaita, who acted as my agents for logistic support. Fathers Jan van der Riet, Joseph Kluwen, and Louis Morosini of the Roman Catholic missions at Takwa and Ususue were always kind. Belo of Kofiloko and Father George Kiriau (Anglican priest of Fouia) were Lau Lagoon people who handled my supplies and mail while I was in the hills. My Baegu friends, helpers, and informants are some 1,800 strong. I cannot mention them all by name, but I do want to cite a few of the many who were so helpful and understanding: Sedea, Lebefiu, Dongofoa, Meke, Bauro, Erefiu, and Wane'au of Walelangi; Wanesukea and Buaga of Faukwakwaoa; Sulaofia, Beni, and Labuga of Anoketo; Maefasia of Uradaue; Au'agara of Langane; Beliga of Agia; Ramoegau of Kafokuru; and Rimanu of Oisamaku.

During a brief visit to New Zealand in April, 1967, Dr. Anthony Hooper and Dr. Ralph Bulmer of the University of Auckland did much to clarify some of my problems and to improve my morale.

My wife Kathryn Penstone Ross deserves credit both for helping me get through this inevitably trying period and for collecting a large part of the data. Despite the fact that they constantly embarrassed me because they spoke the language more fluently than I and grasped cultural subtleties more quickly, my small children Edward and Anne Ross also helped in establishing rapport and making life more satisfying.

Kathryn Ross and Laird Starrick did the illustrations, while William Ward and James Baltaxe handled photographic chores. Jody Douglas and Neva Long (assisted by her office secretarial staff) typed one or another of the several manuscript drafts, and Lynn Kauffman did the proofreading. All are with the Department of Anthropology at the University of Illinois, Urbana. Ann Lowry Weir of the University of Illinois Press handled the editorial chores with skill and tact. Mary Kelly Black of Champaign, Illinois, prepared the index.

Finally I thank the Department of Anthropology at Illinois, particularly Professors Edward Bruner and David Plath, for bearing with me while I wrote my doctoral dissertation and transformed it into this monograph.

Foreword

Since I uttered the invocation for the research on which this monograph is based, I suppose it is only fitting that the benediction come from me as well. Moreover, being invited to write a foreword for a former student's first publication also serves as a considerate and gratifying act of filial piety. Less gratifying, however, is the message that this particular juxtaposition of foreword and text reveals: namely, just see how very far the student has progressed past his mentor! For, although I have in the past emphasized that spacing is an important dimension of social relationships, the treatment that Dr. Ross has accorded this dimension goes far beyond what I then had in mind — in salience, in scope, and in scientific rigor.

To begin with, this monograph offers a wealth of data on the life of the hitherto unstudied Baegu-speaking people of inland Malaita Island. As such it is a very welcome addition to the ethnographic literature of the Solomon Islands in general and of Malaita Island in particular. When added to the existing and increasing literature on Malaitan societies, it will help provide an unsurpassable opportunity for generalizing about human behavior by means of the research strategy of controlled comparison.

Dr. Ross's monograph is also important in a wider ethnographic context, in the light it throws on three key issues of Oceanic social organization: on the composition of basic residential groupings (in Baegu the hamlet is more "basic" than the nuclear family household); on the functions and recruitment of leaders (for all its small scale and egalitarianism, Baegu society contains exemplars of most all of the well-known Oceanic types); and on the interplay between an agnatic ideology and a cognatic actuality in the domain of Baegu kinship.

Principally, however, this monograph provides a comprehensive description of where the Baegu reside, garden, interact, etc., with respect to one another (including the deceased but still animate members of their society) and with respect to the physical landscape. And, perhaps its most notable contribution, it attempts (successfully, in my opinion) to isolate the cultural factors which result in that social and ecological spacing.

The author does all these things in a felicitous, unpretentious manner. While documenting his generalizations and arguments copiously, he has also lightened them with humor and with enough disclaimers of omniscience to render his account all the more vivid and credible to ethnographers who have worked in similar settings.

Douglas Oliver

Contents

1. Introduction

This monograph in cultural anthropology is less than a complete ethnography, yet more than a treatise on a single aspect of someone's cultural life. A complete or perfect ethnography has never been written and probably never will be. The extent of ethnographic reportage is limited, because no one can experience a full life in another culture and reproduce it fully while still at acceptable length to communicate it to other minds. A perfect ethnography (one that identifies so accurately the categories and plans of its creators and bearers that a reader could predict or generate appropriate behavior in novel situations) is probably also impossible, since I suspect that a person who learned another culture that thoroughly would no longer have the detachment and objectivity needed to isolate its crucial *eidos* and *ethos* elements. Nor, now that there are no longer giants on the earth, is there anyone who can or cares to pay the incredible amount of attention to single traits or complexes that men like Boas or Lowie did. Given these "uncertainty principles," one has the option of articles directed concisely to a single point, or of partial ethnographies focused on some phase or sphere of human behavior that we hope will provide insights into the culture as a whole. In this latter approach the ethnographer uses a single dimension, following it like a distinctive thread in all its ramifications and interconnections through the tangled skein of the whole culture. That is the strategy of this monograph, which hopes to tell the story of the Baegu people and their land.

Like most ethnographers, I study one group of people but hope to learn something valuable about mankind in general. The people who educated me were the Baegu of Malaita, a community of Melanesian farmers living in the British Solomon Islands Protectorate (BSIP) in the southwestern Pacific (Map 1).

The practice of going so far and into such exotic locales is sometimes hard to justify. While I suppose I may have been at least in part pursuing the anthropologist's recurring romantic fantasy, the will-o'-the-wisp of an unspoiled humanity, there are persuasive practical reasons as well. Scientific generalizations depend upon adequate comparative data, which depend in turn upon the existence of ethnographic descriptions of diverse cultures. Second, we can learn something of real value from people like the Melanesians who, despite a truly primitive technological repertoire, have in some ways achieved a happier adjustment to their physical and social environment than we have. Third, both as Americans (citizens of a great world power deeply involved in foreign affairs) and as human beings (members of a worldwide global community of men), we have positive obligations to come to know and to create ethically appropriate relationships with other people, no matter how exotic.

Traditionally monographs begin with a "statement of the problem." While it seems a trifle silly to talk about "the problem" of a largely descriptive monograph, one still should define his field and modes of inquiry. Because no one has ever described the Baegu before, I have tried to do as complete a job as possible. Naturally I have had to concentrate on aspects that interested me most: social organization and ecological relationships. Since residential behavior and land tenure are common factors in both social organization and human ecology, I have chosen to expend much of my effort upon those two (and some other closely related) topics.

My strategy (if you can dignify it by that pretentious name) has been to concentrate research efforts upon one aspect of Baegu cultural life (a single cultural dimension), to follow that through to develop a more comprehensive ethnographic description of Baegu life focused upon this one dimension, and finally to generalize from my Baegu experience to draw certain conclusions about human nature and behavior. My starting point has been the relationship of the people to their land: the complex of tropical farming ecology, demography, settlement patterns, land tenure, and residential behavior. This is not an arbitrary decision, for it is obvious that land is the principal resource of a farming people. Local residential groups and land-owning groups are truly fundamental social units. They are figuratively bridges from observable natural reality to the social and cultural principles that anthropologists seek to know. Men are social and cultural animals, to be sure, but society is largely an abstraction and culture exists only in the mind. We learn about these from overt behavior and tangible artifacts. I have

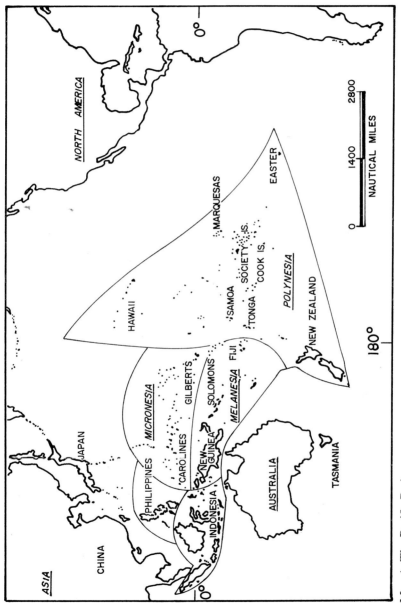

Map 1. The Pacific Basin

reasoned that the natural facts of farming and population could lead me into the more humanly variable patterns of land ownership, land usage, and residence that together are the interfaces between the natural and the sociocultural realms; and that in trying to understand these, I could come to grips with abstract principles of social organization and the cultural categories and rules behind them.

In the course of my field research and subsequent analysis I have had in mind certain questions or concerns and have reached tentative conclusions. These questions and conclusions impose the framework and set the parameters for the resulting monograph. My orienting questions or concerns have been:

A. For the Baegu of Malaita specifically:
1. The nature of their residential and spatial behavior;
2. How this develops and operates; and
3. How it is functional or utilitarian;

B. For mankind and anthropological science in general:
1. The nature of human residence rules and settlement patterns;
2. How human populations space themselves; and
3. About the efficacy of a single-dimension approach (such as this) to ethnographic description.

To anticipate the conclusions, first, the land of the Baegu is composed of named districts, having imprecise borders but focused about ancestral shrines, said to belong to patrilineal clans but actually used by a group of agnatic kinsmen plus their affiliated cognatic relatives. They live in tiny, widely separated hamlets of some eight to sixteen people, an optimum size in their terms big enough for cooperation and social solidarity, yet small enough to reduce competition and the dangers of supernatural contagion. The hamlets (which are frequently moved) usually contain a group of related males sharing a semi-sacred men's house. There is a distinct separation of the sexes; the hamlets and gardens are neatly maintained and sharply delineated from the surrounding forest.

Second, from my Baegu observations I have inferred that the Baegu people make residential decisions (where to settle, when to move, and whether to split a hamlet or maintain its integrity) not on the basis of discrete residence rules, but through complex decisions guided by a whole series of value standards considering economics (resource distribution and site characteristics), social factors (mutual cooperation, solidarity, and kin or client obligations), personal or psychological considerations (ambitions, rivalries, privacy, and aesthetic standards), and supernatural factors (ancestral dieties, filial piety, ghosts, sorcery, and fear of contagion). These decisions in effect jointly maximize the potential benefits accruing from given settlement patterns or residential behavior.

Third, a related deduction is that Baegu settlement patterns and residence rules, together with the norms, values, and decision-making processes accompanying them, are a single system functioning as a human spacing mechanism. This system creates a satisfactory ecological adjustment of population to territory by reducing competition, providing general access to resources, maximizing production, minimizing natural pollution and magical dangers, and minimizing the hazards of natural disasters by hedging and spreading the risks.

Leaving the Baegu and turning to humanity in general, one can deduce (using Baegu data for support), first, that there is a sociocultural system of residential or spatial behavior. Men have (subject to cultural variation) norms or values about their land, their relationship to it, and their relationships to one another where space or land is concerned. Residence rules and decisions express these values. Observed settlement patterns result from cumulative residential rules and decisions, and settlement patterns create and maintain a satisfactory human ecological relationship.

Second, the spatial and residential behavior system (that is, a human spacing mechanism having adaptive value) operates in the quasi-linguistic way that seems characteristic of all human cultural behavior. Residence rules are its grammar, with the relevant values, norms, beliefs, and assumptions its contextual constraints. Residential decisions are utterances in this grammar, conforming to transformational rules that make it possible to talk of cultural competence. Observed settlement patterns are the corpus of data. This residential behavior system communicates "correct" behavior within the society, communicates to the ecosystem itself (through cybernetic or goal-seeking reorientation), and communicates to the ethnographer (who tries to grasp the essence of social or cultural structure).

Third, although evaluation is by no means complete, it would appear that an approach to the phantoms of society or culture pursuing a single tangible dimension or theme (providing, of course, that it is a good one) may have some value in anthropological inquiry.

While it certainly helps to clarify a monograph, I should point out that stating the conclusions at the beginning as well as the end is largely a literary device. As a beginning student I was always amazed at the way professional anthropologists invariably proved their hypotheses with crystalline clarity and almost ruthless efficiency. I had to struggle through the experience myself to realize that one goes into the field with certain preconceptions (usually wrong) and ambitious plans (usually unworkable). Serious hypotheses come only after the ethnographer begins to experience the culture he is studying, learns something, and begins to think about it. In my own case, I left the United States for the Solomon Islands in 1966 with a neat research strategy and a battery of tactics I planned to use to elicit information on points I hoped to prove. But most of these failed. My scientific hypotheses (altered or modified many times, as it turned out) really developed during breaks from fieldwork in 1967 in New Zealand and in 1968 while briefly back in the United States, when I had time and perspective to think about Baegu life. I tested these in both instances after I returned to Malaita during the latter halves of those years and really refined them while analyzing my field notes and records. Now I can state a proposition, check it against my data and experience, and conclude that it is more or less proven or rejected: scientific method in textbook style. But I am embarrassed to go back and read my original research proposal, for it is so different from my eventual results that one might believe they refer to separate projects. As an aid to professional reputations, perhaps we should invent the custom of ceremonially burning all research proposals before publishing our results.

The monograph is really a general ethnography of the Baegu, organized about the twin themes of social organization and ecological adaptation. The problem to which it is addressed, then, is twofold: (1) to explain Baegu social organization in its ecological setting; and (2) to examine what this means for our understanding of human nature and anthropological science.

2. Fieldwork in Malaita

Lying in the southwestern corner of the Pacific Ocean more than 6,000 miles from North America are the Solomon Islands (Map 1). Although the Solomons are not, as Mark Twain said of Hawaii, the loveliest fleet of islands anchored in any ocean, and although they most certainly are not the South Seas of myth and romance, they have a peculiar exotic charm of their own. Being in the tropics — and the wet tropics at that — the islands bear a dense, tropical rain forest that some of us from more austere lands find fascinating or even beautiful. The terrain is rough and high, and during daylight hours massive towers of cumulus clouds build up over the mountains. When seen from a distance at sea the islands have a somber grandeur that is easy to experience but almost impossible to describe; and from the air, when distance mellows the greens of the forest, the aquamarine of the lagoons, the silver and gray of the clouds, and the deep blue of the tropical Pacific, they are beautiful by anyone's standards.

By and large they have been spared the worst excesses of Western civilization. Malaita Island, near the southeastern end of the archipelago, is both literally and figuratively at the end of the line (Map 2). Thanks to its unstrategic location, the virtual absence of important natural resources, and its conservative population, European influence in Malaita has been, comparatively speaking, minimal. The island's Melanesian inhabitants continue in their own traditional fashion. Their conservatism reflects either admirable common sense or perverse stubbornness, depending on your point of view.

Although the British government has maintained posts on the island since 1915 and various Christian denominations have proselytized there for over seventy years, modernization and development schemes have

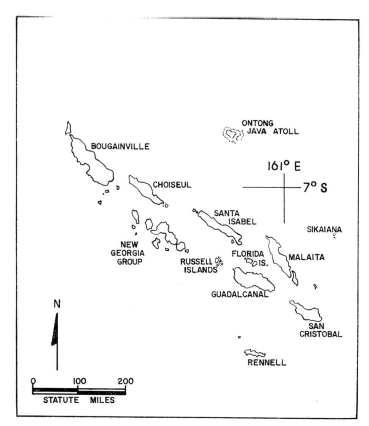

Map 2. The Solomon Islands

been less than resounding successes. Many communities are now Christian, of course, and many people are now lusting after European-style wealth and power. But throughout the island traditional communities rationally and consistently reject change, maintaining their pagan religion and their indigenous social organization. There are few places in the Pacific basin where native peoples have done this. In a way Malaitan conservatism is harder to understand than is, for example, that in the New Guinea highlands. New Guinea highlanders may remain pagans, but they do so largely out of ignorance. They have been contacted and brought "under control" only recently and are largely unaware of our civilization. Malaitans, on the other hand, are aware of the West; they have seen progress and change, but they reject it.

The Baegu of Malaita form one of these enclaves where the traditional Melanesian way of life survives. They are taro and sweet potato farmers living in the rain forest on both slopes of the central mountain massif near the northern end of the island. Once they were famous warriors, but British pacification put an end to native warfare during the 1920's, and only memories and their reputation for fierceness persist today. About half of them are still pagans, venerating the ancestral spirits and sacrificing pigs to them; but even the Christians retain their traditional lore, social organization, and subsistence patterns.

My family and I spent most of the period from mid-1966 through mid-1968 living with the Baegu. They are the most delightful bunch of truly fine people I ever hope to meet, and I owe them an inestimable debt of gratitude that I can probably never repay. From them I learned more, both about an exotic life-style and about the human condition generally, than I feel I could have learned from a decade of formal schooling. In a very real sense, they were the masters and I the pupil. Actually the Baegu have gotten along very nicely for millennia without an ethnographer, and it is a good thing that they had no crying need for such attentions, for Europeans[1] of all descriptions have tended to give the Malaita bush country a wide berth. There are some valid reasons for the unwholesome reputation of the Solomons. The climate is warm and extremely wet. Rain forest, rugged terrain, and unbelievably slippery mud make travel more than routinely difficult. Malaria, dengue, and blackwater fever were endemic diseases; even today minor cuts and scratches blossom into repulsive ulcers if they are not carefully treated. Besides, most Europeans object to lice, flies, mosquitoes, cockroaches, scorpions, and centipedes as companions.

Solomon Islanders and particularly Malaitans had a bad press from the start. Refusing to take any nonsense from anyone, they soon came to blows with Alvaro de Mendaña's troops when that first Spanish expedition arrived in 1568 (Beaglehole 1966:43-48). Aggravated by callous treatment from trading ship or whaler crews on rest and recreation leave, and by blackbirding labor recruiters in the nineteenth century, Melanesian warriors made martyrs of the first Christian missionaries, dealing out in proper ecumenical spirit the same treatment to Protestants and Catholics alike (C. Fox 1967:27-31). Europeans found headhunting in New Georgia and cannibalism in Malaita equally repulsive, and Melanesia acquired an unsavory reputation. Compare this with the long love affair between Europeans and Polynesians, undoubtedly based at least in part on the hospitality European visitors from Wallis and Cook to Paul Gauguin and beyond received in Polynesian parts of the Pacific.

This character assassination of the Solomon Islands and Islanders went

---

[1] I follow Solomon Islands local practice by referring to all white people (including Americans) as "Europeans."

beyond objective reality and became a literary device used to titillate European and American readers. Jack London (1923) agonized about his difficulties there, and Martin and Osa Johnson (1944) hinted at the lurid details of cannibal feasts on Malaita. This tradition of the "Savage Solomons" persisted and was even refurbished by American journalists during World War II, who (to please home-front editors) wrote of steaming jungles and the "Green Hell" of Guadalcanal; this despite the fact that most of the fighting was done on Lever's coconut planta-tion or the kunai prairies of the northern Guadalcanal Plain.

Be that as it may, this sort of nonsense was part of my own intel-lectual impedimenta, and I was forced to overcome a certain amount of personal reluctance before I could participate in a project requiring an extended stay in the Solomon Islands. In other words, I was dragged there kicking and screaming. In the fall of 1962 my advisor at Harvard, Professor Douglas Oliver, first broached the idea that the Solomons would be a good place for my first ethnographic fieldwork. I had just started graduate school after more than four years in the U.S. Navy (where I had been a submariner, so presumably I was not a complete coward). Nevertheless, I mumbled something noncommittal, went home, and tried to forget he had mentioned the possibility. Some four years and several academic dead ends later, I found myself in Malaita with Dr. Albert Damon's biomedical research expedition from Harvard, ready to pick my own village and "do" Melanesian ethnography.

Needless to say, my fears were groundless. Not only did the Malaitans spare me from the cooking pot (white men's flesh supposedly doesn't taste very good anyway), but they took far better care of me than most American communities would. All of us came through only a little the worse for the wear. My two children still nag me that they want to go back to Malaita, because it is so much nicer there than it is in America.

THEORETICAL FRAMEWORK AND METHODOLOGY

After the easy part of ethnographic research is over, there comes the sometimes awesome task of telling people about it. Early in my stay among the Baegu, I came to realize that whatever else he may be, "Primitive Man" is a poor ethnographer. Since he lives it, he does not have to worry about how his system works. But scholars do. The Baegu organize their social life in a number of ways. They recognize named patrilineal descent groups that own the land. At the same time, most rights and obligations apply bilaterally to both agnatic and uterine kinsmen. Frequency of interaction is highest within territorially defined communities or neighborhoods that may be (but usually are not) named. Along with all this comes the social importance of the Big Man, Melanesian-style, as a charismatic political leader.

This coexistence of multiple institutions and principles for social organization is not unduly complex, nor is it unique. After nearly a century of social anthropology, we have adequate methods and impressive theories for dealing with societies that are considerate enough to be decently unilineal. Even refractory cognatic social systems are yielding to anthropological analysis, as we develop more sophisticated approaches. What we have yet to create are efficient, satisfying ways of analyzing and describing people whose social system and ideology may be complex, irregular, inconsistent, or simply messy. This to an extent is Baegu society. They insist on the importance of agnatic or patrilineal descent, yet they stress vigorously the rights of cognatic kinsmen or coresidents.

Idiosyncratic wants and specific conditions or events can at times subvert principles or systems. The task of the ethnographer is to sort these facts out, to fiddle with them until he understands them, and then to put them back together in a description that makes sense to a reasonably intelligent reader. One hopes that scientists of the future can replicate the analysis and results.

Given parameters of intellectual interest and empirical constraints, my basic research strategy has been to simplify Baegu society by projecting it conceptually onto a single dimension, that of men's spatial relationships to the land and to one another in terms of space and land. This is Oliver's (1958:802) "spatial dimension," conforming in a silly but commonsense way to the in-group adage (popular among some anthropologists today) of concentrating on how society shows up "on the ground." Social systems are multi-dimensional, to be sure, but one must begin somewhere. As Goodenough (1951:12) began with property on Truk, because he had to have a convenient and useful entree, I have used the spatial dimension as my initial point of entry. Social relationships among people are fluid, or at least relativistic. It is easier to see these if they can somehow be fixed against something solid, such as the land itself. Reaching the same conclusions that Goodenough (1955) did, I decided that local residential groups and land-owning groups were fundamental to the social organization I was trying to understand, and I chose to begin with a focus upon these.

Ethnographic description does not begin with Locke's blank slate. We all carry distinctive loads of previously acquired facts and theories. In my own case this begins with a prejudice in the direction of ecological relationships, adaptations, and interpretations rooted in biological nature. I use an essentially structural and transformational approach to the categories and plans that are culture, learned from the late Clyde Kluckhohn and indirectly from the traditions of Lévi-Strauss and Chomsky. I take a modified systemic view of social organization and social relations, assuming at least some degree of structural-functional integrity within the social system itself (following Radcliffe-Brown, Malinowski, Parsons, and Geertz) ; but I reject the tautological conservatism implicit in an orthodox functionalist model, because I have been so deeply influenced by the pragmatic social anthropology of Douglas Oliver and Raymond Firth, who never forget or ignore the facts of conflict and individual initiative. Between the cultural or social system and its natural environment, I assume a great deal of adaptive consistency (following Steward, White, Shimkin, Sahlins, Service, Vayda, and Harris). From Douglas Oliver I acquired a strong bent toward practical ethnography with an empirical base; and as an anthropologist specializing in Oceania, I am of course affected by the work of Goodenough (1955), Firth (1957), Davenport (1959), Barnes (1962), Langness (1964), Pouwer (1964), Scheffler (1965), and Keesing (1965) on the problems of non-unilineal social organization.

A word about empiricism and inductive reasoning as components of the so-called scientific method may be in order here. Judging from my own experiences, purely empirical-inductive ethnography does not seem within the realm of possibility. Empirical observation is essential for initial comprehension of a situation, and inductive reasoning can help an ethnographer find some sort of order in the chaos of his early observations. Again, empirical testing of ideas pays off handsomely later in a research project; but in between comes a lot of intuition and deductive reasoning from one idea to another. Hence, call it art or science as you prefer, the heart of ethnography is something more than simple empiricism.

Methodology is a horrible word, reeking of scholasticism and pedantry, but since methods affect both the substantive direction and technical validity of finished research, an ethnographer ought to let people know how he went about his work. Methods and techniques are in large measure predetermined by a scholar's own training and theoretical assumptions. Having the conceptions I do about what culture and society are, I was more or less forced to use the by now standard anthropological participant-observer technique, supplemented by more rigorous investigation of linguistic insights. In other words, I simply settled down to live with my research subjects; to observe their lives, to learn their language, and to participate (as fully as an uninformed but sympathetic alien ever can) in that life.

PARTICIPANT-OBSERVER ETHNOGRAPHY

This is not as easy as it sounds. The problems that a frightened novice anthropologist has in making initial contact and deciding on a semi-permanent research station are well worth a book in themselves. Basically he must choose the right people, choose the right site, and do so in a way that satisfies research requirements, personal desires, and environmental and logistic problems. Of course, the decision has to be made when he has only the haziest idea of what is happening.

After spending a couple of weeks talking with mission officials and Western Pacific High Commission Secretariat personnel in Honiara on Guadalcanal (Map 2), talking with British officials and local Melanesian clerks at Malaita District headquarters in Auki, and tramping about the bush following up contacts they and Roger Keesing (who had done anthropological research further south in Malaita two years previously) had passed on to me, I finally made arrangements in September, 1966, to have a house built for me near a village named Ailali on the eastern side of the island (Map 3). It was in the hills on the left bank of the Sasafa River, about two miles inland from the sea (Urasi Cove) and at about 500 feet elevation. It was a pleasant site with a beautiful view of both sea and mountains and had adequate fresh water for both drinking and bathing. I felt that I could land bulky shipments over the beach at the cove, and there were good (a relative term at best) trails to landings opposite Sulufou and Foueda in the Lau Lagoon where I could meet the once or twice monthly around-the-island shipping services for mail and supplies.

There was a large (200-300) Christian Baegu population in several big villages very nearby and an equally large pagan population within a few hours walk in the hills around me. I wanted to live among a large number of people, as I felt this would make it easier for me to learn their language and to observe their daily routine. For these and for logistic reasons I hesitated to set up shop in a more isolated region, such as the very crest of the central ridge, where the people would be more "untouched" but also fewer. In retrospect this was a groundless fear. I suspect that even had I settled all by myself miles from anyone in the midst of the forest, I would still have had plenty of subjects. I was in fact deluged with prospective informants. They came in the morning before I was awake, talked with me all day, complained about my laziness when I did not feel like working, and stayed at night until I turned out the lamps and went to bed.

On the other hand, I chose not to live immediately in any one village. I feared becoming too involved with a single local political figure,

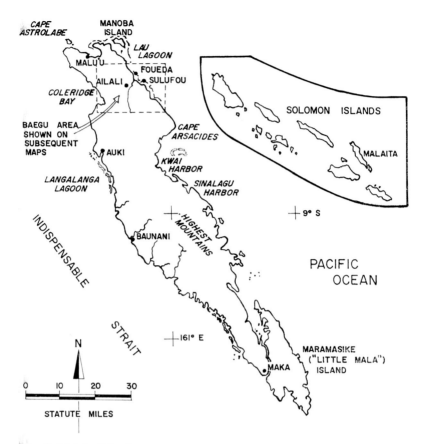

Map 3. Malaita Island

or being too closely identified with one sect. In this I think I was fairly successful, partly by design and partly by fortuitous accident. I picked the site because it was on the trail from the central hills to some of the market sites on the coast where the hill people went (two days a week to each market) to trade their produce with the coastal people. As it turned out there was a good network of trails radiating out into the hills that made it easy (again, a relative matter) for the outlying population to come to me, or for me (not so easy) to visit them. There were also several influential Neo-Marching Rule (an incipient nativistic movement) cargo cult leaders living nearby and a couple of their meeting places in the vicinity. Thus I had a wide range of contacts and a potential research sample of about six hundred people living in the Sasafa River valley and in the hills on both sides overlooking it.

For better or for worse I had selected a base and had contracted for a palm-thatch house. In October, 1966, I moved in and began my fieldwork. I might add that despite my careful reconnaissance and planning, when I arrived on the beach with a smile and what seemed like a million tons of supplies and equipment, my house (as wiser men might have predicted) was less than half finished. So I spent the first month totally dependent on Baegu hospitality in one of their houses.

Eventually my house was finished (although ironically a hurricane demolished the first one a few days after we moved in), and my family and I lived there (with one break for an April holiday in New Zealand) until late in 1967. We went back to the United States for the spring semester of 1968 at Harvard, but I again returned to Malaita for the summer (northern hemisphere reckoning) of 1968. All told I spent sixteen months actually with the Baegu in the field.

The observer half of the participant-observer role in ethnographic research is by far the easier half to fill, although it does take energy, perserverance, and considerable gall. Novelty is soon gone, and despite the exotic surroundings an observer must exert more and more effort as time passes to stay alert during routine activities such as children's play, betel-chewing sessions, household chores, and interminable gossiping. Gardening and marketing were more stimulating, simply because of the change of scene required. The Baegu were very sympathetic to what I was doing, interpreting my interest in their customs as a compliment (it was). Most of them were in fact eager to have me around to observe weddings, funerals, religious sacrifices, feasts and "custom meetings" (cargo cultist assemblies). Although I would dearly love to believe that it was my innate charm that made me such a welcome guest, I should point out that, in current cargo cult thinking in Malaita, there is an urgent feeling that "custom" (the Pidgin word for traditional Melanesian beliefs and practices) ought to be written down in order to make it official. I am afraid they loved my notebooks more than they loved me.

Thus it was incredibly easy to observe Baegu life. I was for the most part limited only by my ambition and stamina. There were of course some exceptions. In an all too human way people were sometimes reluctant to give me the juicier details of quarrels and scandals or other situations they might find embarrassing. But after I had come to know the people better, and to know them as individuals, I was usually able to circumvent this because (again, in an all too human way) there were always incorrigible gossips who could scarcely wait to pass on the latest dirt. In some cases I failed completely. Some people simply did not like me or were suspicious of what I was doing, and these never would have anything to do with me. On the whole, though, my task

Plate 1. Gugumae of Walelangi, said to be the first Baegu man to own steel tools.

was an easy one, and I encountered far fewer "none of your business" attitudes than I feel I would have in an American community.

The participant half of the participant-observer role requires more explanation. As a white man from an urban background with a university education, I could never participate fully in what was essentially a Neolithic subsistence-farming way of life. I could never "be one of them." They knew that, and I made no pretense of it. I learned their language, learned from them, lived with them, and traveled with them. We had a little garden, but it was in miserable shape and I was obviously no farmer; I might make token contributions at their festivals or weddings, but I was certainly not an important part of their social or economic system; and whether Christian or pagan they were devout people, while I was a gentle skeptic. They and I were friends — good ones, I think — but I was always the white man who lived with them.

Inasmuch as I participated in their lives and culture, it was in their mental life. In learning their language and customs, I made a sincere effort to come to grips with life on their terms, to think the way they thought, and to see the world the way they saw it. Participation in this sense (in mental life) involves several activities. First, one must try to enter into the spirit of what is going on around him, to pry into the rationale of beliefs and actions, and to try to understand what these mean to the people themselves. Second, the ethnographer must find knowledgeable and sympathetic informants who can teach him.

Finding suitable informants proved harder than I had anticipated and caused me to alter radically my own assumptions about anthropological fieldwork. Before, I had imagined fieldwork to be a constant parade of new faces, visitors coming and going, and had assumed that quality of research was roughly proportional to the number of subjects processed. This may be true for some problems, but for my purposes I could not have been more wrong.

In the first place most people are too unaware or too inarticulate to be useful informants. A good informant must be in effect a good amateur ethnographer. He must have a broad and deep knowledge of his own people's customs and traditions. He should have a keen, analytic mind so that he can himself discern patterns and anticipate the ethnographer's problems. He must also be articulate enough to explain things clearly and to be a good teacher. In the early stages of ethnographic research there is, in addition to all other difficulties, a language barrier so that one must find a bilingual informant who can translate for him. Finally, an ethnographer must find someone who is sympathetic both toward the project and toward him. Learning and explanation take many hours, and the informant has to be willing to spend this time.

Second, the ethnographer-informant relationship is a highly personal one. They have to know and like each other well, and they must trust each other well enough to relax and be at ease. Casual acquaintances do not make good informants. They are too reserved, and conversations with them never get beyond the banalities of the weather, health, each other's children, and how the crops are doing.

After struggling for weeks to learn something by questioning almost everyone I met, I surrendered to the inevitable and began to cultivate a few more intimate friends to use as primary informants. This sounds more rational than it really was; I virtually gave up in despair, and the friendships grew of their own accord. I never had the good fortune to find a single reliable informant suitable in all respects. If a man were informed and sympathetic, he knew no English; if he were interested and spoke good English, his knowledge was meager; or if he were wise and spoke English, he soon grew bored and avoided me. Eventually the logical answer worked itself out, and I established a fairly effective procedure combining the first two kinds of informants.

Again through one of those fortunate chances, there was a wealthy and respected old man (I judged him to be in his eighties) living near me. He had an incredibly vast knowledge of and love for his own Baegu traditions. He had worked as a houseboy in Tulagi (the old capital in the Florida Group) before World War I, and although he knew virtually no English, he passionately wanted his own customs and traditions to be recorded so that the world would know that the Baegu were not ignorant savages. Living near him was one of his younger kinsmen, a one-legged man of about forty who did speak adequate English. As a result of the loss of his leg and numerous youthful sicknesses, this younger man had spent several years in British hospitals, where he had learned to speak English and even to write. Using these two as my primary informants, I managed to get on with my study of their language, culture, and society.

Besides this pair, there were other intelligent, important people whom I got to know well and who proved to be invaluable informants in depth. Four "Custom Chiefs" (leaders of the ongoing nativistic movement), some Anglican church elders, and three pagan priests in particular spent much of their time tutoring me. Besides having deep insights into aspects of their own customs, these men significantly broadened my range of information and enabled me to check statements and opinions against other sources.

Although intensive work with a few learned informants may be the most efficient way to learn the shared ideas and norms of a society, there are other circumstances where larger numbers are preferable.

Statistically valid descriptions depend ultimately on a sufficiently large sample to make generalizations meaningful. Thus censuses, marketing or garden surveys, opinion surveys, and descriptions of settlement patterns all require a large sample population. An empirical approach

Plate 2. The octogenarian Sedea of the Walelangi clan, a major informant and teacher.

to social structure also assumes observation of large numbers of inter-actions from which patterns and rules are to be inferred.

As time went on I found that, without really planning it, I could use the general population as a sounding board to check ideas I had or conclusions I had reached from serious study and conversation with my "full-time" tutors. As a result of these sessions I would come to believe that I understood certain ideological points, conversational phrases, or behavioral mannerisms. More or less as a means of showing off, I would try to use these in proper context during casual inter-action with other people. If they accepted my speech or behavior as appropriate, I felt I could presume that my interpretations were in-deed correct.

Then, too, I am indebted to dozens of Baegu for letting me quiz them about who lived in their households or hamlets, and who their kinsmen were; for letting me poke into their market baskets; for letting me measure and map their settlements and gardens; and for letting me be an inquisitive busybody in general. They never did fully understand what I was trying to do, but I think they did come to accept me as an incomprehensible but harmless eccentric.

LEARNING THE LANGUAGE

As any anthropologist knows, it is impossible to do adequate field-work without learning the local language. I did not really have much choice in the matter, for there were so few people who spoke satisfactory English. Most of the men had been away from Malaita as plantation laborers, and these knew some Pidgin, a neo-Melanesian *lingua franca* using a basically English vocabulary and a set of simplified pan-Melanesian grammatical transformations. This helped to simplify my language learning problems, but since Solomon Islands Pidgin is no one's native tongue, it was scarcely a suitable vehicle for my sort of scientific inquiry.

Thanks to the efforts of my Baegu mentors and to the attitude of the general population (ranging from genuine helpfulness to amused tolerance), learning the Baegu language was not too difficult. It is a simple language both phonologically and grammatically, and although I have no great aptitude for languages, it took only about four months to acquire enough competence for ethnographic fieldwork. Essentially all my research was done in the Baegu language, for what I learned in the first two or three months was minimal and mostly wrong at that. After some six to nine months I was able to converse in a fairly normal manner. By the end of my fieldwork, my level of skill was what one

Plate 3. Lebefiu of Walelangi in the ceremonial dress of a war leader (*ramo*).

would call competent, but not fluent. My accent was atrocious, and my grammar was careless at best, but I could communicate and people were both amused and flattered by the spectacle of a white man speaking a Malaitan hill dialect.

Learning the language itself was one of the most productive means I found to approach the task of learning about culture or society. New concepts required new words or phrases, and these had to be explained to me. The idea of using linguistic material to discover and explore cultural differences is the basis for the techniques of ethnoscience, or if you prefer, the New Ethnography. Perhaps this is something we have always done, but it has been only in the past fifteen years that ethnographers such as Conklin (1955), Frake (1962), Sturtevant (1964), and Goodenough (1967) have begun to put the procedures on a formal, rigorous footing. In my own research I found ethnosemantic techniques to be useful on at least two levels. The first of these is the principle of looking at a language (and presumably also at a culture) in its own terms, rather than in terms imposed on it by an outside observer, Pike's (1954) familiar emic-etic distinction. It involves isolating and identifying relevant components of definitions and discovering how native speakers classify and create taxonomies of related items within a semantic field. From these linguistic phenomena, so the reasoning goes, we can, as Sapir (1921) and Whorf (1956) have urged, come to understand the world-view and the mental processes of the native speaker. At this level ethnoscientific concepts are again useful. Continuing with a linguistic analogy, by looking at a variety of these taxonomies we can discover complex but recurrent patterns. If we are clever enough or wise enough, we have a chance of discovering fundamental rules that are basic to the language or culture and that generate more complex patterns in a theoretically infinite variety of contexts. These are what Chomsky (1957) is thinking of when he writes about syntactic structures, and what Levi-Strauss (1962a) is looking for when he talks about the structure of culture or society.

Unfortunately, ethnoscientific techniques are not all that useful for my own work. Despite their promise, their rigor and formality have thus far been applied in strictly limited and frequently trivial cases. The bigger, more general problems of life and death, marriage and reproduction, earning a living, and building a village have not proved amenable to formal analysis of this kind. But in specific instances the New Ethnography can be highly effective, and I use it where I can, as Goodenough (1951:63-64) did in Truk. I prefer, however, to deal with a larger slice of human life, and like Keesing (1965:5) I choose not to sacrifice relevancy for accuracy.

3. The Island Environment

Since the Solomon Islands are located about 6,200 miles from the western coast of North America and about 3,000 miles from the South China coast (Map 1), they are far removed from the commercial and cultural centers of the northern hemisphere. They are only some 1,000 airline miles from Australia's southern Queensland coast, but because of a long tradition of loyalty to the Empire (whose major interests lay in Europe, Africa, and India) and a preoccupation with holding off the teeming masses of Asia, official Australia has historically tended to ignore her maritime Pacific neighbors.

As most geographic descriptions tell us, the Solomons are a double chain of large continental islands (Map 2) beginning in the northwest with Bougainville, due east of New Guinea, and ending with San Cristobal at the southeastern end. The northeastern (or Pacific side) chain consists of Choiseul, Santa Isabel, and Malaita Islands; the New Georgia group, Guadalcanal, and several smaller island clusters compose the southwestern (or Coral Sea side) chain.

Malaita (Map 3), where the Baegu people live, is in the southeastern Solomons, lying between 8°S and 10°S latitude and exactly on the 161°E meridian of longitude. Ailali village in the Baegu area of northern Malaita, where I lived and worked, is approximately at coordinates 8°26.5'S and 160°48'E. Malaita is a thin island about 102 miles long (116 miles, if you count both Malaita and Maramasike or Little Mala Islands, separated by a narrow channel, as a single unit) and 23 miles across at its wider points. Elevations are not precisely known, but the central mountain massif rises to something like 4,700 feet in the south-central part of the main island where the Kwaio and 'Are'Are people live, and to about 3,200 feet in the northern part where the Baegu live.

Malaita's long axis actually has a northwest by southeast orientation, but local custom and the Western Pacific High Commission (representing the British government) have cognitively skewed it around to make description of directions simpler. Thus the northeastern coast, fronting on the Pacific Ocean, is said to be the "east coast"; the southwestern coast facing Indispensable Strait and the Solomon Sea becomes the "west coast." In like manner Cape Astrolabe and Manoba Island are the "northern end" of Malaita, while Maka and Maramasike Island are at its "southern end."

Although things have improved since World War II, Malaita is still more isolated than the rest of the Solomons, with the exception of the eastern outer islands (the Santa Cruz group) and small outliers. As of late 1970, Fiji Airways had dependable thrice-weekly flights from Fiji to Henderson Field on Guadalcanal, and Trans-Australian Airways flew from New Guinea to Guadalcanal twice a week. Burns-Philp shipping connects the capital of Honiara on Guadalcanal with Australia every five or six weeks, and several European, New Zealand, Hong Kong, and Japanese navigation companies call occasionally at Honiara.

BSIP Marine Service and local charter vessels make weekly runs between Honiara and the Malaita District administrative headquarters at Auki on Malaita's west coast. Since the government completed an airstrip at Gwaunaru'u near Auki in 1964, the local commercial airline, Solair, flies light planes five days a week from Honiara to Auki.

Rural Malaita remains inaccessible. There is a single gravel road along the west coast now connecting Auki with Kwailabesi on the northern mainland opposite Manoba Island. People dream of roads to the south and across the island, but money to build them is not available. The District Administration provides a once-a-month mail service around the island by "ship" (about forty feet long) that calls at villages along the east coast. Various government officials (district officers, medical staff, and agricultural officials) make regular tours by sea to various parts of the island, so that any given east coast port will see about two government vessels per month. To get into the interior, one walks.

CLIMATE

It is extremely wet, but for the most part Malaita's climate is a pleasant one. The major factor influencing climate or weather on Malaita is simply geographic position. Being near the equator, the coefficient of solar radiation reaching the earth's surface is uniformly high throughout the year with no marked seasonal changes in mean temperature. At sea level, temperatures are nearly always warm.

Because it is so near the equator, Malaita also periodically feels the effects of the intertropical convergence zone (ITCZ) or doldrums. This is a low pressure frontal area where air masses stirred by prevailing trade winds in each hemisphere meet at low latitudes. Winds are fickle, cloud formation and thunderstorm activity are frequent but erratic, and in the changeable weather pattern sudden squalls alternate with dead calms. The ITCZ migrates on the earth's surface according to the position of the sun on the ecliptic relative to the celestial equator. Essentially, the intertropical convergence zone forms approximately where the sun's rays are perpendicular to the earth's surface: to an observer on earth, when the sun is directly overhead. Thus, when the sun appears to move southward in October, November, and December, the ITCZ moves southward, too. It is most closely associated with the earth's equator about the time of the vernal and autumnal equinoxes. The weather conditions associated with the ITCZ, therefore, would have the most effect on Malaita shortly before and after the winter solstice (November and February).

The tradewinds, another result of geographic position, also affect Malaitan climate. As air masses in the tropical zones drift toward the low pressure area near the equator, they are deflected away from a direct course according to the Coriolis effect. In the southern hemisphere, they follow a curving course to the left, becoming a strong, steady breeze that we call the Southeasterly Tradewinds. The tradewinds shift with the seasons, according to the apparent movements of the sun, as do all climatic zones, reaching their furthest northward extent in late June and July, and their furthest southward in December or January. For Malaita, the regime of the tradewinds comes during the southern hemisphere's astronomical winter. From April through August the Southeasterly Trades blow steadily. Moving almost unimpeded across vast stretches of open water, these winds form impressive wave systems; rough seas during this season can make travel by small ship along Malaita's eastern coast an uncomfortable experience, as thousands of wretched voyagers have learned over the years.

As climatic zones shift southward during the Antipodean summer (after September), Malaita experiences still another climatic regime. From September through March the winds are undependable, unlike the tradewinds. Frequently during this time the fringes of the northwest monsoon, set in motion by warm, low pressure conditions over Australia combined with cool, high pressure conditions over the Eurasian land mass, blow over the Solomons. The alternation of variable ITCZ winds with an attenuated northwest monsoon means that seas along the east coast are calmer, but that Indispensable Strait to the west may have rougher waters than usual. Old hands in the area say that the months of October through March are warmer and drier, but my own impressions were that they were simply more irregular.

As seen from Malaita these climatic regimes cycle through the year (Figure 1), with a regular annual progression from tradewinds through

Figure 1. Pacific Basin Climatic Zones Diagram

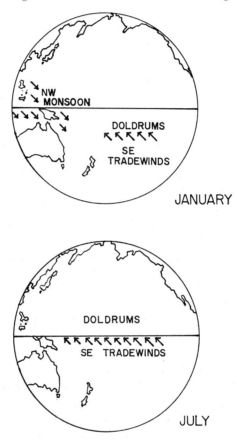

doldrums and the monsoon back to tradewinds as these prevailing weather patterns shift north or south on the earth's surface following the seasonal apparent movement of the sun.

But there are other factors influencing weather; chief among these is the sea. The sea, of course, is the great climatic stabilizing mechanism throughout the world. The relatively high specific heat of water means that greater totals of energy are required to heat water to a given temperature than would be required to heat the same mass of land equivalently. The sea then warms more slowly than do land masses. Conversely, water also tends to retain its heat, so that the sea chills more slowly, staying warmer than land areas when temperatures are falling.

Maritime or coastal regions rarely experience the temperature extremes of continental areas at the same latitude. Malaita, an island, is greatly affected by the sea and has a typically maritime climate, a stable one, with diurnal temperature variations exceeding seasonal ones. The average difference between daily maximum temperature and daily minimum temperature is 13.6°F. The mean maximum daily temperature for the warmest month differs only 3.4°F. from that of the coldest month.

A second general effect of the sea in Malaita is wetness. Rainfall is heavy, cloud cover thick, vegetation lush, and trails usually muddy. Mosses, algae, and fungi thrive in the high humidity. Even light work produces torrents of sweat, clothes mildew, and metallic objects seem almost to rust before your eyes. As a result of frequent showers and many scattered clouds, I have never seen more rainbows, or more perfect ones, than I saw in Malaita.

The juxaposition of land and sea creates a characteristic diurnal variation in weather conditions. Assuming there is no widespread pattern bringing rain over a large area, mornings are usually clear and relatively calm. During the forenoon, differential warming of the land and sea creates a local convection cell (Figure 2) with rising air currents over the land that is by mid-morning warmer than the surrounding sea. Warmer rising air over the land generates a low pressure area, and air from cooler, higher pressure areas over the sea moves inland toward the local atmospheric low above the island. Hence by late morning there is usually a strong sea breeze blowing in from offshore. Offshore or sea breezes are typically marine air, carrying a heavy load of water vapor. As the moisture-laden air moves into the low pressure area over the land, it warms and rises as a convection current. But as it rises it loses its ability to hold its previously absorbed water vapor, and the freed moisture partially condenses as clouds. Shortly before noon fluffy clouds begin to form above the mountains, and during the afternoon cumulus and cumulo-nimbus formations grow over the island. As the cloud build-up continues, more water vapor is chilled and condensed in the atmosphere, and afternoon showers occur. The bases of the cloud pillars envelop the mountains, and evenings in the hill country are often cool, foggy, and drizzly, with wisps of cloud drifting by in the valleys below.

This sequence occurred nearly every day regardless of how clear the

Figure 2. Diurnal Weather Pattern Diagram for Typical Pacific Island

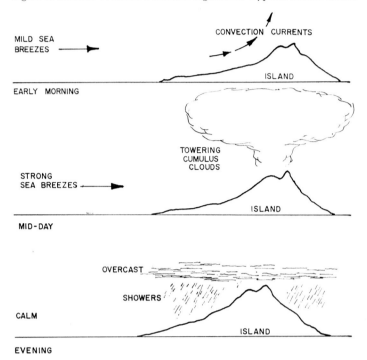

sky was in the morning. I noted only half a dozen days in sixteen months of residence there when the sky over the mountains remained cloudless in the afternoon. There were, of course, other days when rainfall was widespread and lasted all day.

During the night the process at least partially reverses (Figure 2). In darkness the land cools faster than the sea, and the day's clouds dissipate. Winds at higher altitudes sweep the top parts of the clouds away. Cooling of the atmosphere after sunset soon reaches the saturation point, and precipitation further attenuates the clouds. Showers, drizzle, and heavy dew are characteristic of Malaitan nights. As the land cools more rapidly than the surrounding sea, the atmospheric convection cell reverses. Descending air in the higher pressure region over the island warms adiabatically, increasing its water vapor carrying capacity. Remaining water vapor is reabsorbed, and the air over the island gradually drifts out over the now relatively warmer ocean.

After the cloud cover is gone, heat loss by radiation into the clear sky further chills the mountain area during the night. This, combined with a normal lapse rate of air temperature with increased elevation, can make nights in the hill country unpleasantly cold. It is especially chilly

Plate 4. Borofunga Mountain landscape in its usual cloudy state.

just before dawn, when people begin hacking and coughing, slapping or rubbing themselves to keep warm, and trying to coax some life out of dead fires. Because of the nighttime cold, the hill people build their houses on the ground rather than on piles, fill the chinks in the walls with bark and leaves to prevent draughts, and keep a fire smoldering inside for warmth. Dirt floors and smoky interiors may not be sanitary, but when there are no blankets, how else can one avoid the chill?

Temperatures in Malaita are bearable or even pleasant. Tropical days with a temperature in the seventies, tempered by sea breezes or tradewinds, are idyllic. Nighttime temperatures around 60°F. make good sleeping conditions, if one has blankets. The heavy rainfall is at first appalling, but one quickly learns to adapt and not take a drenching too seriously.

Tropical cyclones, the only violent weather in an otherwise equable climate, are something else again. These huge storms, called typhoons in the western Pacific or hurricanes in the Caribbean and South Pacific, are rotating air masses with radii of fifty miles or more around extremely low pressure centers. They invariably originate over tropical seas at low latitudes. Typically they move toward the poles in curving paths, carried first westward by the easterly tradewinds, then recurving to the east when they enter the zone of prevailing westerlies. The low pressure center is crucial to their etiology, since they begin as easterly waves of low barometric pressure. Somehow the air begins to rotate around this low pressure center as a vortex; clouds and heavy rains appear, and high winds develop. The whole rotating mass carries an unbelievable amount of energy. Most of these storms eventually die out over continental areas or dissipate as amorphous gales in high latitudes. South Pacific hurricanes seem to be less predictable.

Hurricanes are popularly supposed to be less frequent and less destructive in the South Pacific than they are in either the western Pacific or Caribbean. Weather records for the South Pacific are sketchy at best (because of vast areas, isolated populations, and unsophisticated technology), so statistics for the region are unreliable (Freeman 1951:16); but during the two-year span when I was there, hurricanes occurred with what I consider respectable frequency. In November, 1966, a vicious and unexpected one crossed northern Malaita. In late March, 1967, another one hit Guadalcanal and San Cristobal, skirting Malaita. In November, 1967, Gizo in the New Georgia group and Santa Isabel Island suffered through a hurricane that again only slightly affected northern Malaita. April, 1968, saw another hurricane pass out to sea after doing a little damage along Malaita's eastern coast, and in December, 1968, still another appeared over Ontong Java atoll, roared across central Malaita, and then hit San Cristobal.

In a technologically primitive area it is difficult to assess ac
how much damage a tropical cyclone does. When it hits a lo\
atoll, its effect, such as Lessa (1964) described for Ulithi, can b
astrous. Damage is not as critical on high continental islands like
laita, for some sheltered areas always come through in fair shape.

The November, 1966, hurricane is a good example. Although it had
been raining for several days, no one expected a storm. It had been
gusty all day but, lulled by heavy rain on the thatch roof, I went to
sleep that evening in blissful ignorance. During the night the wind increased and occasionally heavy gusts shook the house. This partially
awakened me; but, not knowing any better, I quickly drifted off to
sleep again. About 4:00 A.M. I was jolted rudely and fully awake when
the entire roof collapsed. It is hard to be nonchalant in a wrecked house
in pitch darkness. Gathering up a couple of useless blankets, two children, and a box of kittens, we fled through the bush to a neighbor's
house and spent the rest of the morning cowering from the storm. After
the sun came up, as we watched trees crashing down and the roof
of the house next door blowing away, I finally realized that we were
seeing a hurricane from front-row seats. Heavy rains continued for
three days after the storm passed. The British agricultural experiment
center at Dala, twenty miles away across the island, recorded 15.54
inches of rain on Monday, November 14, the day of the hurricane,
with heavy rain also on Sunday and Tuesday. The meteorological station in Auki measured winds of 80-90 knots with gusts of 100.

It is not these objective facts but the effects of the hurricane on
human affairs that are important. Roughly one-fourth of the houses
in the hills were seriously damaged or destroyed. Trails were blocked
for days by fallen trees or branches, until passers-by cleared away the
rubble or cut a detour around large logs. Whole orchards of young palms
were flattened, and the work of propping them up took days. In the bush
many such economically valuable trees as the canarium almond, Malay
apple, and breadfruit were felled by the winds. Perhaps even more
significant damage than outright felling was the wind's stripping of the
immature nuts. It was almost a year before eating or drinking coconuts
were again plentiful, and copra production was practically nonexistent
in 1967 Canarium almond nuts (when dried, smoked, and stored in
bamboo joints) are a useful supplementary food and an important
trade item in the local markets. These are a seasonal crop, ripening in
August, September, and October. Informants estimated later that the
1967 crop was less than half the normal size, presumably as a result of
wind damage by the November, 1966, hurricane.

Heavy rains accompanying the hurricane also wreaked considerable
havoc. The Sasafa River flowing through the center of Baegu country

filled its valley from wall to wall. Flood stage reached some ten or fifteen feet over its normal bank level, and at places the channel was displaced as much as a hundred yards across the valley floor. Naturally, gardens in the inundated valley were completely washed away. In the hills, rock slides (*totole*) loosened by soaking swept down the steeper slopes, carrying away whole groves of trees and leaving the surface barren. Because of drainage problems people usually build their gardens on slopes. The torrents of rain simply eroded many of these gardens away during the week which the rains lasted. In other instances, hillside gardens with heavier and richer brown soil simply absorbed too much water, passed their equilibrium point (given an angle of repose based on dry conditions), and slumped into the valley.

Being subsistence rather than cash crop farmers, the hill people suffered more inconvenience than disaster. It takes four to six months before a new taro or sweet potato garden can start providing food, and people began clearing and replanting immediately. Since gardens are so widely scattered, not all were destroyed. Lucky farmers loaned planting stock to their less fortunate kinsmen and helped feed them in the interim. Most people supplemented these emergency rations with extensive foraging and gathering. The interior pith of the sago palm and cycad are edible, though not highly valued. Swamp taro (*Cyrtosperma* sp.) grows wild in moist places in the hills. There are wild yams, a species of giant grass with an edible pith, and numerous edible ferns, green herbs, and fungi. On the whole people can do rather well on wild foods, although it takes considerable effort.

Before leaving the subject entirely, it might be wise to summarize climate and weather conditions. Malaita's climate is a maritime tropical one, humid and warm.

Heavy rainfall is its most striking feature. In a one-year period (including the unforgettable month with the hurricane) I recorded 309.84 inches of rain. This would imply a monthly average rainfall of 25.82 inches. November, 1966, with its hurricane produced 56.12 inches. For normal months lacking hurricanes January, 1967, was the wettest with 36.53 inches, and September, 1967, the driest with only 13.02 inches of rain. The monthly average for the eleven "normal" months without hurricanes was 23.07 inches, implying that a typical yearly rainfall would be about 277 inches. Days with more than an inch of rain were routine, and I recorded twenty-one normal (non-hurricane) days with more than three inches of rainfall within twenty-four hours, besides the day of the hurricane itself when 15.54 inches of rain fell. There was some measurable precipitation on 322 days of the year, leaving only 43 totally dry days. Tables 1 and 2 give actual precipitation summaries.

TABLE 1. RAINFALL IN THE BAEGU AREA

Month and year	Rainfall in inches	Days of measurable precipitation	
		Yes	No
November, 1966	56.12	29	1
December	25.61	25	6
January, 1967	36.53	29	2
February	22.18	27	1
March	26.59	29	2
April	18.87	21	9
May	22.48	26	5
June	21.46	30	0
July	26.05	28	3
August	22.36	29	2
September	13.02	20	10
October	18.57	29	2
Yearly totals	309.84	322	43

Monthly average (including November, 1966, hurricane): 25.82
Monthly average for eleven "normal" months: 23.07
Estimated total for "normal" year: 276.84

Data were recorded at Ailali in northeastern interior Malaita. The weather station site was about two miles inland from the east coast at an elevation of about 500 feet.

TABLE 2. DAILY RAINFALL IN BAEGU COUNTRY DURING THE YEAR NOVEMBER, 1966-OCTOBER, 1967

Daily rainfall in inches	Days
More than 9″	3
8″	1
7″	0
6″	0
5″	3
4″	4
3″	10
2″	19
More than 1″	53
Less than 1″	229
No measurable precipitation	43

TABLE 3. MEAN AND EXTREME TEMPERATURES IN BAEGU COUNTRY

	Mean temperatures in °F.		
Month and year	Daily maximum	Daily minimum	Average daily range
November, 1966..................	75.10	61.00	14.10
December.......................	77.26	62.23	15.03
January, 1967....................	74.84	63.13	11.71
February.......................	75.64	65.54	10.10
March..........................	75.48	62.74	12.74
April...........................	77.67	61.00	16.67
May............................	76.94	62.19	14.75
June............................	74.93	62.50	12.43
July............................	74.26	62.26	12.00
August..........................	74.68	61.94	12.74
September.......................	77.03	61.40	15.63
October.........................	76.68	61.86	14.82
Yearly average................	75.88°F.	62.32°F.	13.56°F.

Highest maximum: 82°F. on December 9, 1966
Lowest maximum: 65°F. on July 12, 1967
Highest minimum: 66°F. on April 9, 1967
Lowest minimum: 58°F. on April 14, 1967

TABLE 4. PREVAILING WINDS IN THE BAEGU HILLS

	Days per month with wind blowing from a given direction									
Month	W	NW	N	NE	E	SE	S	SW	Calm	Variable
November, 1966.......	3	8	3	1	2	1	1	2	4	5
December............	0	5	0	11	10	1	0	1	3	0
January, 1967.........	1	16	1	0	2	1	4	1	5	0
February.............	1	17	0	3	0	0	1	1	5	0
March...............	1	6	1	1	1	9	1	0	9	2
April................	0	2	0	0	2	14	2	0	7	3
May.................	0	0	0	0	2	17	2	0	9	1
June.................	0	0	0	3	6	12	0	0	8	1
July.................	0	0	1	0	6	13	0	0	10	1
August..............	0	2	0	0	11	14	0	0	4	0
September...........	0	13	2	2	4	3	0	0	2	4
October.............	1	13	1	4	1	1	1	2	4	3
Yearly totals......	7	82	9	25	47	86	12	7	70	20

TABLE 5. WIND FORCE ALONG THE EASTERN COAST OF NORTHERN MALAITA

		Days per month with wind at a given force			
Month	Calm	Mild breeze	Small craft warning	Near gale force	Hurri- cane
November, 1966............	4	17	7	1	1
December................	3	25	3	0	0
January, 1967.............	5	23	2	1	0
February.................	5	19	4	0	0
March...................	9	16	4	2	0
April....................	7	15	8	0	0
May.....................	9	14	8	0	0
June....................	8	16	6	0	0
July.....................	10	10	9	2	0
August..................	4	17	8	2	0
September...............	2	22	6	0	0
October.................	8	22	1	0	0
Yearly totals..........	74	216	66	8	1

Chances for error are significant, since, in the absence of an anemometer, wind force was estimated according to the Beaufort scale by observations of the sea.

TABLE 6. CLOUD COVER OVER THE BAEGU HILLS

	Days per month having cloud formations obscuring the sky at given percentage levels			
Month	Overcast >90%	Broken 50-90%	Scattered 10-50%	Clear <10%
November, 1966...................	14	10	6	0
December.......................	13	8	10	0
January, 1967....................	17	7	7	0
February........................	14	9	5	0
March..........................	14	10	7	0
April...........................	13	9	6	2
May............................	13	9	9	0
June............................	10	14	6	0
July............................	10	17	4	0
August.........................	14	4	12	1
September......................	8	9	12	1
October........................	13	10	7	1
Yearly totals.................	153	116	91	5

Daily temperature variations at 1,000 feet elevation are marked; they are even greater higher in the mountains, where daily maxima are about the same due to vertical convection currents but fall off much more sharply at night. Daily temperature maxima averaged 75.9°F. and nightly minima averaged 62.3°F., for a mean daily temperature range of 13.6°F. change. As Table 3 shows, there was little seasonal variation.

In the hills, prevailing winds were nearly always from the sea, affected by the diurnal pattern of sea breezes. During the tradewind (ara) seasons, April through August, these were strong and veered to the southeast. In the rest of the year they were more unpredictable. Cloud cover was almost always present, particularly in the higher mountains. Tables 4, 5, and 6 give tabular data on prevailing winds and cloud cover on a monthly basis.

GEOLOGY

The whole of the Solomon Islands area is supposedly derived from an ancient Melanesian continent which may have at one time stretched from New Guinea to areas as far east as Fiji or Tonga, but which subsided beneath the western Pacific during the Mesozoic era (Freeman 1951:22-23). Hence the Solomon Islands, like most other land masses west of the so-called andesite line, possess geological structures and rock types more characteristic of continental areas than of the ocean basins proper. Lying near this andesite line that approximates the western border of the "true" Pacific basin as defined by oceanographers, the Solomons are part of the luridly named Pacific "Ring of Fire." Virtually encircling the Pacific basin from Antarctica to Alaska and from Peru to the Philippines, there are a series of active or recently dormant volcanoes lying in a series of crescentic arcs convex toward the basin. In these arcuate mountain regions vulcanism, thermal activity, and earthquakes occur frequently. Within the Solomons there are active volcanoes in Bougainville and Santa Cruz; Simbo in the New Georgia group and Savo off the northern coast of Guadalcanal are dormant but have hot springs and bubbling mud pools. In late 1968 a new submarine eruption occurred between the Russells and New Georgia.

Although Malaitans say earthquakes are common, and that there are times when even "the mountains dance," only one earth tremor happened while I was there (and I almost missed that). I woke up about dawn one morning in August; roosters were crowing, and everything seemed to be jiggling and lurching about in a nauseating way. My first thought was a pang of remorse that I had got myself such an awful hangover. It was only when the alarm clock bounced off a table onto the floor, and I had awakened sufficiently to remember that I had not had anything to drink the previous evening, that I realized it was an earthquake.

Most islands in the area have an igneous core or basement complex of basalt or granite. Overlaying this is a layer of soft sedimentary rock, mostly limestones, resulting from shallow submergence of land areas under warm seas during the Cenozoic Era. In Pleistocene and recent times crustal warping has caused some of this land to reemerge from the sea, and consequent or subsequent folding and faulting of the rock strata have created the characteristically mountainous continental islands one sees in the Solomons today.

The basic structural feature of Malaita is a linear central ridge, broken or separated by rolling hill country lying between Auki and the Kwai Harbor area on the east coast in the north-central part of the island. On both sides of the central ridge are flanking linear ridges and a few outlying hills and knolls. In the north, maximum elevation of this ridge is about 3,200 feet; in the south it rises to 4,700 feet. There is little evidence of any igneous activity at present on the island. Some Baegu folktales mention hot springs with water warm enough for cooking food, and in 1968 government prospecting parties tentatively confirmed the existence of thermal springs in the Kwara'ae bush country northeast of Auki. An aerial geophysical survey conducted under contract by a Swedish company in 1966 discovered a number of geomagnetic and gravitational anomalies in Malaita's mountainous interior. These anomalies sometimes indicate the presence of metallic mineral deposits, but all subsequent ground party exploration has failed to discover any metals in economically significant concentrations.

According to geological survey reports, Malaita has a basaltic intrusive core, but this core is not plainly evident in northern Malaita. I found few basaltic outcrops, but both fine and coarse-grained basalt occur as pebbles or cobbles in stream beds.

Overlying the basaltic core at the northern end of Malaita are strata of sedimentary rock. The dominant surface rock is a poor quality, easily broken, soft limestone. It becomes extremely slippery when wet — part of the island's conspiracy to make me look ludicrous by slipping and falling constantly. ("Soapstone" is the rural American folk name for rock of this sort.) It is rich in fossils indistinguishable from living marine forms of the present lagoon and barrier reef offshore. Fossilized shells of the giant clam (*Tridacna* sp.) are particularly abundant. Large chert nodules are common in the limestone, occurring in three color forms: red, blue-black, and white.

All the limestone strata appear to be relatively water soluble. Streams frequently go underground, popping into and out of the rock, and springs are common. In level areas there are many sinkholes with rock shelters and shallow caverns in the hills. Since it is so soft, almost rotten, this limestone is subject to fractures, slumps, slides, and rock-falls. The entire eastern face of the central ridge in the north, along the left bank of the Sasafa River before it curves eastward to the sea, has slumped, leaving an almost sheer escarpment rising precipitously some 2,000 feet from the river valley to the crest of the ridge.

Malaitan hydrology is characteristic of youthful drainage patterns. There are thousands of small streams, rivulets, and springs. These join into five large river systems in the Baegu area (Map 4). The four that mark the borders of Baegu territory (the Kwainafala, Taeloa, Ataa, and Takwea) flow fairly directly from the central ridge to the sea. The Sasafa runs generally northward parallel to the dividing ridge, then bends sharply eastward emptying into the sea at Urasi Cove. All of these streams have a steep gradient in their upper reaches. Rapids, cascades, and waterfalls are commonplace; the water is clean, very clear, cool, and swift flowing. In some places it has cut steep limestone cliffs or canyons.

Plate 5. Kwanafia, Mikaila, Singiala, and Lebefiu in the Sasafa River gorge.

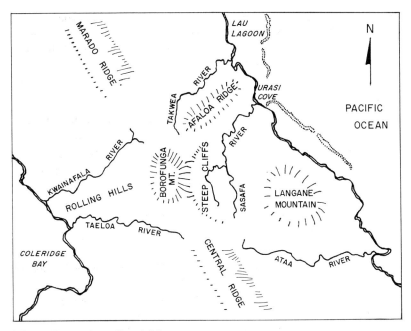

Map 4. Baegu Area Sketch Map

In the lower reaches rivers are slower and deeper. Here they are brackish and subject to tidal ebb and flow, with mangrove swamps near their mouths. One can pole or paddle a canoe for a quarter mile or so upstream, and the area looks the way a classic tropical jungle is supposed to look.

Predictably, given the sudden change from steep to level stream gradients, there are deep alluvial deposits of gravel, sand, and mud near the river mouths. In places there are soft shale strata and some loosely compacted conglomerate. The coastal plain itself is extremely narrow, if it exists at all. Near the beach it is sandy or rocky, and it tends to be swampy or muddy along the river valleys.

The people understand their local soils well and have preferred types for different uses. Sandy coastal soil is best for yam gardens or coconut plantations. Inland soils appear to be of three types: wet black (or brown), dry black, and red. The wet black soil is too heavy and poorly drained for gardens, but some taro is grown there. This type of soil is largely confined to valley bottoms and the feet of slopes. Dry black (or brown) soil, well-drained and friable, is easily worked and makes the preferred garden site. Red soil (possibly lateritic) does not absorb water well, has a rapid surface runoff, and forms a hard crust. Villages or hamlets are built on red soil, because it is firm, does not (because of the hardpan) hold water, and is easy to keep brushed clean. Because of the heavy rainfall, "soil" is perhaps a euphemism; most of the time the surface of Malaita is mud.

VEGETATION

As in all high continental islands there are several rather distinct vegetational zones, each having its own unique floral assemblage. The coastal biome, of very shallow depth, appears in two facies. One is a sandy phase where there is a definite beach. Here pandanus, Barringtonia, coconuts, and pulpy vines predominate. In the swampy phase near river mouths mangroves grow directly on the coast, with sago palms near the brackish or fresh water further inland. The Indian almond or Pacific chestnut (*Terminalia* sp.), or in Baegu *alite,* grows in drier areas near the coast.

The lower slopes, up to about 2,000-2,500 feet, bear a hardwood forest. Along the rivers and in areas of the hills not intensively cultivated there is a primary rain forest of banyans, canarium almonds, and Indo-Malayan hardwoods. Rain forest groves are relatively free from undergrowth, although strangler figs and aerophytes appear on the trees. Where people have cleared the hardwood forest for gardening (and this includes most of the island) a dense, secondary bush forest develops. This is an almost impassable tangle of fast-growing softwoods, woody shrubs, ferns, and annual weeds. At higher elevations bamboo is common.

At altitudes somewhere above 2,500 feet, where cumulus clouds block the sunlight almost every day, there are small patches resembling moss forest. Cycads or tree ferns (*kwae*) are the dominant tall plant, and a dense carpet of mosses, lichens, and liverworts covers the ground to a depth of two to four inches.

ANIMAL LIFE

Like most Pacific islands, Malaita has a somewhat impoverished fauna. Mammals are notable in their scarcity. Man himself introduced the domestic pig and dog, and nowadays there are European cats. The only native mammals are the woolly cuscus opossum (*futo*), the giant rat *Mus rex* (*furingale*), a small wood rat (*kiki*), the giant fruit-eating bat or flying fox (*sakwalo*), and several varieties of smaller insectivorous bats (*tarawedi*). There are dugong (*ie tikwa*) in the mangrove swamps, and porpoises (*kiriau*) sometimes enter the lagoon.

Birds appear in great abundance and variety. Man introduced the domestic jungle fowl or chicken, and some people now keep muscovy ducks. Malaitans capture and keep as pets several species of parrots, sulphur-crested cockatoos, and owls. Almost every family of bird life is represented here, according to Ernst Mayr's (1931:1-26) survey of the Malaitan bird population. A few species are sacred or figure prominently in myth. The sea eagle (*no aabu*), hornbill (*bina*), and frigate bird (*kaule*) are sacred to one group or another and recur as art motifs. Terns (*anakwe*) and a small yellow-breasted sunbird (*diki*) are favorite characters in legend. The migrant New Zealand cuckoo (*korokoro*) is an omen of death or disaster.

Reptiles and amphibians are common, but luckily noxious species of these classes are rare. Crocodiles (*kwasa*) were once abundant in the rivers, but they have been so intensively hunted for their hides that they are now almost extinct. There are venomous sea snakes and one poisonous land snake (*baekwa i tolo*) that is probably a member of the krait family (neurotoxic). Fortunately its bite is not usually fatal, inducing a local paralysis that passes after a week or so. The arboreal Pacific tree boa (*tafo*) is a common intruder in houses. Although it steals eggs, it also is a rat killer and is sacred to some clans. Another large ground-dwelling brown carpet-snake (*loi*) is also semi-sacred. People do not usually kill snakes, since they believe they are in communication with the ancestral spirits. There are some large monitor lizards (two feet in length) and some good-sized pseudo-iguanas. Skinks and geckos are ubiquitous. My field notes and books are literally peppered with gecko droppings. Toads, frogs, and peepers occur in about twelve varieties from tiny dime-sized tree frogs to giant six-inch toads.

Fishes and aquatic invertebrates are typical of the Australian version of the Indo-Pacific marine faunal region. Freshwater species are not numerous. In brackish parts near the sea, there are mudskippers (*akwakwa*) and mangrove crabs (*karu*), and lagoon species come upstream with the tide. I recorded eight species of freshwater teleost fishes, none exceeding six or eight inches, and most rather smaller. River eels do reach a length of three feet and are delicious when smoked. Coconut crabs (*karu*) are not common, but some are caught in the lowlands. Prawns and edible snails live in even the smallest streams.

Arthropods, particularly insects, are plentiful to say the least. There are centipedes and scorpions, but their stings are more painful than dangerous. Spiders reach an appalling size; the *lakwa*, with a leg-spread diameter of six inches, spins webs up to eight feet across in the forest. Large, hairy, wolf-spiders that seem to come with any house reach a size of four inches. All the common orders of insects are present. Butterflies and moths (*bebi*) are spectacular. The black, white, and yellow Victoria butterfly is the world's largest (nine-inch wing span); the blue or green birdwing butterflies are among the world's most beautiful.

Children tie them on strings to use as toys. Large black beetles up to four inches long occur. Ants and termites are unbelievably aggressive, moving into a new house as soon as it is built. Malaitan ants continually outsmarted me, finding a way to get into every conceivable food container. Flies are a ubiquitous nuisance. The anopheles mosquito is unfortunately all too common, and vivax malaria is endemic. Lice are simply a fact of life, and people spend hours picking each other's hair.

HEALTH PROBLEMS

As far as man is concerned, microorganisms and their associated pathologies may be the most significant portion of the natural environment. Malaria, usually the vivax variety, is something everyone in the hills has had, and people simply learn to live with it. Nearly all children have enlarged spleens. Yaws was once a common disease, but since the World Health Organization's yaws eradiction campaign in Malaita in 1958, it is rare there. There is some leprosy, but it is largely under control, and the Anglican Melanesian Mission runs a leprosarium at Fauabu on the west coast.

Malaitans seem to have an undue susceptibility to respiratory diseases. Children always have runny noses, and colds are virulent among adults. Tuberculosis is the Protectorate's second major health problem (after malaria). Active TB is common among hill populations but rarer in the more populous coastal villages, where atypical or more benign forms of the disease may generate some immunity or resistance. Pneumonia, influenza, and related diseases are a recurrent, serious health threat. Major epidemics occur every few years and are greatly feared. In 1966 and 1971 epidemics of this sort killed hundreds of Malaitan hill people. People fear these epidemics but are resigned to them, interpreting them as afflictions caused by the anger of the ancestral spirits.

Diseases caused by poor hygiene or waste disposal problems are also potential killers, but they affect primarily the very young and very old. Dysentery is common, particularly among infants and young children who crawl about and are not exactly exemplars of personal cleanliness. It kills frequently enough so that parents worry if their children show symptoms of diarrhea. Dysentery can, and does, attack people of any age, but it is less apt to be fatal in otherwise healthy adults. Typhoid fever may well be present in Malaita, but I did not have either the experience or the clinical facilities to make diagnoses separating it from other febrile diseases exhibiting diarrhea. Hepatitis may also occur, but theoretically it should not be a problem for people who have grown up in the area.

Bad eye infections are another all too common health problem
the hills. House interiors are tightly enclosed and smoky from the fi
kept smoldering inside. Smoke irritates the eye membranes, and ii
rubbed with dirty hands, infections naturally result. Once started, these
infections seem highly contagious and work their way through an entire
residential group. During the canarium almond season (August through
October) the fly population in the hamlets explodes, attracted by the
sticky, sweet hulls of the nuts that accumulate by the thousands where
people are shelling them. The incidence of eye infections goes up
markedly at this time, spread from one person to another by the flies.

Fungus infections are routine. Nearly everyone in Malaita had a few
signs of tinea versicolor. This, on brown skins, may be unsightly, but it
does no serious harm. Tinea imbricata affects a few people to a marked
degree. These are usually the more slovenly members of the population,
who make a fetish of wearing too many European clothes.

The head louse population is astronomical, but the people do not
worry about them. (Typhus does not seem to occur in Malaita.) Some
children do develop bad cases of scabies, sometimes resulting in nasty
secondary infections.

As among all active agricultural peoples, traumatic injuries occur.
People are always cutting themselves, because they do so much forest
clearing and have such a cavalier attitude toward knives and axes. In
Malaita's hot, humid, and muddy conditions, cuts or scratches that are
not carefully cleaned and treated can develop into tropical ulcers.
These are almost impossible to cure, since a layer of saprophytic organisms protects the bacteria causing the basic infections. Most adults
show scars from childhood ulcers. Burns often happen at night, because
people sleep on the ground next to a fire for warmth. Shortly before
I arrived in 1966, an adolescent girl died from burns received by rolling
into the coals while asleep. Sprains and broken bones are fairly rare,
since the hill people tend to be graceful, agile, and in good condition.

If, as Wallace (1961:174) suggests, cultural patterns affect the expression of mental disorders, it is perhaps futile to look for mental illness as such. As in all human populations, there were a few cases of
mental deficiency. I knew of two retarded Baegu children and of three
cases of obvious senile dementia. There was a single mute woman in
the village nearest where I lived. These unfortunates do not attract
much attention. People are decently compassionate, feeding and caring
for them without making a fuss, protecting them from injury, and acting as if the condition were nothing unusual.

There is a more or less conventional manifestation of spirit possession.
Either men or women can go into a withdrawn state and deliver oracu-
lar pronouncements. The community assumes that in these cases it is

the ancestral spirits (*akalo*) who are speaking through the voice of the possessed one.

Adolescent girls and young women show a pattern of hysterical symptoms called *babatana*. In classic cases, they become weepy and apt to faint, they babble and walk in their sleep, and they run away from their homes to wander in the bush. These seizures are said to occur during the full moon. The consensus of opinion is that *babatana* results from love magic performed by a man who has seen the girl at market or in some other public gathering and who desires her.

In the hill villages, there were few other deviant or abnormal persons. There was one middle-aged woman living in a Christian village near the road on the west coast. She was obviously seriously disturbed, wandering onto the road and the runway of the Gwaunaru'u airstrip oblivious to traffic, and unable to speak coherently. There is no specific word for this condition, however; she was simply described as *oewania*, which also means stupid, vulgar, or common. One pagan man spent time in the mental hospital on Guadalcanal after police apprehended him when he ran through several mountain hamlets chopping down coconuts and areca palms (a classic symptom used by the Baegu to define serious mental or emotional abnormality).

The Baegu recognize persistent bad temper as something out of the ordinary. People who are frequently or unreasonably angry are said to have "dark minds" (*gwauna bobora*), literally "a black head." Since the traditional Malaitan seat of emotions is the gut, this is probably a post-contact innovation. Once, after I had blown up and roundly cursed an entire village and most of Malaita for a series of trivial annoyances that in a field situation seemed magnified into near disasters, a would-be peacemaker sought to ease things by remarking that, after all, "Malaitans sometimes have dark minds, too." When the implications of the "too" finally got through to me, a saving sense of the ridiculous took over. In traditional times before British pacification, ungoverned bad temper was characteristic of the *ramo*, a semiberserk war leader.

Otherwise, Malaitan hill society was a tolerant one, defining harmless neuroses and idiosyncracies within the range of "normal" behavior. Those people who were in fact deficient or disturbed were tolerated and cared for within a routine social context. It would seem, as Bruner (1968) contends, that traditional non-Western peoples may have a more than adequate means of dealing with mental or nervous problems by extending the range of their definition of "acceptable" behavior by providing appropriate roles for potential deviants, and by handling truly serious cases with as little fanfare as possible.

4. The Baegu People

The blessings of Western civilization, such as they are, came late to the Solomon Islands and even later to Malaita. Today Malaita is almost unique among Pacific islands outside the interior vastness of New Guinea in that it has a significant pagan population still trying to maintain a traditional way of life. There are, to be sure, pagan groups in the Santa Cruz region, perhaps some quasi-pagans on the Weather Coast (south) of Guadalcanal, and in the New Hebrides. What distinguishes the Malaitan pagans is, first, that there are so many of them; and, second, that they so consciously reject so much of Western civilization.

Along with Malaitan prejudice against the West, there has been a consistent Western prejudice against Malaitans. Partly the result of the historical accidents of early contacts, there may well be a degree of latent racial prejudice involved, too, since Melanesians are dark-skinned people very unlike the smiling Polynesians so long idolized by ethnographers and romantic novelists alike.

But, even by general Melanesian or Solomon Island standards, Malaitans have had a bad reputation. When European control first began, Malaita was seething with wars and feuds. First ritual, then epicurean cannibalism developed to exaggerated proportions. These, following the pattern that developed in Fiji and elsewhere, were no doubt partly the result of early European trading activities. Labor recruiters and traders seeking quick profits had distributed rifles and shotguns to islanders. These facilitated warfare, made human life cheap, and created a class of professional bounty hunters. Whatever the causes, the pacification of Malaita was a difficult process, and British officials still remain somewhat suspicious of Malaitans.

They share this attitude with other Solomon Islanders. Malaitans working on other islands as plantation hands, houseboys, or stevedores are often taciturn toward outsiders, have a fierce pride, and adhere to a surprising degree to their own unique, local customs. Their sexual puritanism, the readiness with which they react to insults or perceived improprieties, and the vigor they show in pursuing quarrels and vengeance do not endear them to other Melanesians who tend to regard Malaitamen as gratuitous troublemakers.

More or less inevitably, I was influenced by these attitudes. I need hardly add, I hope, that in time I came to admire and even to love the Malaitan people.

RACE

Although very little proof is yet available, the ancient ancestors of the Malaitans, like those of most Pacific islanders, came ultimately from southern and eastern Asia. Coon's theory of an Australoid racial stock going back to the Middle Pleistocene and a population like that of the Pithecanthropines (*Homo erectus*) of Java suggests that mainland and insular Southeast Asia, Australia, and parts of Melanesia were once populated by this genetic strain. The Aitape fossil from the northern coast of New Guinea and early Australian skeletal discoveries (Keilor, Cohuna) make this idea a plausible one (Coon 1962:371-427). Once established in New Guinea and adjacent island Melanesia, this early population evolved into a distinctive local race, the Melanesian-Papuan. "Local race" is here used in the sense that Garn (1961:18-20) uses it, as opposed to wider geographic race or microgeographic population. The relationship of Melanesians to neighboring populations in Indonesia, Australia, Polynesia, and Micronesia are at present poorly understood.

So far as Malaitans are concerned, they are best described as a population with a highly variable phenotype. They are beautiful people — handsome, well-built, strong, and graceful. Their brown skins vary from a rich chocolate to tawny. Most are clearly darker than Polynesian groups. On the other hand, they are not nearly as dark as people of the Western Solomons and Bougainville, whom even Malaitans call "black men." Partial depigmentation occurs in a few individuals. These have light tan skins, blond hair, and brown or blue eyes, but they are definitely not albinos. I knew two of these people, a man of about forty and an adolescent girl. They lived about fifteen miles apart and, as far as I know, were not related. People hotly denied that they were racial hybrids.

Most Malaitans have dark brown or black bushy hair, but again

THE BAEGU PEOPLE   47

both texture and color vary. Hair form is sometimes wavy rather than frizzled. Hair color ranges from a reddish blond to a dark ebony black. Some dandies peroxide their hair, and children are often bleached blond by sun and sea-water, but a natural reddish-blond occurs even in adults. Pattern balding is common among middle-aged and even some young men, although it is not as frequent as in European populations. Body hair is also highly variable. Most men have smooth skins, but others grow respectable beards or have relatively hairy arms, backs, legs, or chests.

Physiognomy and casual somatotyping are certainly not accurate scientific techniques, but it is possible to make impressionistic descriptions of Malaitans' appearances. Although not as short as Negritos (Oceanic or otherwise), most Malaitans are shorter than average European or American populations. I know only three men as tall as I (six feet, one inch), and my impression is that usual male heights run between five feet, three inches and five feet, nine inches. Relatively robust or stocky constitutions are more common among coastal populations; hill people tend to be leaner and more gracile. In general facial appearance, Malaitans have finer features than most other island Melanesians. If one cares to amuse himself by looking for racial types, it is possible to pick out individuals that could pass as Papuans (very fuzzy-haired, with Negroid features), Polynesians (wavy hair and even finer features), or Australian aborigines (wavy hair, pattern balding, heavy brow ridges and sloping foreheads).

LANGUAGE

All Malaitan languages are members of the Malayo-Polynesian family of the Austronesian linguistic phylum. Whether or not "Melanesian" as a whole is a valid linguistic category of equivalent taxonomic rank with "Polynesian" or other subunits, Malaitan languages together with languages of San Cristobal, Guadalcanal, Santa Isabel, and the Florida Islands form a Southeastern Solomons branch of related Melanesian languages. Capell (1954:82-93) speaks of a Melanesian language family, while Grace (1959) and Dyen (1965) do not treat Melanesian as a single comparative linguistic unit. My own purely subjective impression, based on simply listening to other languages, is that Malaitan languages have more in common with Fijian or even Polynesian languages than they have with Melanesian languages in other parts of the Solomon Islands.

All Malaitan languages are clearly related, and diversity is not nearly as great as earlier descriptions and classifications indicate. In particular, dialect differences were overemphasized, and what are in reality dialects of a single language (measured either lexicostatistically or simply in terms of whether or not people understand one another) were promoted to independent language status. Hogbin (1939:16) pointed out that northern Malaitan dialects were precisely that, but many expatriates in the Solomons continue to talk of eighteen or twenty "languages" on Malaita.

Lexicostatistical data and glottochronological interpretation are probably not very reliable for Malaita. Word play is common, with metathesis (inversion of sound sequences) a source of humor and a sign of cleverness. Word-tabooing is widespread, based on the principle that sounds resembling the names of ancestral spirits or used in certain ritual contexts should not be used in common speech (Keesing and Fifi'i 1969:159).

Using rather imprecise standards of whether or not people understand each other, there are between four and eight languages in Malaita (Map 5). Going from north to south, there is a single Northern Malaitan language covering the northern quarter of the island. Its

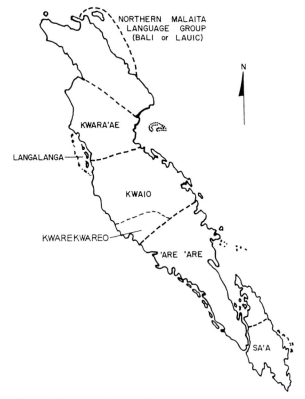

Map 5. Linguistic Map of Malaita

dialects are Lau, Toabaita, Baelelea, Baegu, and possibly Fataleka, which some ethnographers believe to be a separate, albeit closely related language. There is no local name for this language, but Murdock (1964:120) calls it Lauic, and some members of the government call it Bali, as Russell (1950:3) labeled it. *Bali* means literally "side," and in this context it means "us" as opposed to "them." Next to the south, and again extending clear across the island, is the Kwara'ae language. Langalanga, spoken by the lagoon people along the west coast, is said to be quite different from Kwara'ae of the neighboring mainland. Farther south are a number of Kwaio dialects, again a single independent language. Kwarekwareo may be a Kwaio dialect or a language in its own right. In the far south are 'Are'Are and Sa'a, whose precise relationship is unknown. On Maramasike Island or Little Mala there is a colony that speaks the Lau dialect of northern Malaita.

Northern Malaitan (Map 6) is a cluster of several dialects recognized as such by the people themselves. The best-known of these is Lau, spoken by the coastal and artificial island dwellers of the lagoon on the east coast. Ivens (1930) has described Lau in considerable detail, and both the New Testament and the Anglican Book of Common Prayer

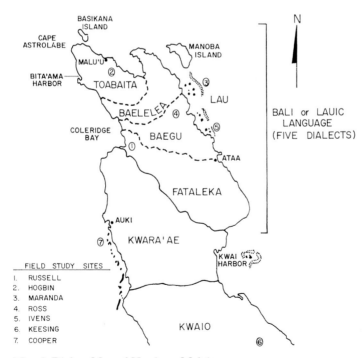

Map 6. Dialect Map of Northern Malaita

have been translated into that language. Besides Lau, the other recognized dialects are named after characteristics or peculiar speech habits of the users. Toabaita, near Cape Astrolabe and the village of Malu'u where Hogbin worked, means "big (or important) people," the name being derived from the fact that these people, particularly those around Bita'ama village, were traditionally the suppliers of porpoise teeth widely used as a form of money (Hogbin 1939:2). Baelelea, spoken in the far northeast of the mainland, comes from the native speakers' habit of reduplicating the word "to go" (*le-le-lea*). *Bae* means "to speak" or "to say." The Baegu dialect, extending through the hills all the way across the island, has a more complex derivation for its name. The Baegu language makes frequent use of a particle *gu*, signifying among other things "some" or "of something." Thus *lau gu* is "more" or "also," and *nao gu* means "nothing." *Gu* occurs frequently in normal speech, but it is remarkable in one context. There is no Northern Malaitan word for "hello," and people customarily greet passers-by by asking them, "Where are you going?" The Baegu, a hill people considered taciturn even by other northern Malaitans, according to local stereotypes usually respond "*nao gu*," meaning "nowhere" or really "I do not wish to say." Hence, to their northern Malaitan neighbors, they are the people who say "*gu*" all the time. Fataleka, the southernmost dialect (or perhaps an independent language) of the Northern Malaitan group, derives its name from the fact that their words for "to say" and "to go" are aberrant. In the Fataleka dialect, "to say" (*bae*) becomes *fata*, and "to go" (*lea*) becomes *leka*.

Linguistic quirks are widely understood, and people identify one another by reference to speech habits. These five major dialects are the most common classificatory scheme, but I should add that even subtler distinctions exist, and people can if necessary make even finer identifications by means of speech habits that appear as isoglosses and dialectic clines.

There is enough trade and intermarriage around the area so that people understand and recognize other dialects. When speakers of different dialects interact, each for convenience uses his own dialect but understands the other's. In describing the interaction, however, Malaitans will say, "I do not talk his dialect." As it came out in Pidgin English, this remark caused early European observers to believe that different, mutually incomprehensible languages were involved.

Although all the Northern Malaitan dialects share essentially the same grammar, there are regular phonological and vocabulary differences between dialects that go beyond the peculiarities leading to their names. An initial position /s/ phoneme in Baegu for example is sometimes /h/ in Toabaita and Lau. Baegu makes far less use of the glottal stop /ʔ/ than do other Malaitan languages or dialects. Vocabularies differ for no apparent reason, with different dialects using completely unrelated forms. "To see," for example, is *rikia* in Lau but *suai* in Baegu.

Fortunately for ethnographers. Baegu is a relatively easy language to learn. Its phonology with few exceptions is not difficult for Indo-Europeans. Initial position for the nasal /ng/ phoneme and for glottal stops /ʔ/ cause some difficulty, but initial glottal stops are frequently phonemically redundant with the following vowel length being shortened. Vowel length itself is sometimes phonemic. Voiced consonantal stops /b/, /d/, and /g/ are prenasalized in Baegu, but this too comes easily with practice. Appendix A and Figure 3 give a more detailed description of Baegu phonology.

Figure 3. Schematic Paradigm of Baegu Phonology

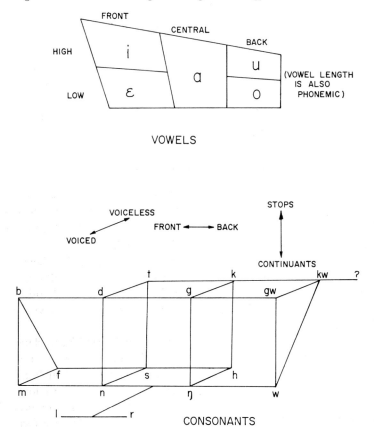

Word order in formal speech is a standard subject–verb–object–indirect object sequence, but in colloquial or informal speech (perhaps as a passive transformation) this can be changed to an object–indirect object–direction construction. Thus a request for tobacco, "Give me some tobacco," is in formal usage *'oe o falea firi fuaku,* but becomes an informal *firi aku mai* (Figure 4).

Figure 4. Baegu Word Order Diagram

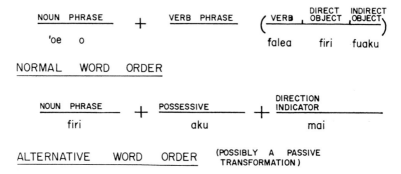

Where I cite Baegu words or names, I use the orthography described in Appendix A. For most names of peoples or places I have used the Baegu form. The exceptions to this result from the Protectorate government's Commission on Geographic Names, which specifies standard forms for official usage.

THE RUDIMENTS OF SOCIAL ORGANIZATION

As this is the heart of the matter, there is no need to dwell on social organization at this time. All that is needed now is to sketch a preliminary outline, so that new ideas or themes can be fitted into a generally appropriate context as they are introduced.

The Baegu live in the hills of northern Malaita, making their living as farmers. They practice a form of slash-and-burn horticulture, growing primarily taro and sweet potatoes. Settlements are small and widely dispersed through the forest. Most hamlets contain only a few nuclear families.

Baegu society is divided into large, named, patrilineal clans, the biggest having several hundred members. These clans claim land ownership rights over districts bearing the clan names. Although agnatic ideology is important in land litigation, and is indeed the idiom used for discussing or explaining most social relations, people emphatically recognize cognatic rights and obligations. Bilateral kindreds form the effective groups at weddings and funerals, and people adamantly insist that both patrilineal *and* matrilineal descendants have a right to use ancestral land. At the same time, people recognize local or neighborhood groups that may or may not be kinsmen. They are usually grouped around and led by an important man who, in typically Melanesian Big Man fashion, has formidable economic and political power. Formal friendships, *kwaimani,* join trading and social partners.

Veneration of ancestral spirits by means of pig sacrifice and observance of a strict taboo system is the essence of Baegu religion. Religious life focuses about spectacular mortuary feasts honoring the ghosts of the dead and is in accordance with the agnatic ideology accompanying lineage and clan organization.

BAEGU PERSONALITY

The Baegu, like other Malaitan hill people, are in the eyes of their neighbors (both brown and white) taciturn or even sullen. Other Solomon Islanders, including even the coastal people of Malaita itself, stereotype the hill people as humorless and belligerent. This is not so.

Personality description is at best an imprecise affair. There are semi-objective tests such as the Rohrschach or TAT, but I did not have access to any of these while in the field. My impressions of Baegu personality are totally and unashamedly subjective.

Ever since "Culture and Personality" was a gleam in the eye of Kardiner or Sapir, anthropologists of that persuasion have had a difficult time defining what they are trying to describe. We all recognize that a person has a personality, but what does a culture (that exists only in the mind anyway) have? To escape from this dilemma and to enable themselves to describe a culture in psychological terms that can be related to the individual personality, Culture and Personality theorists have invented the concepts of basic and modal personality. Basic personality has only a limited usefulness, for it is modeled after the mathematical concept of a mean or average, and average people do not really exist. Modal personality is a more satisfactory tool. Its starting point is the statistical idea of mode, also a measure of central tendency but one defined as the maximum value of a distribution curve rather than the center of gravity of the area under the curve. In simple English, mode is the single value that occurs most often.

A given society will have a constellation of modal personality traits — that is, those traits that are characteristic of the largest number of people in the society or that are the most popular. The beauty of this concept is that as a theoretical statement it can accommodate deviant but recognized roles. There can, for example, be secondary modes representing personality traits shared by a minority of individuals, who may still be of high repute — such as priests or warriors — even though they differ from the majority of the society (Figure 5).

The modal personality for Baegu men is the Good Man, solid and respected but not ostentatious or pushy. He is pleasant and kind, yet not extroverted or ambitious. These people respect one another's privacy and adhere to a general live-and-let-live personal philosophy. They are hard-working and honest. Baegu men tend to be rather sensitive, intensely aware of their environment, and not always stoic about showing pain or sorrow. They complain when hurt, weep or brood when friends or relatives die, and openly love children. They are a kind and

Figure 5. Basic and Modal Personality

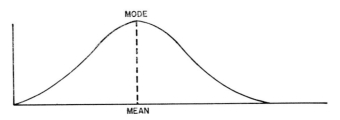

Modal and basic personalities would be the same in a perfect normal distribution.

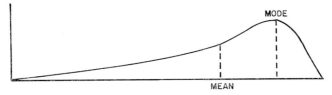

Modal and basic personalities differ if character traits are asymmetrically distributed. Basic personality is related to the idea of a mean or center of gravity of the area under the distribution curve. Modal personality uses the idea of a mode or most frequent single value.

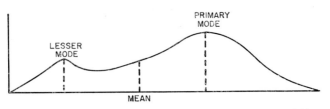

Modal personality constructs can account for the coexistence within a single population of deviant but acceptable personality types; basic personality constructs cannot.

hospitable people. Travelers or visitors with valid credentials are enter-
tained freely; they consider the European custom of hotels, where one
pays for board and lodging, to be barbarous. But along with this comes
fear and suspicion of strangers whose business they do not understand,
or of innovations.

There are of course variants or secondary modes. Leaders, real or
potential Big Men, are like Good Men only more so. These are ambitious people who want to dominate. They are hospitable and generous
to a fault. They are much more outgoing: loving activity, definitely
extroverted, and addicted to display. These leaders as dominant persons
can be highly charismatic. Along with these traits, there is both less
demand for privacy and less fear of strangers.

Priests tend to be more stable. Quiet, dignified, even-tempered, and
knowledgeable, they are almost scholarly in comportment. Priests are
elected by consensus, one of the criteria being that they behave as
priests are supposed to behave. Exceptions occur, of course.

War leaders (ramo) no longer exist, but people still recognize the
personality type. These men are wilder, have quick tempers, and are
said to be immune to pain or fatigue and to show no fear of danger
in battle. People cheat a little here, wearing magical belts said to make
warriors invulnerable. Physically, war leaders tend to be domineering
mesomorphs.

Then, too, there is the less than common man (wane oewania).
These unfortunate souls tend to be lazy, dirty, and ignorant. The dis-
reputable few who bear this stigma are quiet, unaggressive, and withdrawn.

Modal personality for Baegu women changes through time. Girls are
supposed to be shy, graceful, and very modest. Most of them are rather
giggly. Married women ought to be modest and hard-working. Older
women, roughly those past menopause, become much more extroverted;
they are openly friendly and mildly bossy. These did not hesitate to order
me around or to scold me if I annoyed or insulted them.

Baegu children are a joy. Infants are constantly fondled and nur-
tured, but as they grow older they become self-sufficient and spend
most of their time in juvenile play groups. A few are spoiled, but most
are quiet and well-behaved, leaving adults alone. They obey well, but
this is at least partly because no unreasonable demands are made of
them.

From my descriptions, the Baegu appear as paragons of virtue, and
there remains the problem of why they have such a bad reputation
throughout the Solomons. One important factor is that they are terribly
afraid of making fools of themselves. They are conservative and avoid

new things they do not understand. They are somewhat suspicious and fear strangers, appearing in these situations to be sullen and uncommunicative. When confronted with a novel situation where they feel insecure, their response (acting on Lincoln's aphorism that it is better to remain quiet and be thought a fool than to speak and remove all doubt) is to become taciturn.

Exacerbating this condition is the concept of *tolo* prevalent in northern Malaita. The Lau people of the east coast lagoon area are sophisticated, receptive to innovations, and able to move with ease in business with strangers, including Europeans. The bush people are not. Hence, in the Lau dialect, anything that is inferior or stupid is labeled *tolo* or "hill-like." The Baegu and other hill people are sensitive to this, and they take great pains to avoid ridicule. I should add that there is also a certain amount of reverse snobbery; hill people describe themselves as much more virtuous, hard-working, and honest than the coastal folk.

When Malaita men from the hills leave their island to work in town or on plantations, they are ill at ease because, having had little contact with European or other Melanesian ways, they do not fully understand their novel situations or roles. Instead, they seek to excel and still keep their self-respect in traditional roles as hillmen and warriors. Even quiet, unassuming chaps become flamboyant when among their own kind in the towns. They are in effect assuming warrior (*ramo*) personality traits. Men put fern fronds in their hair, in Baegu country the traditional badge of having recently killed a man. They carry a bushknife, club, or gun with them constantly. They become loud and truculent, quick to anger. Because they insist so zealously on maintaining traditional standards of conduct, they are constantly involved in quarrels and court cases. Most of this violence involves women or traditional curses. I was in Honiara, the capital city on Guadalcanal, for only one brief week in 1968. During that time the police arrested a Baelelea man who had killed a Langalanga man for patting the first's "sister" (to us, a parallel cousin) on the rump at the Honiara market, and two Malaitamen working on a plantation (one Kwaio and the other Baegu) drew long jail sentences for severely mauling a fellow from the western Solomons who had told them to "eat shit," a grievous offense in traditional Malaitan terms.

HISTORY OF CONTACT

European contact began with Alvaro de Mendaña's expedition from Peru in 1568. Although Mendaña was in some ways remarkably humane for a sixteenth-century Spanish gentleman, his forces fought with

Melanesians wherever they landed. This was the first of a long history of excesses, warfare, and cruelty. Whalers and traders put into Melanesian ports, taking what they wanted by force. The worst of the blackbirding labor recruiters literally kidnapped, or recruited with lies, Melanesians for forced labor in Queensland or Fiji. Predictably, Solomon Islanders responded with violence, killing even well-intentioned European visitors. Eventually the eastward bulge of northern Malaita came to be called Cape Arsacides, or Cape of the Assassins.

To put things into a more accurate perspective, the situation was not uniformly this bad. Some labor recruiters were decent and honest, treating Melanesian workers kindly, and some Melanesians voluntarily returned for second periods of indentured service. On the other side, one castaway white sailor lived peacefully for more than a decade among the Lau people of northeastern Malaita (Ivens 1930:53).

Missionary activity began in earnest during the late nineteenth century. Early Anglican and Roman Catholic missionaries, Bishop Patteson and Bishop Epalle, were martyred, but the missions kept on trying (C. Fox 1967:28-32). Toward the end of the century, Christianity arrived in Malaita. Hogbin (1939:174) reports that native South Seas Evangelical Mission adherents, who had been converted to fundamentalist Protestant Christianity while working as indentured laborers overseas, began proselytizing in northern Malaita before the turn of the century. The Roman Catholic Marist fathers established a mission in Auki on the west coast in 1909 (Keesing 1965:18). The Melanesian Mission of the Anglican Communion has had notable successes since the 1890's in northern Malaita (C. Fox 1967:28), particularly around its hospital at Fau'abu in the northwest, and near Sulufou in the Lau Lagoon on the east coast. In recent decades, Seventh Day Adventists and Jehovah's Witnesses have begun work throughout Malaita.

Governmental control for the Solomon Islands began only in 1893 with the United Kingdom's proclamation of a British Solomon Islands Protectorate, excluding Bougainville but eventually including the Santa Cruz Islands (Allan 1957:36). Prior to that date each local group of people was, within the limits of its own power, completely independent. In the absence of any institution even remotely resembling a central authority, Solomon Islanders (using introduced European weapons) did their best to destroy each other, and unscrupulous whites gave the labor trade its notorious reputation. By establishing the Protectorate, the British government was acting to control and regulate local warfare and the South Pacific labor trade. Some cynics suggest that the action of imperial Germany in claiming northeastern New Guinea, the Bismark Archipelago, and Bougainville, and also the expansion of

French interests from New Caledonia into the New Hebrides, may have had some influence on the British decision.

From their administrative headquarters at Tulagi in the Florida Islands the British moved (with surprisingly meager forces) to establish and maintain order and to extend their control into the remoter parts of the Solomons. In 1909 they laid out a government station in Auki on the west coast of Malaita to serve as headquarters for a district administration. Malaita was at that time in a state of virtual anarchy resulting from mass importation of war-surplus rifles that enabled local strongmen to terrorize whole districts. With admirable coolness and efficiency the new administration began to pacify the island, registering or confiscating firearms, collecting a head tax, and breaking the power of the war leaders. One of the more impressive figures of that era was District Commissioner Bell, who (before he was killed by the Kwaio at Sinerango in 1927) had successfully pacified northern Malaita and earned the respect of the local war leaders. This he did with only a few Melanesian constables, personal bravery, and an apparently overpowering will (Keesing 1965:19). During the Pax Britannica that followed, conditions slowly changed. Senseless killing declined, trade increased, the missions made a little headway, and Levers established a coconut plantation on the west coast near Baunani.

World War II was a cataclysmic experience for much of the Solomons, but it had little direct effect on Malaita. Although the Japanese occupied Tulagi, the Protectorate government did not flee precipitously or abandon its responsibility to govern. The seat of the government moved to Auki, and district officers in outlying areas went to ground in the bush country, some of them performing bravely as coastwatchers for the Australians or in liaison roles after American forces arrived (Colonial Office 1946:17-21). Almost no actual fighting took place on Malaita. The Japanese briefly raided Auki while government officers retreated to the forest. Japanese army personnel set up a weather station on Cape Astrolabe that was wiped out during the Guadalcanal campaign (Colonial Office 1946:21).

What did affect Malaita was the exposure of Malaitamen to the enormities of Western wealth and power. Previously Malaitans had seen only the attenuated margin of Western civilization, and they were not overly impressed by what they saw. But during the fighting on Guadalcanal in 1942-43, and later when Guadalcanal served as an advance base for operations in New Georgia and Bougainville, thousands of Malaitans served with the Americans in labor battalions and as armed scouts in a BSIP Defense Force. Greatly impressed by the Americans, Malaitamen returned home after the war, bringing with them a new movement called Marching Rule that had begun in wartime

Guadalcanal. Partly the heir of prewar nativistic movements, partly cargo cult, and partly a nationalistic political movement, Marching Rule quickly spread throughout Malaita. Participants concentrated in large, nontraditional fortified villages, refused to pay taxes or to co-operate with the British government, and demanded a measure of autonomy (Keesing 1968:277). Firm action by British authorities eventually ended Marching Rule, and governmental reforms appeased some of the movement's membership. But there is still much Neo-Marching Rule ideology to be found in a quiescent state in Malaita.

Besides missionary activity and governmental authority, Western civilization advanced into the Solomons on a third front, that of commerce. The giants of European trade in the South Pacific (Burns-Philp, W. R. Carpenter, Breckwoldt's, etc.) have come late to these islands. For decades the bulk of retail trade has been controlled by Chinese merchants. Operating from headquarters in Honiara or other government towns, they establish general stores in outlying areas, dispatch small ships with trade goods to call at remote places, and serve as middlemen supplying small bush "stores" (usually of suitcase size) operated by Melanesian villagers. So far as Melanesian villagers are concerned, Chinese traders are *the* source of Western goods.

European-owned and operated plantations are another channel for commercial penetration. These have been the most important sources of cash income for Melanesians, and 95 percent or more of adult Baegu males have been away to earn money on these plantations. The combination of highly desirable Western goods and plantation labor as a means of getting the necessary cash has proved irresistible, and Solomon Islanders are now thoroughly enmeshed in a material goods–oriented cash economy. Men leave home to work on plantations for many reasons, but the two most obvious and pressing are the desire to buy things and to accumulate cash to pay the annual head tax or "rate." Unfortunately, far too many men acquire expensive tastes while away from home and spend much of their wages in company stores at or near the plantations. Since most plantations are in Guadalcanal or the Western Solomons (only one is in Malaita), plantation labor gives many Malaitans their only chance to travel. Malaita, being the most populous island, is the leading source of labor for the entire Protectorate, and major plantations make regular annual or semiannual voyages to rural Malaita to recruit workers.

ACCULTURATION: THE MISSIONS

Although the Baegu are certainly not the untouched pagans they once were, Christian missions have been only moderately successful. It

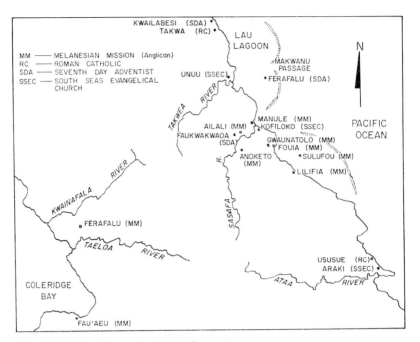

Map 7. Mission Penetration in the Baegu Area

is impossible to say exactly, but roughly half the northern Malaitans are
now nominally Christians.

The Anglican Church's Melanesian Mission (MM) has been highly
successful among the Baegu. From Fau'abu Hospital on the west coast
(Map 7), the Anglicans have moved in to establish a large Baegu village called Ferafalu in the Taeloa River Valley. From Sulufou Island
in the Lau Lagoon, they have moved to Fouia on the east coast of the
mainland, and then on to form two large Anglican settlements at Anoketo and Ailali in the Sasafa Valley. There are Anglican schools at
Lilifia and Gwaunatolo serving the Lau Lagoon. The Anglican priest
serving these places is a Lau man, Father George Kiriau, as is the suf-
fragan bishop for Malaita of the Diocese of Melanesia, Bishop Leonard
Alufurai.

The South Seas Evangelical Church (SSEC), successor to the South
Seas Evangelical Mission (SSEM) of Hogbin's time, has been most
successful among the Baegu of the Ataa Valley some ways south of the
area where I lived. They also have several small hamlets along the coast
and in the lower Sasafa Valley. The SSEC exercises less central control
than does the Anglican church. There are no resident clergymen in the
area, and hamlets are led by church-appointed local headmen. There

are SSEC schools at Araki, near Ataa, and at Unuu, near the mouth of the Takwea River opposite Makwanu Passage in the Lau Lagoon. At the time I was in the field, both of these had schoolteachers from New Zealand.

The Roman Catholics have a major mission station at Takwa on the mainland across the lagoon from Manoba Island, and a lesser one at Ususue near Ataa. These have been moderately successful, attracting numerous Baegu converts particularly around Ataa. Dutch or American Marist priests have in the past run these missions, but there was (1968) a recently ordained priest from 'Are'Are in south Malaita at the Takwa mission.

The Seventh Day Adventists operate in northern Malaita from a modest school and dispensary at Kwailabesi, just north of Takwa. They have made considerable progress in the Lau Lagoon but have not been too successful in the hills. Their Baegu converts are mostly former Anglicans who have been attracted by the millenarian aspects of the SDA faith. In effect, the Adventists are almost a European-led cargo cult. There was one small SDA village near where I lived, and another in the Ataa Valley. Other Christian hamlets conform to traditional practices in that residents tend to be kinsmen, but the SDA village I knew personally (Faukwakwaoa) was a composite affair with unrelated converts from three different clans.

Although they do not actively participate in the others' rituals, Christians and pagans have developed an acceptable accommodation to one another. Each believes the other's theology. To Christians the pagans' ancestral spirits (*akalo*) are dangerous ghosts, earning the Pidgin name "devils." But no Baegu would question their existence; they are, after all, ancestors of Christian Baegu, too. *Akalo* can either punish or reward their descendants, and Christians rely upon Jesus or Mary to protect them from the anger of these ancestral spirits. The fact that Christians do not have to sacrifice valuable pigs to keep ancestral spirits happy is, I suspect, a point that makes Christianity more palatable to some people. Hogbin's (1939:191-95) description of Malaitan Christianity is still a valid one.

On the other hand, pagans never question the existence or power of Jehovah, Jesus, Mary, or any of the saints, who are neatly fitted into a familiar framework as spirits belonging to Europeans. Arguments between Christians and pagans are frequently a debate about the relative power of the two sets of spirits. The pagan's position grossly simplified is that Malaitan spirits are apt to be the more powerful where Malaita or Malaitan worshippers are concerned. As Keesing (1967:92) has pointed out, Christian nonobservance of menstrual and birth taboos restricts Christian-pagan interaction. Exposure to these polluting influences would, in the pagan view, be too dangerous and the consequent purification rites too expensive. However, my impression is that the Baegu must not take these observances as seriously as the Kwaio. Although they are not active participants, Christians go to pagan festivals to hear the music and watch the dancing, and pagans sometimes join their Christian kinsmen at feasts connected with church holidays such as Christmas or Easter. Pagans from deep in the interior regularly spend the night with Christian relatives living along the trails to coastal markets. Christian and pagan kinsmen continue to help one another in secular activities such as house-building, and both congregations continue to assert their claims to jointly owned land.

All of these factors make conversion or apostasy intellectually easy, and some missionaries have tried to make the transition to Christianity an easy one. Anglicans and Roman Catholics have been especially willing to accept traditional customs whenever possible, such as the performance of old songs and dances at church festivals and the incorporation of bride-price payments as part of the marriage ceremony. A few congregations even use taro and coconut water rather than bread and wine for Holy Communion, so that the symbolism of the rite will be more appropriate for Melanesian conditions.

The single most important factor causing people to become Christians is the fact that nearly all local schools are run by the missions. Malaitans are fully aware that Europeans control the best jobs and highest incomes, and that some education is needed to get high-paying jobs. Thus pagans are in many cases willing to send their children to mission schools, even at the risk of having them baptized. How effective these conversions are is not certain, for there have been a number of reversions to paganism once the schooling ended.

It seems, in fact, as if the proportions of Christians and pagans in the population may be almost at a point of equilibrium. The Baegu people are about equally divided, half affiliated with missions and half remaining faithful to the ancestral ways. There is considerable movement in both directions. Among the people I knew best (the population sample area) since the beginning of 1966, nine pagans moved to mission villages, while seven Christians returned to paganism (Table 7). One in each of these categories is an adolescent boy who decided he wanted to learn to read, enrolled in an Anglican school, found it harder than he expected, and went back to the hills. Conversion and apostasy are easier for women and adolescents than for men, who have to sacrifice pigs to the *akalo* for their Christian days of error if they return to paganism.

It is hard to judge long-term trends accurately. Extrapolating from

TABLE 7. BAEGU CONVERSION/APOSTASY RATIO DURING THE PERIOD
SEPTEMBER, 1966-AUGUST, 1968

	Pagan conversions to Christianity	Christian apostasy to paganism
Anglican............................	3	6
SSEC...............................	5	1
SDA...............................	1	0
Roman Catholic......................	0	0
Jehovah's Witnesses..................	0	0
Totals..........................	9	7

the usual post-contact pattern of events in Oceania, it would seem logical to predict an accelerating swing toward Christianity. But Malaita's may be an atypical situation. Hogbin (1939:247) predicted an early end to paganism, yet thirty years later there are still pagans in northern Malaita who have much the same relationship with their Christian kinsmen as they had in Hogbin's time. The religious situation in Malaita may be more stable than is sometimes believed.

ACCULTURATION: GOVERNMENTAL CONTROL

Headquarters for the British Solomon Islands Protectorate are in Honiara on Guadalcanal. In charge is a High Commissioner for the Western Pacific, appointed from London, who relies upon a civil-service secretariat to conduct government business. There is also a Governing Council consisting of both appointed and elected members, that should, if constitutional development goes as planned, eventually assume both legislative and executive responsibility for self-government.

The entire Protectorate is divided into four districts: Western (New Georgia and Choiseul), Central (Guadalcanal and Santa Isabel), Eastern (San Cristobal and Santa Cruz), and Malaita. Malaita District, consisting of Malaita Island itself, Maramasike or Little Mala Island, Sikaiana, and Ontong Java, is the most populous.

The district commissioner (DC) has, in managerial terms, "line" responsibility for Malaita. As his line assistants, he has two or three district officers who are responsible for a particular part of the district (north or south) or who assume general executive functions as directed by the district commissioner. Along with these come a number of "staff" officials with authority to perform specific functions: agricultural officers, police, posts and telecommunications, medical, marine, or whatever special units may be temporarily assigned from Honiara such as forestry, lands and survey, or geology. Nearly all of the district admin-

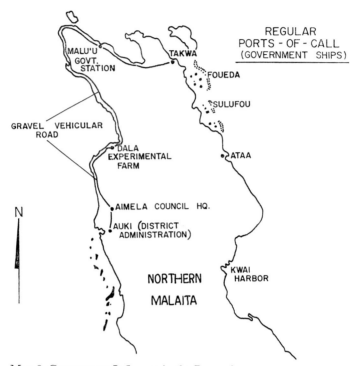

Map 8. Government Influence in the Baegu Area

istration lives and works near Auki (Map 8), but there are three small outstations: an experimental farm at Dala in the northwest; an agricultural office, a police barracks, and a hospital at Malu'u in the far north; and a police barracks at Maka in the south.

There is an elected Malaita Council, with its own president, that has considerable autonomy and authority, although the DC does retain veto and budgetary powers over council decisions. Malaita Council is an institution resulting from a compromise over Marching Rule demands for self-government, with its own offices and some staff at Aimela near Auki. The Council levies taxes (called "rates") and has been active in providing rural health clinics, some schools, and one road along the northwest coast.

The legal system on Malaita is a hybrid one. The administration relies heavily on local consensus and traditional norms to maintain order. There are a number of thatch courthouses around the island, built to provide a formal setting for customary law. Disputants can argue their cases there, and (theoretically, at least) interested parties guided by elders can reach a suitable consensus. Of course, most disputes never get to these courthouses; they are resolved at the hamlet or village level. Really serious cases, or disputes that reach no consensus, are heard at Magistrate's Court conducted by the DC or one of his district officers. The High Court in Honiara has jurisdiction over serious felonies and serves as an appellate court. Police constables are sometimes available as bailiffs in the native courthouses and for bringing serious cases to Auki for Magistrate's Court.

The district administration exercises fairly effective control over the areas near Auki and, considering the lack of funds and personnel, it seems to have a surprisingly good informal intelligence input from the rest of the district. However, direct contact between government and people in rural Malaita is only marginal. The district commissioner and medical and agricultural officers make periodic tours along the east coast by boat. On rare occasions, one of these officials will take a walking tour in the bush, but it is obviously impossible for such a few men to maintain any regular contact with interior areas.

Malaita is divided into a number of subdistricts or wards (usually having a headman and one or more clerks appointed by the Malaita Council or one of the governmental agencies), and since 1968 the government has established several postal substations, but again these officials are concentrated on the coast. Their influence, too, is only marginal. Traditional status carries more weight than government appointments, and people on occasion explain, "He is the Headman, but these others are our 'real' leaders."

People in the hills credit the government with more power than it actually possesses. There is only a small force of regular police constables (usually about thirty) and a small paramilitary group called the Melanesian Field Force. These probably could not control a serious insurrection or determined lawbreakers, but parents conjure them up as bogeymen to scare recalcitrant children. (A detachment of Field Force troops was coincidentally camped at Uru in 1965 when a Kwaio man speared an SDA medical assistant, the last time a white man was murdered.) When minor crimes do occur, people seem to assume that the police will do something about it.

Malaitans are divided in their attitudes toward the Malaita Council. Some see it as a patriotic group working for self-rule; others believe council members have sold out to the British. Participation in council elections is desultory, partly because people are not interested, and partly because electoral rolls are woefully inadequate. In the hills there is formidable but quiet opposition to the Malaita Council. There is some latent cargo cult thinking that sees political activity of this kind as useless. People everywhere resent paying taxes, and there is much grumbling about the council's annual "rate." Among the hill people this is aggravated because they realize so few benefits from the taxes they pay. Council schools are nonsectarian, but they are always in coastal villages where mission schools are already available. Health clinics are always on the coast, and the road is a coastal one. Why, the hill people ask, should they pay for amenities for coastal folk? There is also considerable suspicion about council motives stemming from honest doubts, simple misunderstanding, and perhaps even a bit of paranoia. There were always rumors about someone running off with the tax money. Many hill people misunderstand official copra and cocoa development schemes, seeing them as a kind of forced labor, or believing that the Council is trying to get people to plant cash crops as a pretense to raise taxes. In 1968 the Baegu were positive that land survey and mineral prospecting projects were blatant attempts to steal their land.

Not all development schemes are seen in this grim perspective. People are eager for the coastal road now running from Auki to Kwailabesi to extend along the east coast.[1] It will bring the bright lights of "metropolitan" Auki closer and make it easier to get European goods. Young men talk of getting Hondas or bicycles, but I fear they will have trouble getting the cash to realize their dreams. They are also making sporadic efforts to organize cooperatives (called "unions") modeled after the government-sponsored fishing, farming, or marketing cooperatives now developing in other parts of the Solomons. Unfortunately, the Baegu have little to sell but their labor, and few will buy that. They also have only hazy ideas about how they will use the money they hope to earn.

ACCULTURATION: COMMERCIAL INFLUENCE

Desire for Western material goods is in Malaita (as it is almost everywhere) the strongest force drawing people away from traditional rural villages toward a new style of life. But to participate in the novel lifestyle, one must have money. The only way the people from the Malaitan hills can get money is to work on plantations, since they have few saleable resources and lack technical or clerical skills. There is only one plantation on Malaita. It is at Baunani in the south and hires people from that area, so Baegu men must leave Malaita to work. Commercial coconut plantations are concentrated on Guadalcanal, the Russell Islands, and the New Georgia group. Over 95 percent of all adult Baegu males have been to one or more of these places. Only the very old or

---

[1] This road was extended to Fouia by 1971.

those with a physical handicap have never left Malaita. Many men go back for another tour every few years.

This causes some domestic crises. Malaitans believe that the rest of the world is peopled by scarlet women and libertine men, and women sometimes accuse their husbands of going away to philander. Some plantations permit wives and children to accompany the men who come as laborers, but very few Baegu women go. Men fear that they will learn bad habits from foreigners. Sexual standards are looser in the western Solomons, and western Solomons women do not work as hard as Malaitan women do.

Most trade goods reach the Baegu hills indirectly. Plantation workers bring home many things when they finish their contracts, of course. There are Chinese trade stores at Auki and Malu'u, and new cooperative general stores with a small range of merchandise at Dala and Matakwalau (Map 9), but all of these are two days round trip by foot.

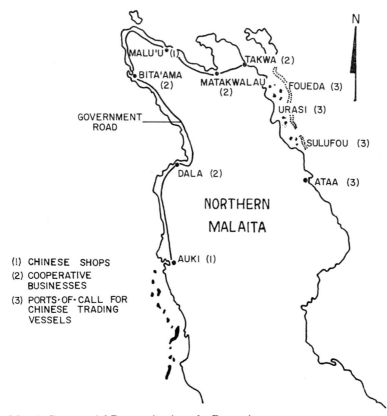

Map 9. Commercial Penetration into the Baegu Area

Chinese traders call irregularly at ports along the east coast, but their prices are outrageously high, and by the time hill people can get to the shore, the boat is usually gone. A few ambitious men operate small "stores" in the bush. These are usually illegal in that they have not paid the government's hawkers' or vendors' fees. They usually consist of only a suitcase full of soap, flashlight batteries, needles, salt, curry powder, and miscellaneous small items that the would-be storekeeper buys from the Chinese trading vessels to resell in the hills.

The situation is a painful one, because expectations and wants exceed resources. People want more and better things, but they do not have the cash to buy them. So they are rapidly being tied into a foreign-dominated mercantile system.

STATUS OF ACCULTURATION

Predictably enough, changes in material culture have been the most extensive and the most noticeable. Steel tools have almost completely replaced stone ones during this century. Only the oldest men can remember using stone adzes. Clearance of land for gardens is done exclusively with fire, steel bushknives, and steel axes. On the other hand, the traditional wooden digging stick is the only planting implement, and people still make nutcracking hammerstones and drill points from chert. There is limited use of iron nails, steel needles, and imported cordage; but these are highly valued, salvaged and reused until they are decayed almost beyond recognition. Most fastening is done with traditional fibers and cordage.

Nearly everyone has some Western clothing. A few old men in the hills go naked, but most wear a brightly colored calico kilt or twill shorts. Young men buy shirts with money earned by plantation labor and wear them until they are threadbare rags. All women (except the Seventh Day Adventists) go topless. Christian women wear calico skirts. In the hills near their hamlet some pagan women still wear traditional dress; unmarried adolescent girls are naked except for a red cane belt, married women wear a pubic apron that leaves the buttocks bare. But even these have cloth skirts that they put on when they go to market, so that the coastal people will not laugh at them for being backward. Children of both sexes first begin wearing clothes somewhere between five and ten years of age, and even then some prefer to carry their shorts or calicos over their shoulders rather than around their hips.

In routine situations people can and do still light fires with a wooden fire plow, but nearly all men have cheap cigarette lighters. A few rich men have kerosene lanterns, but kerosene is hard to get and expensive.

Some have flashlights, but replacement batteries are much too dear to be practical. For illumination people rely on fires and torches of dry bamboo splints.

Tobacco is a universal habit (again, except for the SDA's). Both men and women have pipes and, if they can get paper, they roll cigarettes from it. Children begin begging for tobacco at about six years of age, but they rarely get any because most adults have little to spare.

Food, ornaments, furnishings, and toys remain overwhelmingly traditional; however, most families have a single metal cooking pot. When they can afford it, people may buy salt or soap. Mirrors are also popular. Rich men may have blankets, an old army cot, some U.S. Army pans or water canteens, and even a portable radio (usually lacking batteries), but these are obviously luxury items used only to entertain distinguished visitors.

Cash (Australian currency) supplements but has not replaced barter in the market place, or the traditional shell and porpoise teeth valuables. Most people keep a small hoard of silver shillings to use at the markets, for some coastal folk want cash if they can get it. The bride-price at weddings may include some Australian pound notes, but the bulk of the bride-price is still strings of shell money.

In the social system some change has been inevitable. Warfare has ended, although feuds linger on. Because of a decline in the use of traditional sanctions, observance of taboos is not as stringently enforced as before. Capital punishment, execution of troublemakers, and revenge by assassination are no longer common, although killings still occur occasionally. The courts and churches provide alternate means for redress and punishment, and payment of fines or "compensation" is now routine. Many older people claim that standards of behavior are deteriorating.

Along with these changes comes a certain amount of cynicism about both traditional culture and human nature in general. According to local custom, if a taboo were seriously breached, angering the ancestors, the guilty party must sacrifice a pig. One old man grumbled to me that priests decide a sacrifice is necessary whenever they (the priests) are hungry for pork.

On the other hand, much of traditional culture remains vigorous. Christians as well as pagans recognize and respect the same kinship obligations and land-tenure principles. Christians, too, try to keep the old art forms, dances, music, and epic legends alive. Only the Seventh Day Adventists want to give these up. The pagans make a vigorous, conscious effort to keep the old ways vital and the traditional ritual communities intact. "Custom" has acquired a degree of functional autonomy, with rites performed as ends in themselves. There is a strong sense of duty in this; people feel they owe it to the ancestors not to forget the old ways. One man about my age has assumed the priestly duties for a rump congregation of less than a dozen clansmen who remain pagan, even though the rest of the group have recently become Anglicans. He explained to me that when he grew old, he too would join the church, for there would be more food and medicine available from the mission. But, he went on, it would be very sad now if everyone forgot the ancestors.

Thus pagans resist Christianity not out of ignorance but by choice. There is no reason at all to assume that either congregation has a monopoly on good judgment or intelligence. Since pagans and Christians share so many customs and supernatural beliefs, paganism becomes almost as much a conservative political party as it is a religious community.

THE ETHNOGRAPHIC PRESENT

As is the style among ethnographers, I write as if the conditions I experienced are a static reality. Although I am fully aware that conditions have changed and are changing, I emphasize the traditional ways.

This is in some respects quite wrong. There *are* many Christians; much of my data must come from gossip, legend, and hearsay rather than direct observation; and great strides are being made toward acculturation. But I think I have cogent reasons for taking this approach. In the first place, there are pressing reasons for salvage ethnography as well as for salvage archaeology in the face of technological progress. Such traditional non-Western societies as northern Malaita are changing rapidly, and in another generation any sort of work on traditional customs may be next to impossible. Second, it is essential to try to make sense of a culture or society on its own terms, not as it is affected and upset by foreign ideas. Baegu society is in transition, and much that was harmonious in a traditional setting may be discordant or incomprehensible in a modern context. Thus, even though I lived in a changing community, I have elected to try to describe it as if it were a more traditional one. As far as possible, I have used direct observation: watching daily routine activities, following people about, and attending ceremonies and social happenings. To supplement and fill out this information, I have interviewed and questioned knowledgeable old men about Baegu life.

But although I choose to emphasize the traditional system, I cannot altogether ignore change. I cite Christian or acculturation data whenever it is useful for comparison or illustration. It is also certainly worth remembering that the study of change is a valid end in itself and may in some ways be even more worthwhile. As I gain more knowledge of the Baegu over the years, I hope to follow the process of acculturation, but the details of traditional life make a good starting point for research.

The ethnographic present I am writing about therefore is northern Malaita as it was in 1966-68, skewed a bit to emphasize the traditional rather than the modern or the foreign. I think the Baegu would agree with this procedure. Christian and pagan alike had much pride in their own way of life. They showed surprising sophistication about what I was doing, urging me frequently to write everything down so that the world would not forget how the Baegu lived or what they had done.

5. Human Ecology in Malaita

Malaitans, like other men, have developed their own characteristic adaptation for local conditions, and theirs has been a successful one. Malaita is not a rich island, but no one there is poor or hungry. Most significantly, if we accept the Bulmers' date (1964:72) of at least 6000 B.C. for early occupation of the New Guinea highlands, and Palmer's (1968:26) estimate of before 500 B.C. for early settlement in Fiji, they have lived on their island for thousands of years without destroying or polluting it.

SALTWATER AND BUSH PEOPLE

The salient feature of human ecology in Malaita is the separation between coastal and interior populations. This classification is not something imposed on the facts by outside observers, but a fundamental part of the peoples' own world-view.

The saltwater people (*wane asi*), literally "people of the sea," live in coastal villages or on offshore islands, either natural cays or artificial ones constructed of coral blocks in shallow lagoon waters (Map 10). These people are fishermen, although they eat large amounts of vegetable produce and most of them have small gardens on the mainland. The essential point is that their primary interests and self-identification are directed toward the sea. They are consummate fishermen — they swim like dolphins (using the Australian crawl actually invented in the Solomons), and even small children handle dugout canoes as if they were extensions of their own bodies. They have a flattering self-image, believing themselves to be smarter, more worldly, and more personable

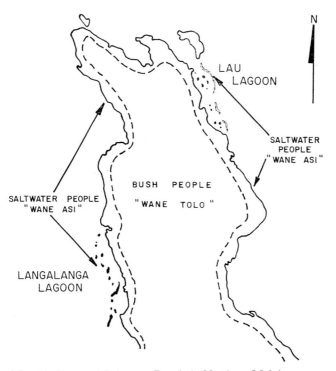

Map 10. Bush and Saltwater People in Northern Malaita

than the bush people. In northern Malaita the largest bloc of saltwater people are the inhabitants of the Lau Lagoon on the east coast.

The bush people (*wane tolo*) live in small hamlets in the interior, usually above an altitude of five hundred feet (Map 10). They are farmers, growing sweet potatoes and taro and raising pigs. Their name means literally "people of the hills." They are indefatigable walkers and know the forests intimately, but they have little interest in or aptitude for maritime skills. The saltwater people look down upon the bush people as hillbillies, backward and a bit slow. From the other point of view, the bush people see themselves as purer, simpler, more honest, and morally superior. The Fataleka, Baegu, Baelelea, and some of the Toabaita form the bush populations of northern Malaita.

ECOLOGICAL ZONES OF NORTHERN MALAITA

If one could cut a slice through Malaita from east to west and then look at the profile from the north, he would see a number of ecological zones dependent on altitude and distance from the sea (Figure 6).

Figure 6. Ecological Zones in Northern Malaita

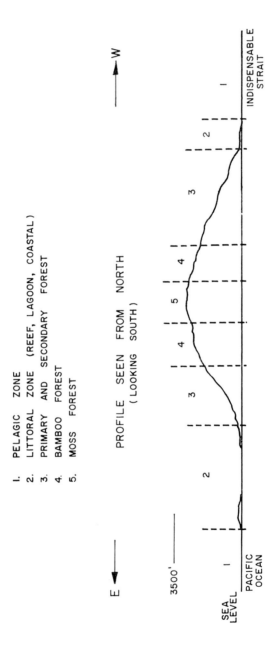

1. PELAGIC ZONE
2. LITTORAL ZONE (REEF, LAGOON, COASTAL)
3. PRIMARY AND SECONDARY FOREST
4. BAMBOO FOREST
5. MOSS FOREST

PROFILE SEEN FROM NORTH
(LOOKING SOUTH)

Distribution of these zones east and west from the island's central ridge is asymmetrical. The classification of people as bush or saltwater depends, obviously, on the ecological zones they exploit. The distribution is not a completely neat one; there is some overlap, but each has a monopoly over an extreme part of the continuum. Saltwater people exploit the sea and lagoon regularly, while bush people do not. Bush people, on the other hand, extensively use the mountains, where saltwater people simply do not go.

The outermost ecological zone, the pelagic zone or open ocean seaward from the reef, is used exclusively by the saltwater folk. While they do not depend on the resources of this area, they do occasionally catch bonita, tunny, mackerel, sailfish, and flying fish there. Porpoise drives begin there; the animals are driven ashore, where they are killed by clubbing.

The littoral zone includes reef, lagoon, and coastal areas. On the east coast there is an offshore barrier reef with a broad, shallow lagoon. The reef is broken by deepwater passages formed where fresh water from major rivers inhibits the growth of coral polyps. The west coast has (in the northern quarter of the island) mainly fringing reefs along the coast. Reef and lagoon areas belong to the saltwater people, and pools or sections of the reef are owned by individuals or lineages. These waters yield most of the species habitually used as food fishes. They catch some crayfish or langoustes (*ura*) and crabs (*karu*) here, but Malaitans do not prize these as greatly as the outer world's gourmets do. The saltwater people quarry block coral for building stone or rubble fill on the artificial islands. They crush and burn staghorn coral to make powdered lime for their areca nut and betel pepper leaf quids.

Inland from the reef and lagoon is a beach and coastal area including both marine and land resources, where the rights of saltwater and bush people overlap and where there is some competition between them. Sandy-bottomed shallow areas of the lagoon have their own distinctive species: flounder, anchovies, sardines, sharks, and rays. Bush people claim right of access to the lagoon, but few of them ever use it. Saltwater people do not fish for sharks, these being at least semisacred, but occasionally a bush man will try to spear or hook one. Men from the hills now and then use a dip net to fish in shallow water for shoals of tiny fish that the saltwater people disregard as rubbish. Hill people also collect clams, beche-de-mer, and crustaceans from shallow, sandy lagoon areas. Hill women carry bamboo joints to market to fill with seawater for seasoning food. Sandy beach areas have groves of coconuts; many pandanus (*tare* or *kaufe*), Pacific chestnut (*alite*), and Barringtonia (*fuku*) trees grow wild, but these invariably belong to saltwater people who use them for mats, edible nuts, and fish poison. Swampy areas of the shore yield edible mangrove seedpods (*koa*), land crabs (*karu*), swamp hardwood timber, and (formerly) crocodiles. On the lower seaward slopes of the hills (below 500 feet) and in the lower river valleys are the gardens of the saltwater people. Their principal crops are yams, sweet potatoes, and swamp taro. They grow considerably more introduced American or European vegetables than do the hill people. There are extensive sago palm groves in this area, used for house thatch and pig feed, and some fruit and nut trees. Hill people claim jural rights over much of this land, but regardless of their claims, the saltwater people have effective possession and use of it.

The bush people enjoy virtually exclusive rights in hill areas above 500 feet elevation, for the saltwater people fear the hills and go there only fully armed and for special occasions. This is the primary and secondary forest zone. The lower hills, roughly between 500 and 2,000 feet, are heavily wooded. In a few places there are small stands of primary hardwood rain forest, usually sacred groves where the ancestors are buried, but most hill areas are garden land or secondary bush forest in a regenerative phase between croppings.

Gardens of the bush people are always on moderate to steep slopes. They prefer friable, well-drained black or brown soil. Principal hill crops are taro (*alo*) and sweet potatoes (*kai rogi*), with bananas (*bou*), sugar cane (*ofu*), and the edible hibiscus (*dee*) the most important secondary ones. People grow a few carefully nursed yams and tobacco, and some people plant small amounts of introduced food crops (pineapple, manioc, maize, tomatoes, cucumbers, papayas, or shallots). Around the hamlets themselves are a few coconuts, areca palms, betel peppers, tobacco plants, and some ornamental or magical shrubs, usually hibiscus or cordyline. One old man has a poinciana that he has transplanted lovingly from Honiara. A few people have started small plantations of coconuts or cocoa, but these do not grow well in the hills, and many hill men regard government-sponsored planting programs as oppressive interference.

In the woods at this intermediate altitude are numerous canarium almond (*ngali*), Malay apple (*kabarai*), breadfruit (*rau'ai*), and other fruit and nut trees. Sago palms (*sao*), essential for thatch, grow only in wet spots at low elevations (below 1,000 feet). The bush forest at these intermediate altitudes has considerable economic value itself. The bush people exploit the forest haphazardly for food, and systematically for building materials and firewood.

Next inland beyond this forest zone, above 2,000 feet but below the region of almost perpetual cloud cover, comes a zone of bamboo forest.

Because of the steepness of the eastern slope, bamboo forests on the eastern side of the island occur in only limited areas, but they are much more extensive on the western slope. Because the land is so steep and the bamboo so difficult to clear, there are only a few gardens in these areas. Although the Baegu do not eat bamboo shoots, they use the plant for some purposes. Large bamboo joints (the hollow space between stem nodes) make good water bottles, containers for storing smoked nuts, and cooking vessels for boiling vegetables or making pig-blood pudding at festivals. Small bamboo joints are engraved for use as lime boxes, and dried splints of bamboo become torches. There are some wild foods at this altitude, the most spectacular a large orange raspberry called *toto*.

Somewhere above 2,500 feet along the central ridge, where an almost perpetual cloud cover keeps everything cool and moist, there are small areas resembling moss forest where aerophytes and Spanish moss festoon tree branches and a dense carpet of mosses, liverworts, and lichens covers the ground. Because of the moss, gardening here is difficult. It would be rather like trying to cultivate wall-to-wall carpeting. But for some obscure reason, a number of the Baegu prefer to live high among the clouds. They say they like the view, the cool breezes, and the privacy. An exhausting, slippery climb up the mountain wall keeps all but serious travelers away. Their gardens, however, are usually some 500-1,000 feet below in the secondary bush forests. When necessary, people use the pith of the cycad (*kwae*), the most evident tree in this high zone, as an emergency food source or for feeding swine.

Freshwater streams, running from all but the highest areas to the sea through all ecological zones, may be said to be another habitat. Stream beds provide chert nodules for the few stone tools still used and limestone blocks for wall-building, cooking stones, and (when powdered) ornamental pigment. As mentioned earlier, people spear fish and eels and gather prawns and edible snails from these streams. Finally, although stream water is essentially a free good, its importance for drinking and bathing should be obvious.

ECOLOGICAL ADAPTATIONS: HORTICULTURE

Regardless of how the earliest settlers made their living, Malaitans of the present and known past have depended on horticulture. Gardens provide the Baegu their staff of life, and gardens have appropriate ritual significance to match their economic importance. Preparation of a sacrificial garden initiates the great mortuary feasts (heart of the public religion), gardens can be harvested only after a first-fruits offering, and sex is forbidden in garden areas. Taro (*Colocasia* sp.) or sweet potatoes (*Ipomea batatas*) are always the major crop in hill gardens, but most people plant a few others, depending upon individual food preferences, the availability of seed or clones, and the physical properties (soil type, shade, drainage, slope) of the garden plot itself.

The surprising thing about Baegu diet is the heavy reliance upon predominantly starchy foods, particularly taro and sweet potatoes (Tables 8 and 9). Analyses of these two food crops by Massal and Barrau reveal that *Colocasia esculenta* taro tubers average 1.9 percent protein by weight (Massal and Barrau 1955a:19-20) and sweet potato tubers 1.7 percent protein (Massal and Barrau 1955b:11-12). Both

TABLE 8. BAEGU FOODS ARRANGED IN ORDER OF PREFERENCE WITHIN CATEGORY

	Domesticated foods (garden or hamlet)	Semi-domestic (owned)	Wild foods
Proteins	Pig Jungle fowl *Beans		Fish and other seafoods Wild birds Wild game Arthropods

Carbohydrates	Taro (*Colocasia*)
	Yam
	Sugarcane
	*Sweet potato
	*Manioc
	*Maize
	*Pumpkin
		Swamp taro
		  (*Cyrtosperma*)
		Bush taro
		  (*Alocasia*)
		Breadfruit
		Sago
			Cane grass
			  (*Saccharum edulis*)
			Wild yam
			Cycad pith
			Pandanus sp.

Vegetables	*Hibiscus manihot* Taro leaf *Tomatoes *Chinese cabbage *Watercress *Cucumbers *Shallots		Fern fronds Wild greens Fungi

Nuts	Coconut	Canarium almond
		  (*Canarium* sp.)
			Pacific chestnut
			  (*Terminalia* sp.)

Fruits	Banana *Papaya *Pineapple *Melon	Mango Malay apple (*Eugenia* *malaccensis*) *Spondias dulcis*	Raspberry *Citrus

* Introduced crops of recent foreign origin.

yield only small amounts of vitamins and essential minerals. Both are mostly water (72.5% and 70.8% by weight), with carbohydrate components of 24 percent and 28.5 percent respectively.

There is little evidence of malnutrition among the Baegu. Both men and women are strong, healthy people with attractive physiques. Children are robust and active; none are obese, and few if any are markedly thin. Apparently people who live on a diet composed largely of starch-rich, protein-poor foods such as taro or sweet potatoes maintain adequate nutritional standards by eating unbelievable amounts of those foods. I refused at first to accept the figures from my quantitative dietary surveys (results reproduced in Table 9), but close follow-up

TABLE 9. BAEGU DIET

	Adult and post-pubertal adolescents			Juveniles (6-14 years)			Weaned infants or small children
	Males	Females	Both sexes	Males	Females	Both sexes	
Gross weight in ounces							
*Protein foods......	1.200	1.778	1.417	1.667	3.333	2.500	.....
Carbohydrates.....	40.600	40.556	40.583	41.000	39.167	40.083	25.667
Vegetables.........	12.000	16.000	13.500	17.500	14.667	16.083	11.333
Nuts..............	7.667	5.111	6.708	4.000	6.000	5.000	.....
Fruits.............	7.267	2.556	5.500	2.167	....	1.083	0.667
Totals........	68.734	66.000	67.708	66.334	63.167	64.749	37.667
Percentage of diet by weights							
Protein foods.......	1.7	2.7	2.1	2.5	5.3	3.9	...
Carbohydrates.....	59.1	61.4	59.9	61.8	62.0	61.9	68.3
Vegetables.........	17.5	24.2	19.9	26.4	23.2	24.9	30.1
Nuts..............	11.2	7.7	9.9	6.0	9.5	7.7	...
Fruits.............	10.6	3.9	8.1	3.3	....	1.7	1.8
**Totals......	100%	100%	100%	100%	100%	100%	100%

* Protein figures may be inaccurate, due to sampling and observation problems.
** Columnar totals do not always equal precisely 100% when added, because of the arbitrary rules to be followed in rounding off decimal figures to significant places.

Portions are in ounces per person per day and percentages of type of food by weight. The dietary survey involved three households for a nine-day span. There were eight adults, four juveniles, and two weaned "infants."

observations convinced me that an adult Baegu male does indeed eat between three and five pounds of taro and sweet potatoes per day. According to my results, children (6-14 years) eat almost as much, but I do not trust these figures. I suspect that the simple fact that I was watching them closely made most of them want to show off by stuffing themselves.

Baegu horticultural practices follow a bush fallow system. This, as Barrau points out, is shifting cultivation in the sense that a garden plot is used for only a year or two, then abandoned in favor of a new site. Although the locus of gardening activity shifts, the farmers themselves may continue to live for years in the same old hamlet. Shifts in hamlet location may or may not be related to the horticultural cycle. From an ecological point of view, what is significant is that by shifting garden plots frequently, abandoned sites regenerate a secondary bush forest growth and presumably during the rest or fallow period regenerate soil fertility; hence the name "bush fallow" system (Barrau 1959:53).

In selecting a site to clear and plant, a gardener has to consider both the legality and the technical suitability of his choice. He must have the right to use the land based on agnatic membership in the proprietary descent groups, cognatic descent from the ancestors associated with the land (buried and worshiped there), or explicit permission granted by the titular owner, the genealogically senior member of the corporate group holding residual title to the land. This is a theoretically complex but practically simple process described in detail in Chapter 8.

Gardeners prefer a site covered by secondary forest growth, saying that the softwood trees, shrubs, and weeds are easier to clear than are areas of primary hardwood forest. This means, assuming that secondary growth follows human clearing of the land, that they habitually reuse sites that were previously cultivated a decade or so before. There is no explicit rule of thumb saying that fields should lie fallow for a given number of years, or even indirectly that second-growth trees should reach a given size before the land is cleared again for gardening. But people do avoid making a new garden on a site where traces of former habitation or use are obvious. Thus the timing of the bush fallow cycle, that is, the time elapsing between use and subsequent reuse of the land, is determined by the natural decay rate of the man-made features associated with gardening: log fences, lean-to shelters, and brush piles. When these disappear, consumed by rot and the jungle, and when human memory fades, a plot can again be used for gardening. Since the oldest clearly recognized former house sites or fences I saw were at least five or six years abandoned, I would guess that cycles run between ten and twenty years.

The rationale for not using former garden sites again is that use takes something out of the soil. Most people have no ready explanation, but a few men told me that old gardens have no "fat" (*rarangana*). Forest soils are rich with a semi-sticky humus, offering an analogy between soil richness and animal fat on the basis of physical properties. Meggitt (1964:223) reports that among the Mae Enga of the New Guinea highlands, "grease" is seen as a common fertility or vigor factor shared by both mankind and the soil. This suggestion of a potential cosmological explanation is intriguing, but among the Baegu it is too vague a concept to be carried further.

Nor are new gardens often built adjacent to old plots. In hilly country with steep slopes much dissected by streams, this is rarely possible. Land is plentiful in the hills, and there is no pressure to use it more efficiently by intensive or regular rotation within a defined area. When it is time to start a new garden, most hill people simply pick the best site available; it may or may not be near their old garden.

Hill people prefer to use sloping land. Hillsides have better drainage and in some ways clearance and tillage are easier on sloping ground, where less stooping is necessary. Most of the land above 500 feet, where the gardens of the bush people are, is sloping, so to an extent the apparent preference for sloping land may be unavoidable. Saltwater people, whose gardens are along the coast and in the river valleys, may use flat terrain. Hill people are aware of this, and explain that hill people simply know better.

Garden fields are initially cleared by classical slash-and-burn techniques. Today steel bushknives (machetes) and axes have replaced stone tools, making the process faster and more efficient but presumably leaving the sequence of events unchanged. Once the gardener selects a site, he fells small trees and clears the underbrush. Cuttings and trimmings lie for a few days to dry; then they are piled and burned, leaving the ground essentially bare. Burning around their bases may kill some large trees, but most of the ones of wide girth survive to shade the garden. Economically useful or magical trees and shrubs are left standing. The next step is to build a fence around the edge of the clearing, enclosing the garden proper. This plot is ideally rectangular, as are house plans, hamlet clearings, and (according to some) the universe itself. The fence is, I believe, largely symbolic. Some people say the fence is to keep pigs out, but most fences are so low or so flimsy that they would not even momentarily deter a seriously hungry pig. Fences do establish and maintain a symbolic and actual separation between the forest (nature) and the well-cared-for garden (a cultural feature). Some people set out a magical cordyline plant (*sango*) in each of the

Plate 6. Kwaomata of Walelangi planting taro with a dibble in his hillside garden.

four corners to ensure the garden's well-being and productivity. Many also build a small thatched shelter for protection from sudden rains and to store planting stock or harvested crops.

Although steel has replaced stone cutting tools, the traditional wooden digging stick or dibble (*kwata*) remains the primary digging and planting tool. With the dibble people open the soil for planting shoots or seeds and build small hills for yams or sweet potatoes. After planting, the garden may require two or three weedings. However, sweet potatoes grow so fast and so luxuriantly that weeds simply do not have a chance. After four to six months, crops are harvested for food as needed, with some shoots saved for replanting.

It is difficult to make any meaningful statement about average garden size. People replant as they go, putting taro or sweet potato cuttings back into recently harvested parts of their old garden or starting a new garden before they abandon the old. Thus the area under cultivation by one person will be at a maximum when his new garden has not yet begun to produce, but he has not yet quit harvesting from the previous one. A man and wife each have separate gardens. Each selects a garden size intuitively, tailored to the terrain, the number of children they have to feed, and his or her own ambition. For what it is worth, the average hard-working parent's garden (based on a sample of twenty-four gardens) covers 21,899 square feet or .503 acres. Thus an individual would have between 21,900 and 43,800 square feet (.503 and 1.006 acres) under cultivation at a time. Considering that both man and wife will have a garden, and given that the average parental pair has 2.7 dependent children, this would mean that it takes between 43,800 and 87,600 square feet (1.006 and 2.012 acres) of garden to support an average Baegu hill family, or roughly speaking 9,319 to 18,638 square feet (.214 to .428 acres) per capita at any one time.

RITUAL AND FERTILITY

Efforts to stimulate productivity and maintain fertility are largely supernatural. Abandonment of a garden after only a year or two restores fertility through secondary forest growth and humus accumulation. This shifting of garden sites is simply done as a matter of custom without any elaborate explanation. Other phases of gardening activity are overtly magical or religious.

The rectangular plan (Figure 7) is one harmonious with other cultural shapes (clearings and house plans) and is assumed to be "proper." The fence, too weak to really keep out pigs, maintains a cognitive distinction between wild nature and cultivated gardens. The magic cordyline plants (sango) in the four corners are explicitly said to keep the forest, insect pests, or blights from encroaching on the garden area within the fence and to promote the growth of the domesticated garden plants. A few people may make a small stone altar at the upper end of the garden, but most people doubt the efficacy of such a shrine because only priests can properly consecrate an altar, and then only in a proper holy place. Such garden altars are primarily aesthetic.

People observe certain taboos in connection with gardening. Old pagan men say one should be continent and avoid contact with women when planting, but younger men insist this is not necessary. Menstruating women can spoil a garden, but since they are isolated in a menstrual hut on the edge of the hamlet, they are not likely to be near one. Gardens are inappropriate spots for love-making, which ought to be done in the house or the bush.

The ancestral spirits expect a first-fruits offering, and it is not right to use food from a new garden until this is made. The owner gives a

Figure 7. Typical Baegu Garden Plan

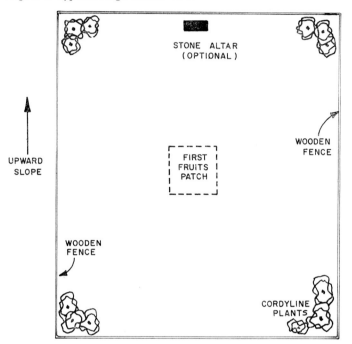

token offering to a priest, who cooks it, prays, and presents the food to the ancestral spirits. The garden, previously "closed," is now said to be "open" (*mole na*) and can be harvested as needed.

Veneration of the ancestral spirits is the heart of Baegu religion. Among the things people hope to achieve by honoring the ancestors are the prevention of crop failure and, conversely, garden productivity. The spirits of the dead can, if they wish, bless their descendants with worldly success: fertile gardens, fecund pigs, a healthy family, wealth and influence. This concatenation of well-being, power, and a further element of truth or legitimacy is labeled *mamanaa,* presumably cognate with the "mana" familiar to students of religious beliefs in Oceania. The ancestors are buried on land still owned by their descendants and are supposed to continue to be interested in the land and the affairs of the lineage. But these ancestral ghosts are neither inherently good nor inherently evil. They can bless, but they can also punish in anger. Religious practice therefore seeks to please the ancestral spirits, to keep them happy, and to supplicate blessings from them. By and large, the *akalo* act in negative ways — promoting well-being by not sending disasters or bad luck. Positive effects on garden growth and yield come from the practice of magic, rather than religious ritual (following Malinowski's terminology).

One technique is the taboo system aimed at avoiding or preventing action that might anger the dead. The other is an elaborate cycle of mortuary feasts in honor of the dead, said to extend if done properly over an interval of sixteen years following the death of an important man. The cycle entails a series of spectacular sacrifices and feasts called *maoma*. At the ceremony, numerous pigs are ritually strangled by priests as offerings to the ancestors. I saw thirteen killed at one, twenty-four at another, and twenty-seven at a third, but "in the good old days" fifty to one hundred pigs are reputed to have been slaughtered. These are roasted and consumed at communal meals, and the ceremony ends with all-night sessions of epic singing and a grand panpipe concert and sacred dance on the final day. But the round of activities leading up to the final sacrifice and dance features the planting and cultivation of a sacred taro garden dedicated to the ancestors.

This ritual garden is seen as an "ideal" or perfect one, symbolizing the religious aspect of gardening and the role of the ancestral spirits in maintaining the productivity of the land for their descendants' well-being. Taboos, ritual sequences, and gardening etiquette are observed scrupulously. When the taro is ripe, people harvest it and roast it as is or make it into a pudding (*lakeno*) with coconut cream to eat with the pork at the sacrificial communal meals.

The essence of success, which for a horticultural people depends on garden fertility, is the remembrance of the ancestors.

OTHER BUSH ECONOMIC ACTIVITIES

Although gardening takes up most of their time and provides almost all their diet, pigs (*boso*) have a crucial ritual and symbolic importance in Baegu life. Not surprisingly, the Baegu have an intense interest in pig husbandry. People make pets of pigs and spoil them greatly. Women and children sleep with piglets at night and feed them cooked (sometimes pre-chewed) sweet potatoes. Some people pen pigs on the edge of a village, but immature beasts usually wander freely about the hamlet and into the houses. Pigs never go hungry, receiving generous daily rations of sweet potatoes. Animals destined for eventual sacrifice to the ancestors get especially lavish and tender care. They are petted, fed constantly, and kept in the house at night to keep them from wandering and becoming accidentally polluted (*sua*).

Pig-stealing is something of a sport, so most people keep a close watch over their livestock. Pigs breaking into gardens cause frequent quarrels,

and the respective rights of pig-keeper versus gardener are poorly defined. Because pigs have so much freedom, some inevitably go wild.
There is a feral pig population that people occasionally hunt, but the
status of these tends to be ambiguous. Some folk insist that they retain
rights over feral swine and ought to have exclusive hunting privileges.

Since pigs are expensive animals (a full-grown one may cost $40.00
Australian), they are not eaten for routine occasions. For pagans, pork
is appropriately served at the great mortuary feasts (*maoma*). Christians kill and eat pigs at weddings or church holidays, but in both communities pork is a sacred, not a secular, food.

Because of their value, both in monetary and ritual terms, ambitious
men invest large amounts of time and energy in feeding and caring for
swine. They are in some ways an investment, a way of accumulating
and storing the produce of large sweet potato gardens, but they do not
have as great importance in this respect in Malaita as they have elsewhere in Melanesia, such as in Bougainville (Oliver 1955:348). Young
pigs are, however, a common gift for younger relatives.

Other livestock have only marginal importance. People keep jungle
fowl (*karai*), feeding them occasionally but making no systematic attempt to control them. If they find an egg (usually half-hatched), they
eat it, and they occasionally roast or stew a stringy old bird.

Dogs serve as companions for children, are valued as watchdogs, and
may be used to hunt feral pigs. A few people keep European housecats
to control rodents, but dogs and cats are seen essentially as liabilities.

Trees have a recognized economic value. Every village has a few
areca palms and coconuts, but the latter do not grow well at higher
altitudes. People claim fruit and nut trees scattered in the forest, and
they actually plant sago palms (used for thatch) in marshy places at
relatively low altitudes.

Foraging in the bush, particularly the secondary forest, provides
nearly all building material and supplements the diet. Sago palms for
thatch are individually owned, but timber for construction, vines for
lashings and fiber, and bamboo for walls or rafters come from the bush.
Bark cloth, made from banyan or breadfruit trees, now has only symbolic rather than utilitarian significance. Forest hardwoods become food
bowls and weapons, bamboo has myriad practical uses, and hard seeds
are used for beads and rattles. Firewood is perhaps the most essential
product habitually gathered from woodland areas. From time to time
people gather fern fronds, edible greens, and fungi to vary their diet.
There is a moderately tall grass (*losi*), the *Saccharum edulis* or "pit-
pit" in Pidgin, that has an edible pith and inflorescence that is not
really cultivated but is highly prized. People eat the heart of several
species of palms. This sort of gathering assumes greater importance in

times of stress (hurricanes or crop failure), when it may be of major significance.

Hunting does not have great economic importance, nor does it have the symbolic or recreational significance that Bulmer (1968:302) reports from the New Guinea highlands. Pig hunts generate excitement but are scarcely profitable. Wild pigs are usually chased down, brought to bay, and speared. Nowadays a few people who have shotguns or rifles may hunt birds, particularly the Pacific pigeon (*bole*). In former times, people netted, snared, or trapped birds. The bush turkey or megapode (*geo*) is valued but rare. Netting birds is said to have been a communal activity, but modern bird-shooting involves only solitary stalking. People kill the large fruit bat or flying fox (*sakwalo*) both to eat and for its teeth, valued as ornaments. The bow and large three-pronged bamboo arrows are the weapons used.

A wide range of slow game rounds out the larder but does not offer much intellectual challenge. People climb trees to catch the cuscus opposum (*futo*), but say they do not eat either kind of rat found in Malaita. Large lizards are occasionally eaten. Two varieties of garden spider are edible, many smooth-skinned caterpillars are table fare, and there is a systematic effort to gather grubs, particularly a large (four to six inches), succulent beetle grub found in rotting sago pith. It is not possible to say how much of these things people eat, but they are probably an invaluable dietary supplement in that they provide specific proteins not otherwise available in the largely vegetable diet.

People do some freshwater fishing. They spear river fish or shoot them with the three-pronged arrows. Nowadays some men buy cheap goggles from Chinese traders and make slings of rubber straps and wire darts to dive for fish. They noodle in holes along river banks for eels and prawns. Occasionally men or boys will dam and divert small streams to gather the prawns and small fish exposed in the dry bed.

Coastal activities are strictly marginal, as far as the Baegu are concerned. In the first place, their right of access to the beach is limited and sometimes contested by the saltwater people. A few hill men make dugout canoes from forest hardwood trunks that they float downriver to the sea. These they sell to the saltwater people or store on the beach for their own use. Hill women collect saltwater to use as a condiment. On moonlit nights, hill people may go to the shore to catch crabs, and when the tide is out they gather clams, snails, crabs, and sea slugs near river mouths. Men from the bush now and then try to spear a shark or a dugong near the mangroves, but this is only an incidental activity. Some men do not eat mollusks or crustaceans, because of taboos and beliefs identifying them as feminine foods. There is also a superstitious fear that eating shellfish may make a man impotent.

NATURAL DISASTERS

Catastrophes are rare. Hurricanes do some wind damage, but their worst damage is soil slump and landslides resulting from heavy rains. Any period of exceptionally heavy rain can be troublesome, causing flooding in the valleys and slippage on hillsides. People fear thunderstorms, believing them to be manifestations of ancestral anger and malevolence. But in all of these events damage is localized rather than general.

Theoretically earthquakes could cause widespread damage from landslides in the mountains, but major tremors are rare events. Fire frequently destroys houses, but thanks to heavy rainfall and high relative humidity forest fires are impossible. Epidemic diseases kill people but do not affect means of livelihood. From an ecological point of view, insect pests or plant diseases could be disastrous. On occasion plagues of locusts or caterpillars have denuded and destroyed entire gardens. During the 1950's a series of taro blights did widespread damage in Melanesia, virtually wiping out taro production in some places; but taro cultivation survived in highland Malaita, perhaps because of the extremely fragmented arrangement of garden holdings.

TRADE AND MONEY

Economic institutions link both bush and saltwater populations into a single ecological and economic system. There are two semi-distinct circulation patterns for goods and services extant in northern Malaita. One operates within a quasi-sacred or at least a nonutilitarian context, while the other is a barter trade system for largely secular subsistence goods.

Basic to the first pattern are the traditional shell valuables or native money. There are several items so used, but the most important are the *tafuli'ae* (meaning ten strings) of red and white shell beads. Bits of shell are ground into discs or spools, pierced, and threaded onto strings almost a fathom (*abala*) or one span (arms extended to the sides) long. A series of tortoise shell bars at intervals connect ten of these strings into a single unit. Other traditional ornaments are also used as formal currency, among them massive necklaces of porpoise teeth (*lifona kiriau*), belts or girdles (*esu*) of tiny shell beads woven into intricate patterns, similar arm bands (*abagwaro*), and beautiful bands (*galu*) of bright red and white shell beads with a pattern of porpoise teeth and hard black seeds in the center. All these and the *tafuli'ae* are worth $10.00 Australian. Porpoise teeth have individual value, going at the rate of an Australian sixpence (five cents in their new decimal coinage) for each tooth of standard size (about one inch long). The Baegu give these as presents, but they prefer not to use them as cash in market situations, believing that such usage is inappropriate.

In the characteristic circulation pattern for these valuables, the people of the Langalanga Lagoon on the central west coast make the beads from shells gathered by diving in lagoons around Malaita. Langalanga people exploit their own lagoon and also send diving expeditions to the east coats. Most porpoise teeth come from the Toabaita people in the far north, particularly those around Bita'ama Harbor who conduct regular porpoise drives. Teeth, beads, and finished ornaments are traded around the coast of Malaita from one saltwater group to another, and from the coast they are traded up the hills into the interior. Once in the hills most exchange follows the longitudinal axis of the island, one hill group trading with another, so an epicyclic pattern within a pattern exists with the hill people operating their own system (Figure 8).

People are eager for these shell valuables, because they are a measure of traditional status (more admired than status conferred by government or churches), and because the valuables are the essential portion of the bride-price. Weddings involve the most spectacular exchanges of those traditional valuables, for a good wife can be fabulously expensive, depending on her familial connections, beauty, temperament, and virtue.

Figure 8. Economic Networks in Northern Malaita

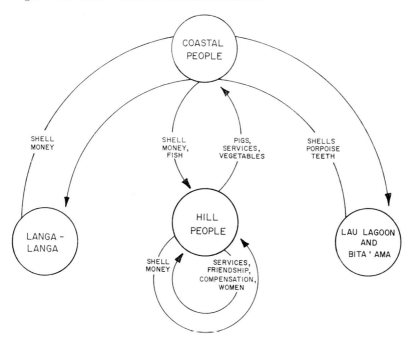

Unable to comprehend that a good bride-price is what gives honor and legitimacy to a marriage, and misunderstanding the transaction as chattel transfer, some fundamentalist missionaries have sought to outlaw the bride-price. This effort is barbarous. In our own civilization, it would be psychologically equivalent if a religious group were to outlaw church ceremonies, forbid white dresses, and insist that all weddings take place in a sleazy justice-of-the-peace's office with papa and his shotgun in the background. Anglicans and Roman Catholics accept the custom but have tried to establish a standard rate of five *tafuli'ae*, to prevent inflation and competition. In reality, bride-prices are variable. Minimum bride-price for an attractive, hard-working pagan virgin from a good family is ten *tafuli'ae* plus an equal value of porpoise teeth and some other miscellaneous goods — roughly speaking, somewhat over $200.00 Australian.

The pattern of marital exchange in the hills follows the long axis of the island, so the bride-price in such marriages usually remains within the hill population. Within the hills there is a *statistical* tendency for what alliance theorists would call patrilateral cross-cousin marriage, or delayed direct exchange, with women going one direction in one generation, the other in the next generation (R. Fox 1967:201). There is no rule to that effect. What appears to make the system work, and it is more a complex than an elementary system, is a feeling among men that bride-price payments between lineages ought to balance. It is expressed as "We paid them for my wife; they ought to buy one of our daughters." But the statistical tendency is only a slight one at best.

There is some tendency for bride-price payments to go from saltwater to bush people, but not the other way. Communication between the two populations involves a differentially permeable barrier. Saltwater women rarely marry hill men, for they do not want to leave the lagoon (virilocal residence prevails) for the hinterland. But according to traditions, when polygyny was more prevalent, rich saltwater men would buy hill girls for second wives because they were less expensive. Hence (theoretically, at least) more bride-wealth would go up into the hills than would come down from them. In effect, hill populations could accumulate traditional wealth by trading away women.

Traditional shell valuables were commonly given as presents to children or younger relatives as a mark of esteem. They were also appropriate currency for compensation payments in cases of taboo violations, insults, curses, and personal injuries. There is no pattern to this circulation other than that gifts, torts, or taboo violations usually involve the people that interact together most frequently. If such transactions took place between bush and saltwater people, the flow was probably a balanced one in both directions.

The other major channel for transmission of these shell valuables is in connection with religous services, where they are used as contributions or payments for services. The mortuary feasts (*maoma*) involve singing of epic tales (*'ae ni mae*) about the deeds of the ancestors, but performance of these is frequently taboo for the lineages involved. Thus outside musicians, singers, and dancers must be hired to perform, and traditional shell monies are the most acceptable payment. Hill people have a great reputation as musicians or dancers, so they frequently perform at saltwater festivals. Here wealth is traded into the hills in exchange for artistic services.

Since it is easier to breed pigs in the bush than it is on the crowded artificial islands, saltwater people may buy bush pigs for sacrifices. Again, this is a means whereby hill people can acquire traditional wealth.

Hill people occasionally contract for large orders of fish for weddings or other ceremonies. This may involve payment of shell valuables in the other direction, but often a fish order is balanced by a corresponding contract for taro from the hills.

Although there are ways for the bush people to acquire traditional wealth, they remain relatively poorer than the saltwater people. Saltwater people, being on the coast, have easier access to resources, and nowadays greater access to wage-labor jobs and Western goods. It is easy to see why today the saltwater people are the richer, but I do not completely understand why this should have been so (the coastal prejudice against hill people indicates it was) in a wholly traditional setting.

There is some pressure to replace the shell money system with Australian currency, but the two are not completely convertible. There is some use of cash among the ancillary goods making up a bride-price, but people still insist that the basic portion be paid in *tafuli'ae* and porpoise teeth. Some men try to buy the valuables with their plantation wages, but the elders (who control the wealth) usually insist that valuables be exchanged or given only in traditional circumstances. Thus cash is not a direct road to traditional status.

BUSH MARKETS

The vigorous barter trade system connecting the bush and saltwater peoples is slowly developing a new cash basis. Along the shore are a series of marketplaces operating on regular schedules. This is today integrated with the seven-day governmental and church week, with markets two days a week in most places. However, since northern Malaitan languages reckon a four-day cycle, I suspect that previously markets occurred every four days.

Plate 7. Baegu girls trading taro for fish at the Sulione market near Urasi Cove.

These markets (*usia*) follow a strictly formal protocol. Market time is a formal truce period, and fighting is supposedly forbidden. Hill people come for miles to attend the market, arriving first and spreading out their produce. Saltwater people usually arrive in groups by canoe. At the larger markets a signal on a shell trumpet or gong signals the formal beginning of trading. Women do the actual bartering, while men supervise or gossip.

Trade is essentially direct reciprocal barter, with garden crops and areca nuts from the hills exchanged in standard quantities for sea produce, although there is some haggling over the quality or size of merchandise. There are some prearranged deals, and some people maintain long-term informal arrangements with trading partners in the other population. But most trading is on an *ad hoc* basis; deals are made simply because each of the two traders has something the other wants.

"Market" as used here refers to the institution and place where barter takes place, rather than the price-determining mechanism or institution. In Malaitan markets, prices are fixed by customary belief shared by both bush and saltwater groups. Goods have a known arbitrary value, at least in the short run, and are traded in standard lots by barter or direct exchange of one commodity for an equal value of another. However, there is evidence of the incipient development of "market mechanisms," in the economic sense (Bohannan 1966:231). In traditional trading there is some haggling — more precisely, griping — about quality and quantity of merchandise. Baegu women complain that saltwater women try to give them rotten fish, and Lau women complain that the hill ladies offer tiny potatoes or taro corms. To resolve such arguments, traders fiddle with the lots of merchandise offered, adding a big tuber to the pile in place of a small one or substituting a fish that does not smell so bad. More important on a long-term basis, frequent quarrels of this sort breed resentment. Unhappy traders seek other sources, and women who habitually offer bad fish or small tubers will not be able to exchange their produce. Since barter traders prefer to trade where they are treated best, the consumer does have a voice. Being responsive to supply and demand, albeit in an imperfect and cumbersome way, Malaitan markets are, in a limited sense, incipient market-mechanisms.

Outside or acculturative pressures also are tending to alter traditional barter trading in the direction of negotiated prices and cash payments. Australian shillings, since they are the means for acquiring Western goods, are in great demand. Many people keep a small hoard of coins and are eager to get more. The saltwater people, having more opportunity to buy from Chinese traders, are especially eager for cash. Lau

Plate 8. Maefasia of Uradaue presenting shell money (*tafuli'ae*) to H. M. Ross (photograph by Don Mitchell of Harvard University).

women in the native markets sometimes ask for payment in silver coins, refusing to exchange goods on a barter basis. There is some negotiating over this, and some hill women are tempted to sweeten the deal by throwing in extra large vegetables, or alternatively to accept a smaller than usual fish.

HUMAN POPULATION: SIZE AND DISTRIBUTION

Unfortunately, it is not easy to describe the Baegu population, or any interior Malaitan population, as a demographer would. Rough terrain, tiny residential units, relatively long distances, and lack of any transportation but bipedal locomotion (alternating with getting up from one's backside out of the mud) make census enumeration inefficient except on a team basis. The large number of men away working on plantations at any given time, lack of understanding by the people about the purpose of a census, and the tendency for people to list foster children and guests or clients as officially resident both in their natal and their present households are social factors introducing potentially large inaccuracies.

According to government figures derived from the 1960 census, Malaita District is by far the most populous district in the Protectorate, having an official population of 54,599 out of a total of 114,000 for the entire British Solomons Islands Protectorate.[1] This census estimates 47,800 for Malaita island proper (this includes tiny offshore islands), 5,700 for Little Mala or Maramasike Island, and 1,099 for the Polynesian outliers Ontong Java and Sikaiana that are administratively attached to Malaita District.

The British government has tried, war and the balance of payments permitting, to conduct regular decennial censuses in the Solomons. These have been well-planned and energetically executed, but they suffer from both physical difficulties and lack of cooperation. Malaitans, never known for whole-hearted cooperation with the government, have consistently opposed census efforts. Either fearing the census as a government plot to extort more tax money, or feeling that it was none of government's business anyway, the bulk of the Malaitan people have reacted in characteristic fashion and met census teams with attitudes ranging from apathy, to sullen resentment, to angry physical obstruction. Unable to cope with the very real difficulties involved, officials have relied heavily on estimates of varying reliability, supplemented by tax or electoral rolls and interpretation of aerial photographs, for producing censuses of the Malaitan population.

During 1967, District Commissioner Richard Turpin made an ambitious and well-conceived attempt to improve the quality of census figures for Malaita. Using volunteer help (young people of the Voluntary Service Overseas organization) in areas around the government stations of Auki and Malu'u where the administration had good control of residential patterns resulting from town plans and first-hand knowledge, he conducted an intensive door-to-door census count. By comparing this information with electoral and tax rolls, he determined that previous population estimates for Malaita were consistently as much as 30-35 percent too low. The actual population in sample areas appeared to be related to rate-payer registrants by a factor of 4.52. On this basis, he estimated the population to be nearer 61,544 than the officially accepted figure (Turpin, n.d.).

If anything, his estimates are still too low, for electoral lists in the outlying wards of rural Malaita are not nearly as comprehensive as those for the relatively well-developed areas he used. In the one local election I witnessed (June, 1967) only 30 percent of the adult male residents of the precinct near where I lived were listed as eligible voters (compared

[1] Preliminary and (as of August, 1972) unpublished results of the 1970-71 decennial census indicate a slightly lower Malaita Island population of 50,659, show that Malaita holds 31.47% of the Protectorate's total population, and yield a population density of 28.95 persons per square mile for the island as a whole. Identification of hamlets and dialect groups is still indecipherable.

with over 50 percent in more settled areas). Taxpayer rolls are more complete but still not perfect. However, the Secretariat in Honiara does not officially accept Auki's revised estimates for Malaita, preferring to wait for the next decennial census in 1970-71 before revising their official figure.

From the official census breakdown, one would guess that there are about 2,200 Baegu, based on figures of 1,500 for East Baegu ward and 900 for West Baegu/Fataleka ward. But these figures are inherently inaccurate, for ward boundaries are for administrative convenience, and in real life distinctions between Baegu, Lau, Fataleka, and Baelelea do not neatly coincide with wards. West Baegu/Fataleka ward obviously contains a mixed Baegu and Fataleka population. Since, geographically, half the ward is Baegu land, probably half the people (450) are Baegu. There are probably about 250 Baegu in the next ward to the northeast, Takwa ward, that is primarily Baelelea. Added to the 1,500 for East Baegu ward, these figures would yield an extremely rough estimate of 2,200 Baegu.

Unfortunately, the 1967 revised estimates are even harder to work with, for they systematically lump Baegu and Fataleka into common subdistrict categories. This recomputation shows 5,853 people in East Baegu/Fataleka subdistrict and 2,536 in West Baegu/Fataleka subdistrict, for a total of 8,389 Baegu and Fataleka. My visceral impression is that the Baegu are certainly not more numerous than the Fataleka; they are very likely at least half the size of the Fataleka population. Fiddling with these proportions would suggest that the Baegu population is in the range between 2,796 and 4,195. But these figures, even if accurate, would still not be fully relevant for anthropological purposes, for they include large numbers of coastal villages that are socially and culturally in a no man's land between saltwater and bush people. Culturally they are saltwater people, but socially (and by descent) they may be more akin to the hill people. To be culturally Baegu is to live in the bush in the interior.

My own information about Baegu demography comes from work done in 1966, when I was still learning by doing, and some excellent information obtained in 1968 after I knew the people and one area fairly intimately. I was thus able to refine my figures (for this small geographic area) to the point where I have genuine trust in them. My sample area of intensive accurate information was roughly the Sasafa River drainage basin and along the crests of the divides to either side of it (Map 11). I did not include any coastal villages, even though these do include numerous Baegu migrants who have chosen to move to the coast. I chose to enumerate and work closely with those people who still lived in the hills on traditional Baegu land as root-crop farmers.

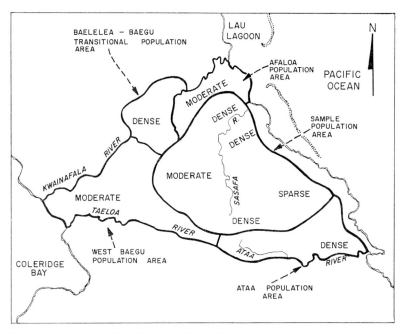

Map 11. Population Distribution in Baegu Territory

Hence my specific data and estimates deal only with people who are still culturally Baegu hill people, not those who are acculturating to the saltwater ecological adaptation.

For my sample area I have good house-by-house head counts. As of the second week in July, 1968, there were 504 people present in the sample area, with 19 men and boys at that time away on plantations or working at government stations in Auki and Honiara, for a total of 523 permanent residents. Tables 10, 11, and 12 break these data down to convey pertinent demographic facts.

Outside the sample area only estimates are possible. My estimates are derived from walks through or visits to other areas, interviews with important local residents, and sample population surveys made by young men to assist me. There are probably about half as many Baegu living to the north of my sample area between the Sasafa and Takwea rivers (Afaloa territory) and in the interior hills toward Baelelea areas (Waleano territory); I estimate there are about 260, most of whom are still pagans.[2] There is a similar number of hill people (mixed Christians and pagans) to the west (on the far side of the central dividing ridge) for another 260. Finally, there are probably half again as many people as

[2] For the location of named districts, refer to Map 17 on page 161.

in my sample area (or about 837 Baegu) living to the south of my area along the left bank of the Ataa River, among its headwaters, and between the headwaters area and the sea. This would mean there are about 1,820 Baegu still living in the hills as subsistence farmers. About half of these are still pagans.

Estimates of population density are doubly vague, for both population and area can only be estimated. Since the Baegu area (Map 12) is roughly triangular (the western side between the Taeloa and Kwainafala River is only a mile long and can be disregarded) with an east-west base of 14.8 miles and a north-south height of 8.3 miles, its area is approximately 61.4 square miles. Using the 1960 census estimate of 2,200 Baegu, this would mean a population density of 35.8 persons per square mile. For the 1967 upward revision, assuming a mid-point value of 3,500 people, there would be 57.0 persons per square mile.

To use my own figures of hill residents only, it is first necessary to lop off the coastal area of lands used by saltwater people and residents of coastal villages. This is again impossible to measure accurately, but saltwater gardens never appear more than a half-mile inland, and hill gardens are rarely if ever within a half-mile of the sea. The Baegu west coast is only one mile long and the east coast 11.2 miles long, so this would remove a saltwater gardening area of 6.1 square miles from the

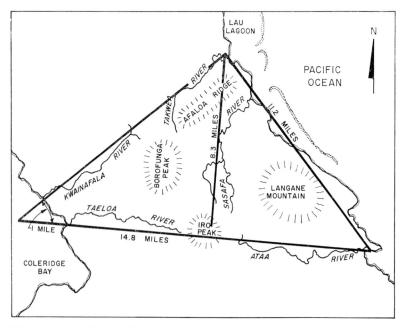

Map 12. Aerial Extent of Baegu Territory

61.4 square mile total, for a net area of 55.3 square miles available for use by the bush population. Using my estimate of 1,880 Baegu still in the hills, this would mean an interior population density of 34.0 persons per square mile. Since there are 640 acres per square mile, each Baegu has potential use of 18.82 acres.

In fact, of course, the population is not evenly distributed over the land, so such figures as these do not fully tell the story. For one thing, the conversion of half the population to Christianity has created significant differences. It is easy to overemphasize these differences, but new trends appear among the Christian population that may have a long-term significance for the whole area. First, there is a tendency for Christians to settle on the coast. Mission officials favor this, because it is easier to keep their congregations on the theological straight-and-narrow here where clergymen can call regularly and where the temptations of pig feasts and pagan dances are less readily available. There is some advantage for the people themselves, for it is easier to obtain

TABLE 10. BAEGU HAMLET SIZE AND COMPOSITION

	Number of hamlets	People	Average hamlet size	Households (Baegu definition)	Households per hamlet	Average household size
Sample area						
Pagans (traditional)..	14	189	13.5	48	3.4	3.9
Pagans (Neo-Marching Rule).........	3	78	26.0	25	8.3	3.1
Anglicans..........	4	151	37.8	36	9.0	4.2
Roman Catholics....	..	..	...	..	..	..
SSEC..............	4	75	18.8	18	4.5	4.2
SDA..............	1	30	30.0	9	9.0	3.3
Totals and gross averages......	26	523	20.1	136	5.2	3.8
*Ataa area**						
Pagans (traditional)..	3	42	14.0	7	2.3	6.0
Pagans (Neo-Marching Rule).........	5	136	27.2	31	6.2	4.4
Anglicans..........	1	39	39.0	9	9.0	4.3
Roman Catholics....	4	335	83.8	87	21.8	3.9
SSEC..............	4	272	68.0	61	15.3	4.5
SDA..............	1	13	13.0	3	3.0	4.3
Totals and gross averages......	18	837	46.5	198	11.0	4.2

* Ataa (southeastern Baegu) area data were collected by a Baegu schoolteacher, Joel Roboalasa, acting as my assistant.

Western products here. Coastal villages become halfway houses to the Lau way of life, and the people living on the shore become fishermen, adopting saltwater customs and techniques and making their gardens along the coastal strip. A second trend is that Christian converts tend to concentrate in large villages, usually near river valleys. Here, except for their new religious practices, they continue much the same old Baegu way of life, growing taro and sweet potatoes in traditional ways, and continuing to farm land traditionally owned by their lineages.

But the new settlement pattern is definitely abnormal. Table 10 showed comparative sizes of typical Christian and pagan settlement. There are serious strains in these new living conditions, and the Baegu do not seem comfortable living in these large, crowded villages. In the

TABLE 11. BAEGU FAMILY SIZE

	Fruitful monog-amous couples	Women married polyg-ynously	Widowers with young children	Widows with young children	Total parental pairs	Dependent children	Dependent children per parental pair
Sample area							
Pagans (tradi-tional)	23	0	10	4	37	105	2.8
Pagans (Neo-Marching Rule).	7	0	6	0	13	30	2.3
Anglicans	19	2	1	2	24	69	2.9
Roman Catholics	. .	. .	. .	. .	. .	. .	. .
SSEC.	12	0	1	2	15	39	2.6
SDA.	4	0	1	0	5	13	2.6
Totals	65	2	19	8	94	256	2.7
Ataa area							
Pagans (tradi-tional)	6	0	1	0	7	29	4.1
Pagans (Neo-Marching Rule).	18	2	2	5	27	65	2.4
Anglicans	5	0	2	1	8	24	3.0
Roman Catholics	38	4	9	9	60	168	2.8
SSEC.	38	6	7	7	58	144	2.5
SDA.	3	0	0	0	3	7	2.3
Totals	108	12	21	22	163	437	2.7

Table includes only presently married couples and widowers/widows with living children under 20 years of age.

TABLE 12. SEX AND AGE OF BAEGU POPULATION

	Under 9	10-19	20-29	30-39	40-49	50-59	60-69	70-79	Over 80	Totals
Males..........	73	63	32	29	42	21	7	6	3 —	276
Females........	63	56	33	35	32	17	7	2	2 —	247
Totals....	136	119	65	64	74	38	14	8	5 —	523
Percentage of total population.....	26.0	22.8	12.4	12.2	14.1	7.3	2.7	1.5	1.0	

Ages are estimates only, based on remembered events near times of birth. Adequate data are available only from my sample area.

decade or two that these large settlements have existed, they have been troubled by constant fission. As frustrations and tensions build and as rivalries develop, would-be leaders take their followers and, although remaining in the church, found new independent villages. During Marching Rule days there were two large settlements in the Sasafa Valley, one on each bank. Since 1955, the SSEC adherents on the right bank left to found three small hamlets of their own. The large village, Anoketo, remained Anglican, but has sent out two tiny off-shoots. On the left bank the Anglicans and the SSEC people soon parted company. The SSEC group later split in half. In the early 1960's a number of Anglicans converted to Seventh Day Adventists and built their own settlement. While I was there, four Anglican families moved out to start another hamlet. An interesting feature in all these cases is that the new breakaway settlements seem to approximate in size the typical traditional pagan hamlet.

Pagans continue to inhabit the interior, farther from the sea and higher than the Christian villages (see Table 13 for comparative distances and elevations). Pagan settlements are tiny, ranging from one to six nuclear families, with smaller ones more common.

There has been differential conversion to Christianity by districts or areas (Map 13). A few areas are almost totally Christian. The Uradaue and Gwaikafo people of the Sasafa right bank are Christians but for a few remnants, as are the Uuo of the lower Ataa Valley and all the people of the Western coast. Others are about half and half, such as the Langane people of the outlying mountain massif between the Sasafa River's upper reaches and the sea, the Afaloa people between the Sasafa and Takwea rivers, and the Kafokuru people of the central massif and the upper Taeloa Valley. The Walelangi people, one of the

TABLE 13. BAEGU POPULATION DISTRIBUTION

Number of hamlets			Approximate elevation	People		
Pagan	Christian	Total		Pagan	Christian	Total
4	0	4	3000'	36	0	36
4	0	4	2500'	65	0	65
5	0	5	2000'	98	0	98
2	0	2	1500'	37	0	37
2	4	6	1000'	31	137	168
0	5	5	500'	0	119	119
				267	256	523

Number of hamlets			Approximate miles from sea	People		
Pagan	Christian	Total		Pagan	Christian	Total
4	0	4	6 miles	36	0	36
3	0	3	5 miles	56	0	56
2	0	2	4 miles	41	0	41
6	2	8	3 miles	116	9	125
2	6	8	2 miles	18	237	255
0	1	1	1 mile	0	10	10
				267	256	523

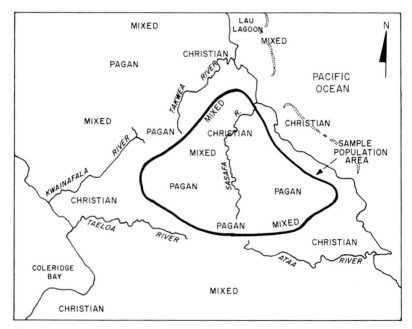

Map 13. Conversion to Christianity in Baegu Territory

largest groups, are split, with mixed Christian and pagans along the left bank of the Sasafa, pagans in the center of the island, and Christians again in the western hills beyond the divide. Other groups are still mostly pagan. These include the Waleano people in the northern interior, Oisamaku and Au'angisia along the Sasafa left bank, and Agia and Masu to the south among the headwaters of the Sasafa and left-bank Ataa tributaries.

This differential conversion has led to different types of settlement patterns or different arrangements of people on the land (Figure 9). In largely Christian districts there are large villages, with much empty land where the people garden. In pagan areas the population is more evenly spread, with small hamlets interspersed among garden lands. In some pagan areas there are larger than usual hamlets, where Neo-

Figure 9. Comparison of Land Use by Pagan and Christian Baegu

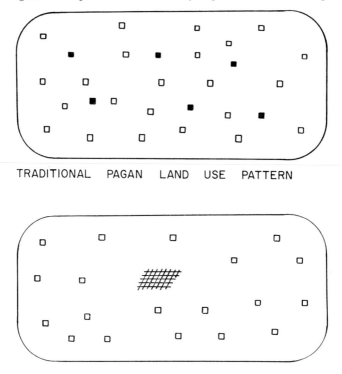

TRADITIONAL   PAGAN   LAND   USE   PATTERN

MISSION   LAND   USE   PATTERN

□   GARDEN PLOT
■   SMALL HAMLET
LARGE VILLAGE

Marching Rule beliefs have caused people to live together in abnormally large settlements. In areas where there has been only partial conversion to Christianity, villages tend to be on the lower slopes and pagan hamlets on the upper slopes and hilltops with both groups gardening in the unsettled areas.

TIME

Time is an important phase of ecology, directly involved with human aging, the natural year, changing residence patterns over the years, and cultural interpretation of these processes. It is a dimension in the sense that it is an indispensable parameter for describing events. Presumably models of time are derived from empirical experience in and of the natural world.

Perhaps the most obvious indication of the passage of time, certainly subjectively the most fascinating one, is the human aging process. This is empirically a one-way, linear process from the fetus in the womb through birth, growth, maturity, and senescence to death. They are not necessarily the same state, but life begins from nothingness and ends in oblivion; in the absence of proof to the contrary, some people postulate an equivalence of the null at both ends of the progression, thereby converting a linear process into a cyclical one (Leach 1961:136). The Baegu, however, have not been seduced by this dream, and life remains a one-way street. Their theories of conception are vague to the point of nonexistence. Copulation causes babies, fertilization resulting from accumulation of semen in the mother's womb. Some say the mother's contribution to the fetal substance is menstrual blood; others say it is the uterine or vaginal mucus. Some say the father contributes the personal soul (*ano*), while the mother imparts the vital essence (*mango*). Most say they simply do not know. After death, the body obviously disintegrates, but the soul may become a ghost or join the ancestral spirits (*akalo*) as a god-like supernatural being. Since these are not reborn, life and time are sequential rather than cyclical.

Stages are more important than age in the life sequence. A married young man has more influence than a chronologically older bachelor. In a way, people are as young as they behave. Chronologically middle-aged men can dance and sing with the youngsters, if they have the agility and the desire. Senescence and retirement are matters of activity and interest, not years. Men become "old" (*wane waaro*) only when they cease to be effective as leaders and advisors, regardless of their actual age. Relative age matters more than chronologically absolute age, which for that matter is scarcely ever accurately known. Rank of siblings stems originally from birth order, but is modified by vigor, skill, and achievement. Birth order is really important only in questions of titular land ownership. But people are aware of birth order, and they usually know who is relatively older and younger among their acquaintances, even if they have only the vaguest ideas of when people were actually born.

Plate 9. The crippled interpreter, Bauro, using an adze to make a wooden vessel (photograph by Kathryn P. Ross).

Plate 10. Aliki and Liuomea practicing the sacred panpipes (*'au*).

This can usually be refined only to the degree of born during Marching Rule, during the War, about the time Mr. Bell was killed, or some other well-remembered event or condition.

People can reckon passage of time in years, but it is rarely necessary or desirable to do so. One of the few exceptions is the cycle of mortuary feasts following the death of an important priest when (ideally) there should be a series of four or eight festivals, one every two years. The apparent change in angular altitude of the sun is not sufficiently marked to be worthwhile as a measure of one year. But there are two seasonal events that are noted and are used to measure passage of cyclical years. One is the fact that the southeasterly trade winds (*ara*) begin in April or May, lasting until about October, with the northwest monsoon (*koburu*) or variable winds prevailing the remainder of the year. Thus the annual onset of the tradewinds marks the passage of one yearly cycle. More important to the hill people is the annual ripening of the canarium almond nuts (*ngali*) during August through October. This period is a recognized season and in fact provides the name for the Baegu year, *faangali*, literally meaning "making of the *ngali* nuts."

There is also a cycle of months progressing through each year. Three of these are named for aspects of the canarium almond season, since this is a festive time greatly enjoyed by the Baegu, who spend much time traveling, courting, gossiping, singing, and dancing during the nutting season. Months are called *madami*, the Baegu word for moon. This way of reckoning time is nowadays rather confused, and people do not seem at all sure of the number of months or their names. The problem arises, I think, from attempts by astronomically naïve missionaries and linguistically naïve officials to translate what probably was a traditional calendar of thirteen lunar months into direct equivalence with the arbitrary twelve-month Western calendar.

There is also an independent four-day cycle in operation. The Baegu can verbally specify three days in advance: today (*tara'ina*), tomorrow (*bobongi*), the day after tomorrow (*fule*), and the day after that (*fokau*). This, I believe, most probably reflects the traditional interval between markets on the coast where saltwater and bush people barter their products.

Passage of diurnal time is reckoned according to the sun. The day begins with first light, and there are twelve or more named periods signifying light intensity and light quality (assuming a relatively sunny, nonrainy day). The most important diagnostic trait for reckoning the stage of time within the day is the altitude of the sun in the sky, not its azimuth.

6. Baegu World-View

Even after accounting for the fact that I had more knowledge of the outside world, whereas they had vastly more knowledge of the rain forest on a tropical island, it was apparent that the Baegu had in some cases radically different conceptions of spatial relations and environmental possibilities than I. Of course, people deal not directly with their environment, but with a cultural interpretation of it. Given approximately equivalent sensory acuity, everyone probably gets about the same input of raw stimuli; but cultural differences result in differing perceptions and cognitive organization. Dissimilar sets of mental categories and plans for coping with life create unique world-views, so that Baegu folk geography and conceptions of real space are not always congruent with ours.

BAEGU COSMOLOGY

Malaita and the sea around it are the world (Figure 10). This world is flat, as the sea is flat, although Malaita itself is mountainous. Malaita is, of course, the center of this world; however, the universe as a whole is three-dimensional, with the heavens above and a netherworld beneath the flat surface of the earth. People are unsure about its shape. Some old men argue that its border is circular, giving the universe a discoidal or spheroidal shape. They say that, since men can walk or sail around Malaita, it must be essentially circular or oval. Others insist that since men make rectagular houses and gardens, the universe must be quadrilateral with square corners.

The Baegu are aware of other peoples and places, but their impor-

Figure 10. The Baegu Universe

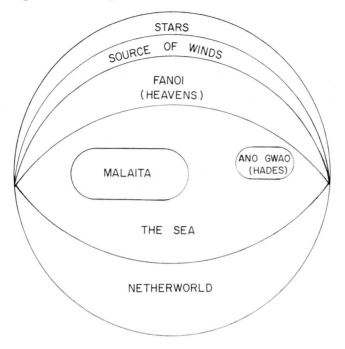

STARS

SOURCE OF WINDS

FANOI
(HEAVENS)

MALAITA

ANO GWAO
(HADES)

THE SEA

NETHERWORLD

tance diminishes as distance increases. Nggela (the Florida Islands) and even Guadalcanal are on clear days visible from the mountains. In the old days, coastal groups raided Santa Isabel, and Isabel has always been the source of *'ai ni gao,* a hard, dark, ebony-like wood. Outrigger canoes occasionally drift in from Ontong Java or Sikaiana, and the latter figures in at least one epic tale.

Despite this knowledge of outside peoples, northern Malaita remains the relevant social universe. The Baegu recognize their linguistic affinity with other northern Malaitan dialects (Lau, Toabaita, Baelelea, and Fataleka). Intermarriage, trade, and other social interaction occur routinely among these northern Malaitan groups and even extend into the Kwara'ae region of central Malaita. The Langalanga people of Malaita's central west coast make and distribute traditional shell money around the island. Central and southern Malaita, although known, fade in importance.

Non-Malaitans, particularly other Solomon Islanders, are seen as morally inferior. Their women are hussies, as failures to observe menstrual taboos or to make bride-price payments prove. The Polynesians of Sikaiana appear in Baegu epics as wife-stealers, debauchers, and moral degenerates of the worst sort. Europeans are so socially distant that, except as sources of cash wages and wielders of police power, they are outside the system. Chinese exist to be merchants and to exploit Melanesians.

America does not fit the pattern of increasing irrelevance with distance. Since the Pacific war and the Guadalcanal campaign, Malaitans have admired Americans. They believe they have special kinship with Americans, and some would like the Americans to return and drive out the British. The British administration, whose home government was trying to maintain a neutral position, was mildly embarrassed in 1967 by a native-led movement to recruit a battalion to go and help the Americans in Vietnam.

The heavens (*fanoi*) exist in several layers above the surface of the earth. Here are the sources of the winds as well as the heavenly bodies. In poetry and myth, the stars are fireflies (*bubulu*) in the outer layers of heaven, and meteors trace the movements of god-like ancestral spirits (*akalo*). Mythological characters enter and return from a subterranean (and subocean) world beneath the one we know. There actually are limestone caves and sinkholes to support these theories, and many small hillside streams pop into and out of the porous limestone strata, lending additional credence to such a hypothetical underworld. Some legends tell of an ancient race of pre-men like the menehune of Hawaii, called *oo,* who dwelt in caves, rock shelters, and pit houses before the ancestors of the Baegu arrived in Malaita.

There are hosts of supernatural beings in the Baegu world. People believe that there are many ghosts and spirits abroad in the forest, and most Baegu are rather apprehensive about traveling at night. *Gosile,* the ghosts of fetal children whose mothers died during pregnancy, are particularly malevolent and greatly feared. One female demon, Orobilia, lives within a rock, traps unwary male passers-by, and forces them to perform oral intercourse with her before she will release them.

Men themselves have several souls. The *mango* is a vital essence or spirit like Bergson's *élan vital.* It is identified with the breath; when breath is gone, so is life. The *ano* is the spiritual or spectral double of a man. People compare it to a photographic image. An individual may have any number of this kind of soul, and there is no fear of soul theft. Photography is in fact greatly appreciated. The *ano* can have its own existence independent of the body, traveling about during dreams in a classic Tylorian manner.

As in animistic systems anywhere, men believe that souls continue to exist after physical death. Through a divination procedure shortly after burial, the soul tells the survivors whether or not death was natural. In most cases people bury the corpse in a sacred grove (*beu aabu*) near the hamlet of the deceased. This is usually on land owned by the deceased's lineage, and where that descent group and the local community have worshiped. Here the soul, if it is contented, remains. The Baegu believe that the *ano* becomes part of the supernatural population, continuing after death an association with the places it knew in life: the hamlet where as a man he lived, the bushland where he gardened, and the grove where he honored his own ancestors. This belief as stated in Baegu is a poetic one; the soul remains with the living as long as they remember him. As a supernatural being, the soul after death can have more power than the living man. Important men can be particularly powerful after death, becoming *akalo,* the god-like ancestral spirits who can either bless or curse the living. They are strong, but morally neutral, and most of the practice of the pagan religion is intended to propitiate and please them. The *ano* of the forgotten journey to a Melanesian Hades called Ano Gwou, usually identified with Ramos Island, an uninhabited coral island lying between Malaita and Santa Isabel. Unlike the Lau people or the Kwaio to the south, the Baegu do not practice secondary burial.

BAEGU FOLK CARTOGRAPHY

When asked where the Baegu live or when asked to describe the extent of Baegu lands, bush people invariably begin by describing a quadrilateral section of Malaita (Map 14). As they see it, Baegu territory extends across the island; the Pacific Ocean defines its eastern limit and Indispensable Strait its western one. Since I (like the bulk of the population) lived on the Pacific or eastern slope, the Pacific is "the sea" (*asi*) while Indispensable Strait is "the other sea" (*asi ruu*). Two rivers, the Kwainafala and the Takwea, form the northern border and another two, the Taeloa and Ataa, the southern. For each of these pairs of rivers people talk as if they arose from adjacent sources and then flowed in more or less straight lines from their headwaters to their mouths, the Kwainafala and Taeloa westward and the Takwea and Ataa eastward toward the Pacific. Naturally, their sources are diffuse at best, and their courses anything but straight.

The pattern formed by these parameters, the two coastlines and straight lines approximating each riverine pair, is in reality almost triangular. The Kwainafala and Taeloa debouch a mere mile apart, while the mouth of the Ataa is almost twelve miles southeast of the Takwea. Yet the Baegu themselves see it as a rectangle and invariably draw it as such on sand or paper, with angles square and opposite sides of equal length.

This tendency to think of space as broken into units enclosed by rectangular borders is widespread. Besides the definition of Baegu ter-

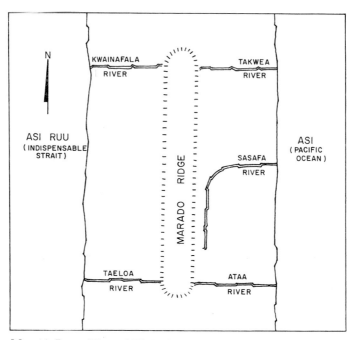

Map 14. Baegu View of Their Own Territory

ritory in this way, I have already described how some informants see the universe as having rectangular or square limits. Districts occupied by descent groups (to be considered later) are also mapped quadrilaterally. Man-made structures repeat the same pattern, with gardens, settlement clearings, and houses all having a rectangular or square plan.

INTERPRETATION OF THE LANDSCAPE

The landscape is more than a collection of topographical features. We all know this intuitively, but in America we tend to forget it. Nonetheless, our personalities and our landscapes interact. We all assume that life-styles and perhaps even the meaning of life itself are different in the midwestern prairies, New England's valleys, and the grandeur of the Pacific coast. "Home" for most of us means certain features that release a flood of nostalgia. We may repress or deny this, or at best consign it to irrelevance, but the Baegu are acutely aware of their landscape and its meaning. Virtually every aspect of their terrain has some social or emotional significance.

For the bush people, mountains are particularly important. Marado Ridge along the central spine of the island contains the holy places where the ancestors first settled (Map 15). Obviously, the first settlers had to land on the coast, but for the Baegu, traditional history began when the ancestors claimed Marado. Marado lies near the northern portion of the central mountain massif; it includes a few prominent named peaks (such as Borofunga and Iro), plus innumerable small sites such as Fau Umu, where the ancestors cooked their first sacred meal. *Fau* is Baegu for "rock" and *umu* is of course widely used in Polynesia for "oven," although the modern Baegu word for "oven" is *bii* in both secular and sacred contexts.

Langane Mountain, a prominent peak on the east coast, is separated from Marado by the Sasafa River Valley. Langane is an obvious landmark, a concentration of bush population, and the site of many pagan shrines not directly connected with the Marado shrines by descent or legend. Some, but not all, of the groups living there claim to be descended from settlers who came there by a different route, Bina a landing spot on the shore. *Bina* means hornbill, and some of these people observe a quasi-totemic affiliation with that bird rather than with the eagle (*no aabu*) that is sacred to the descendants of the Marado settlers.

The Sasafa River itself is a superb waterway cutting through the

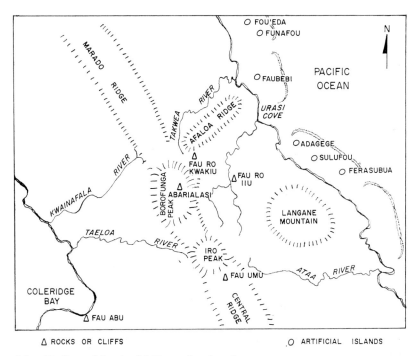

Map 15. Some Meaningful Baegu Landmarks

center of Baegu country. It must be one of the most beautiful rivers on earth, flowing through deep limestone canyons, with giant tropical hardwoods along its banks and dense thickets of ferns and shrubs over-hanging from the slopes rising steeply above it. The water is absolutely clear and quite cold, the current is swift, and there are innumerable rapids and small waterfalls. Malaitan children and hedonistic ethnog-raphers can waste hours there. The Baegu see the Sasafa (it means "thigh") as the center of their land. On the lower slopes of Borofunga Mountain overlooking the Sasafa Valley, not at its actual source but near where it bends sharply to the east and the sea, there is a petro-glyph of a Baegu woman named Abarialasi. She is the central figure in a long Helen-of-Troy myth that relates how she was captured on the beach by a raiding party of lechers from Sikaiana, how her husband and his followers rescued her, and how they ultimately annihilated the vil-lains. Her image is carved on a limestone slab facing along the course of the Sasafa toward its mouth. Her legs are spread, and people say that her left leg represents the people of Marado while her right one symbolizes the others. Unfortunately, there is a hole in the rock where her vulva should be; people snickered like school boys when they ex-plained the carving to me, and I had the distinct impression they were testing my gullibility.

There is no overt dual organization found here, and this cosmological dualism should not be stressed. The classification of people into descen-dants of Marado settlers and descendants of others, while it approxi-mates, does not neatly match the geographic categories based on the Sasafa River. There are subtle dialect differences between the two areas.

Interestingly enough, this cognitive distinction between those north of the Sasafa and those south of it can lead to the conclusion that "Baegu" simply does not exist. There is no distinct limit separating the Baegu from the Fataleka to the south or the Baelelea to the north. In-stead, descent groups living along the rivers (the ostensible boundaries) identify themselves either way, depending on the convenience of the moment. People of the Waleano clan were Baegu when they talked to me but Baelelea when they performed songs or dances at festivals in the Lau Lagoon, where Pierre and Elli Maranda were working and where some hostility against the Baegu existed. For months the Wale-langi people, among whom I lived, told me that I was lucky to be living with them on the left bank of the Sasafa. The south-bank types were, they said, not at all like the Baegu, but more like the Fataleka to the south. After I had been there some nine months, a visitor from the Masu clan on the right bank confided to me that it was a distinct pity I had chosen to live north of the river. The north bank types were, he said, unfortunately not Baegu, but were more like the Baelelea to the north. I have strenuously rejected the obvious conclusion.

TERRITORIAL DIVISIONS

Baegu land is not a single block, but is subdivided into a number of districts (*lolofaa*) claimed by descent groups. Districts are the critical units of the Baegu universe relating three things: people, land, and ancestral spirits. Claims to land derive from supernatural and kinship bases. Early ancestors first settled and claimed the land of a district. When they died, the ancestors were buried in sacred groves on the land. Today their descendants "own" the land, and are responsible for worshipping their own ancestors (who are now god-like *akalo* and who are of course buried on the land).

All districts have certain natural and cultural features. The most important and visible of these are the sacred groves (*beu aabu*) of primary rain forest, where the ancestors are buried and where the community of descendants and coresidents worship. Ritual life focuses upon these readily visible groves.

Borders of districts are most indistinct. Where large streams are the reference line, the border naturally follows the channel. Small streams lie totally within districts, and often the border is the ridge dividing drainage areas. In other places borders are simply connecting lines joining prominent rocks or stands of timber, or even amorphous zones between adjacent focal shrines.

Districts may be informally divided into neighborhoods that are local clusters of settlements (perhaps focused about a single sacred grove or shrine) whose members habitually interact frequently, and who may have some community of interest. There is no native Baegu name for a neighborhood as distinguished from a district.

Districts and neighborhoods are not simply portions of landscape. Rocky outcrops, groves, ridges, knolls, springs, and streams are known and named. Larger streams will be sequentially divided, and each deep pool may have a name of its own. One old man, somewhere over seventy, sat down with me one afternoon and named over 1,000 "places" in his district. His knowledge may be exceptional, but the point is that people are intensely aware of the topographical features they live among. Geographical folklore is rich, and many of the "places" have stories about them or figure prominently in epics.

The concept of "place" as an identifiable part of a district has considerable significance. Kevin Lynch, working among the "savages" inhabiting metropolitan Boston, Jersey City, and Los Angeles, created models based (he believes) on the ways these populations perceive their urban environments. Lynch analyzes cities in terms of paths, edges, districts, nodes, and landmarks (Map 16). As he defines them, *paths* are "the channels along which the observer customarily, occasionally, or potentially moves." *Edges,* in contrast, are "lateral references rather than coordinate axes"; they are boundaries or barriers rather than paths. *Districts* are areas or sections of two-dimensional extent, having a recognizable character, and which a person can mentally feel "inside of." *Nodes* are junctions or foci of travel, where paths cross or concentrate. *Landmarks* are sharply defined physical objects, used by observers as external point-references (Lynch 1960:47-48). Lynch's analysis of urban landscapes in these terms is suggestive and interesting, but it soon becomes apparent that the Malaitan Baegu, a definitely nonurban people, live and work with different images.

Bostonians, according to Lynch, see their city as a series of districts or neighborhoods, each of distinctive character. The collective pattern is connected and rationalized by a network of paths, routes that traverse neighborhoods and go from one to another. Nodes occur where two or more paths intersect. In Boston paths may radiate in many directions from these nodes, and in Paris this sort of star or radial patterning is probably even more important. As Lynch has it, these districts are

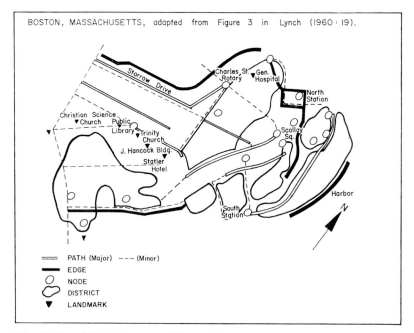

Map 16. Lynch's Environmental Image Components

conceptually more important and more satisfying for their inhabitants if they possess one or more clearly defined edges — that is, if they are highly "legible" or "visible." Happiness for a Bostonian is the Charles River edge of Boston, particularly as seen from the waterfront at MIT where Beacon Hill and the Back Bay appear clearly in profile. Who, for example, could ever picture Chicago without Lake Michigan and the Outer Drive (Lynch 1960:66)?

Like people everywhere the Baegu operate with models of their own environment and landscape. For them a spatial grammar of edges, paths, and nodes does not make sense, but one of landmarks and districts does.

Edges tend to be indistinct, for it is rarely possible to see a distinct boundary between one spatial category and another. Even where the actual boundary is distinct, there is no difference in character between the two tracts, and travelers rarely "see" the edge. They come out of dense wood, cross a stream or ridge, and enter another dense wood. Where districts blend in vague zones between focal shrines or where boundaries are imaginary lines between prominent features, it is quite literally impossible to see an edge except from elevated vantage points or overlooks. Somehow an edge seen in overview as on a map or diorama lacks the mental impact it has to a traveler who encounters it directly. "Boundary" has little if any juridical value in Malaitan land concepts; as Cochrane (1969:340) points out, land rights or privileges have focal definitions, stressing centers rather than peripheries.

Nor are paths all that important for the organization of space. Unlike our own, Malaitan paths do not follow preferred routes or take advantage of favorable terrain. Paths do detour around obvious barriers, for Malaitans, like most of us, cannot walk on water, climb sheer cliffs, or leap tall trees at a single bound. But for the most part Malaitan trails tend to follow straight lines from one point to another, and only in extreme cases do paths follow contours. If the way from here to there requires travelers to go first up and then down steep inclines, so be it. A lifetime of this sort of disregard for relief gives Malaitan bush people a hill-climbing virtuosity approaching that of the mountain goat; it gives ethnographers sore muscles and a nagging sense of inferiority. If trails go directly from one place to another, the actual route of the path itself is not really important. Thus, by logical implication, nodes or intersections of paths cannot have any great significance.

What does matter are landmarks and the known or recognized areas immediately surrounding them. People "know" their environment in terms of readily identifiable, usually prominent or focal features. Besides identifying particular features, such as rocky outcrops, knolls, ridges, or groves of trees, people recognize plots of land (often directly related to a prominent feature). Thus a recognized named area may be the land lying around, above, or below a conspicuous part of the landscape. This sort of cognitive pattern yields a number of fixed points, with elastic circles roughly delineating "districts" (in Lynch's sense, not as I use the term for Baegu settlement units) around them. Landscapes mentally focus upon a number of widely known features. Around these fixed points are circles of varying limits, and between them are plots of varying dimensions. Although the prominent landscape features themselves are definite and fixed, the plots around and between them are not and frequently overlap. Boundaries and extent vary according to current or past human usage; relationships are topological, but anchored to the fixed features. A map drawn according to this world-view would resemble an elastic sheet of chain mail (Figure 11), very different from Lynch's "image" of an American city.

People find their way from place to place much like navigators at sea or, more precisely, like pilots in coastal waters. A man knows where he is relative to one prominent feature. He knows where he wants to go in relation to another prominent feature. He sets out toward that place, taking a path leading in the right direction and adjusting his course through the jungle to maintain a proper heading according to the position of the sun and the relative slope of the ground. If he becomes confused en route (the forest is thick and vision difficult), he may climb a tree or seek a high point to get a new "fix" from another known, prominent feature. Over the years, fairly distinct trails appear connecting points where travel is frequent. But if storms or landslides make old trails impassable, or if a man wishes to go to a spot along an infrequently traveled route, he will cut a new path through the bush and will not fear getting lost.

SEX AND SPACE

Throughout much of Melanesia, the distinction between male and female is an important one. The separation, as Meggitt points out in his comparison of Mae Enga and Kuma material from the New Guinea highlands, can exhibit marked variations in pattern from place to place, but it nearly always appears to be phrased in terms of conflict or of structural opposition. Meggitt's Mae Enga associate the concept "male" with things that are good or powerful, whereas "female" goes into an opposed category along with the valueless and the weak. Mae Enga men fear and avoid women and accept a rather puritanical sexual code. The Kuma of the eastern highlands, although they do not fear women, show "a deep rooted antagonism between the sexes," with men trying

Figure 11. Baegu "Image" of Their Land

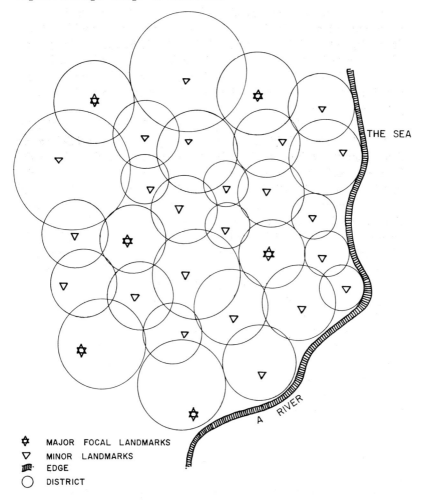

MAJOR FOCAL LANDMARKS
MINOR LANDMARKS
EDGE
DISTRICT

to dominate women, to overcome feminine "unreliability," and to deny female options that might undermine an assumed male superiority. As Meggitt cleverly and accurately puts it, "The one reflects the anxiety of prudes to protect themselves from contamination by women, the other the aggressive determination of lechers to assert their control over recalcitrant women" (Meggitt 1964:221).

Jacques Barrau, dealing mostly with horticultural lore from New Caledonia, extends both the topical and geographical range of this Melanesian male-female dichotomy. Traditional New Caledonian farmers divided their garden crops into male and female conceptual categories, each having its own distinctive techniques, rituals, and symbols. He portrays taro (*Colocasia* sp.) as the paramount female and the yam (*Discorea* sp.) as the leading male crop and equates them with wet and dry ecological conditions (Barrau 1965:337). Although the Baegu likewise characterize their crops as male or female, Barrau's classification is not valid in a literal sense among these Malaitan hill people, who perversely see taro as the male and ritually important crop, with the sweet potato a female and secular crop.

David Eyde (basing his thinking on his own fieldwork among the Asmat of West Irian, Firth's Tikopian material, and Mead and Schwartz's data from the Admiralty Islands) believes not only that this male-female opposition is pan-Melanesian (if not pan-Oceanic), but also that it is expressed spatially as well as socially (Eyde 1968). This would mean, I suppose, that both settlement patterns and social organization (insofar as these express a male-female distinction) derive ultimately from some sort of Levi-Straussian deep structure characteristic of the Melanesian mind (whatever that means). He cites two examples to support his contention. One is the common custom of dividing a residential unit (be it village, hamlet, or household) into male and female halves, or of separating a village into men's clubhouse versus family dwelling-place sections. The other is the use of spatial terms to express social relationships. For example, Firth (1936:213-17, 298-303) notes that the Tikopian word *paito* can apply to a material house, to a patrilineal descent segment, or (as *kano a paito*) to a bilateral personal kindred.

While the Baegu do not use precisely this same metaphor, they do label the collective body of wife's consanguineal kinsmen *lumaa*. For a male ego, these are the people who are affinally related to him by the marital alliance of two kindreds, his own and his bride's. *Lumaa* is fairly obviously cognate with the northern Malaitan word *luma*, which means women's, family, or dwelling house. In the Tikopian case, the "house" reference involves descent or consanguineal kinship, while in the Malaitan one, affinity. These are superficially quite different concepts, but Leach's (1961:7-13) topological or functional (in the mathematical sense) treatment of filiation and affinity suggests that they may indeed be treated as aspects of a single more general system.

MALE AND FEMALE IN MALAITA

If male-female antagonism is a Melanesian idiosyncrasy, it is a Malaitan obsession. The Baegu scrupulously observe distinctly different social and ritual roles for men and women, based on the assumption that the essential natures of the two sexes are grossly incompatible.

Fundamental to this is a fear of female procreative power or fertility: the belief that it pollutes and weakens. Male virility and fertility are good things. They are essentially spiritual blessings derived from the ancestors and are associated with strength, good health, and success. On the other hand, female fertility and procreative power are not necessarily good and (in theory at least) should be avoided. People equate female sexuality with lust and assume that females are the aggressors in illicit sexual relations.

According to the beliefs of the pagan religious system, contact with femininity can cause loss of spiritual and physical vigor. Participants in major religious ceremonies and those planning critical secular projects such as military expeditions therefore think it wise to avoid sexual intercourse. The polluting power of this essence of female, whatever it is, is so great that it acts even indirectly. As an illustration of the ability of femininity to contaminate by even indirect action, pigs that have "seen" the isolated huts where women give birth (*bisi ni lafi*) are unfit for use as sacrifices, so pigs dedicated to the ancestors are carefully watched and not permitted to go wild.

As the Baegu see it, femaleness weakens a man physically, pollutes his spiritual quality, makes ritual impotent, and can also neutralize magical power in general. One folktale relates how a clever woman defeated the villains by stepping over their magical weapons, thereby destroying their power. Baegu weapon imagery is explicitly sexual, and the *alafolo* type of war club is in metaphor a penis. What the girl did to the weapon and the men was to *faakeni* them. *Faa-* is the causative prefix characteristic of Austronesian languages; *keni* is the Baegu word for female. She "made them female."

I should point out that Baegu men do not in real life appear to fear women or contamination by women. Priests or self-important men who have a Malaitan version of the "holier than thou" attitude may avoid women, but an emotion of fear is absent and the word "fear" (*mou*) is never mentioned. Avoidance is based on devaluation of female qualities: the belief that although they may be hard workers and good mothers, women are stupid, lacking in talent and moral fibre, and not to be trusted.

SEXUAL ELEMENTS IN THE TABOO SYSTEM

Taboos, by prohibiting "wrong" behavior, are meant to prevent angering the ancestors. Specific taboos (actions being dangerous or forbidden) are many and varied. While some are peripheral and of little importance, the central structure of the taboo system is the proposition that contact with female reproductivity is to be avoided wherever possible. To belabor the obvious, this can be overdone. Since no human group has yet developed an effective substitute for sexual reproduction, a certain amount of cohabitation with females is necessary if the society is to continue. Baegu men therefore face duty squarely and copulate. I suspect some even learn to like it.

What happens is that female (largely reproductive) and male (by definition "important") activities are compartmentalized and are not supposed to be mixed. Sexual relations in a garden, for example, are improper; people should make love in a dwelling house or in the woods. During menstrual periods women withdraw to huts (*bisi*) on the edge of hamlet clearings. Mothers give birth in isolated huts (*bisi ni lafi*) deep in the forest. The female latrine is well away from the settlement. Men do not go there, and it is a sin for a woman to relieve herself elsewhere. (There is some confusion of genital and excretory organs.)

Along with these beliefs and practices, the Baegu have developed rather puritanical sexual attitudes. In traditional (pre-British) times adultery and seduction were capital crimes. They still involve whopping fines or compensation payments by the seducer to the injured male. There is also a well-developed concept of symbolic adultery or fornication. If a man steps over a woman's legs, her sleeping mat, or her backpack carrying cords, he has symbolically fornicated with her and is liable for compensation payments. People tend to believe the worst. If a man enters a married woman's house, sits next to her, or talks with her in private, the community assumes they are lovers. If young couples "date" without a chaperone, adults accuse them of sleeping together. Thus it is taboo for women to menstruate, give birth, or relieve themselves as part of the community. (Male defecation however, is frequently a social occasion.) It is taboo for men to come in contact with these female functions; it is taboo to make love in close proximity (spatial or temporal) to anything "important"; and it is taboo to have much of anything to do with someone else's wife.

Violation of these sexual taboos is both a tort and a crime. Violators (or those responsible for the violator, if the guilty one is a female or a child) must pay compensation to the "injured" party. A seducer must compensate the cuckolded husband with traditional shell valuables or cash, or pay his unmarried paramour's guardian (usually her father or brother) for taking her innocence. If a woman leaves the menstrual hut when she should not, or if a weak bladder betrays her and she does not feel like taking a long, cold walk in the night to the ladies' room, she "injures" someone; in this case the men of the hamlet, whose ancestors are offended. For this the guilty girl's consanguineal kinsmen must pay the men of the hamlet where the damage was done. Similarly, if lust

overcomes a couple in a garden, they should pay the men whose
cestors (associated with the land) they angered in their impatience.

Besides the personal "injuries" requiring compensation, such trans
gressions are also crimes against the community (perhaps "sins" would
be a better word). Naturally, not everyone is caught. But in times of
trouble when people learn by divination that the ancestors are angry,
there follows a period of strain and suspicion. Usually someone eventually confesses to one of these "sins." Once a sin or crime is acknowledged, it must be expiated by an offering given to a priest for sacrifice
to the ancestors. For serious crimes (adultery, seduction, or injury to a
kinsman) this requires a pig. For lesser offenses, fish or taro may suffice.

Although not strictly taboos, certain activities or things are associated
with one sex or the other. Men are warriors, priests, dancers, musicians,
and singers.[Only men climb the giant canarium almond trees to pick
the nuts.[Both sexes garden, but people believe that taro is appropriately
a male crop while sweet potatoes are suitable for females. Transportation of market produce, household goods, firewood, and water is done
by women. Women conduct the actual negotiations and barter exchange
at markets, while their men look on. This sexual identification of activities and objects seems to be a one-way affair. Men can play at female
roles, but women should not assume male ones. At a Lau Lagoon sacrifice I attended, one of the men in the dance group wore only a married woman's pubic apron (*masa*), much to the crowd's (that included
Baegu spectators) amusement. However, if a Baegu girl tries to dance
or sing in public, men are disgusted or offended.

SEX AND SPATIAL RELATIONS

There is, as should be expected, a certain harmony between sexual
attitudes and normal spatial relationships among persons. Dwelling
houses have an inner (family or women's) portion and an outer (public
or men's) portion. The inner portion is divided into male and female
halves. The fireplace is on the male side; drinking water is stored in
bamboo joints on the female side. Men's houses (*beu*), forbidden to
women, are on one side of a hamlet; family or dwelling houses (*luma*)
are on the other. Off to one side of the settlement will be the men's
latrine; the menstrual huts (*bisi*) and women's latrine will be on the
other. All of these features are oriented to a single concordant pattern
(Figure 12). If the menstrual hut is to the east, the dwelling houses
will be on the eastern side of the settlement, and the eastern half of
each dwelling house will be the female half. Conversely the western
half of each dwelling house will be the male half, and the men's houses
and latrine will be to the west. In larger hamlets, the men's house (*beu*)

Figure 12. Sexual Geography of Baegu Settlements

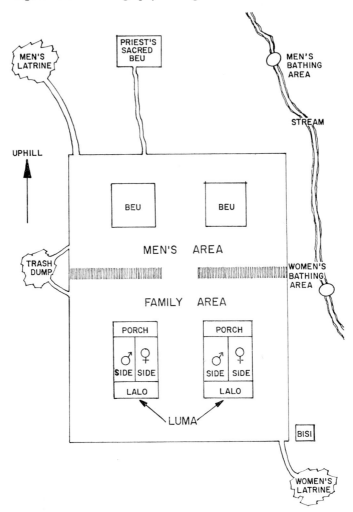

may occupy a central position. Women do not enter the men's house, and men do not go near the *bisi*. Both sexes interact around the dwelling houses.

To a large extent this male-female opposition is interpreted within an uphill-downhill context. This will make sense to anyone who has ever traveled in the Malaitan bush country, where tired legs and short breath soon make it clear that uphill-downhill is a basic fact of Baegu life. The basic proposition of this relatively commonsense model is that the polluting or weakening quality of the female tends to flow downhill.

The men's half of a hillside village therefore will be the uphill side. For villages on knolls, my impression is that the men's half will be to landward and the women's half to seaward. If a settlement is fortunate enough to have two watering places available, the men's washing and drinking spot will be upstream, the women's downstream. If a party of Baegu bathes in a river, the men always pick the upstream position.

This gravitational orientation becomes culturally significant in a number of behavioral contexts. I have previously recounted the *faa-keni* episode from folklore, wherein a woman destroyed the magical power of a man's weapons by stepping over them. In real life women simply do not take a position above men. Women do not step over sitting men, nor do they climb a tree or house frame with men below them. Parties of Baegu walking cross-country seem automatically to assume the correct male-female positions. The narrowness of forest trails forces people to go in single file. Men lead the way uphill, step aside and pause at the summit, and let the women lead the way downhill. The process is reversed in the valley. For what it may be worth, a supposedly knowledgeable acquaintance tells me that sex with northern Malaitan women is no sybarite's dream. The girls have never read Malinowski, and most of them apparently believe that the ventral-ventral male over female position (the so-called missionary position) is the only way decent people make love.

If women do not go above men because of the danger of contamination to the men, men do not stand or pass immediately above women because the sexual connotations of this position make it improper. The importance of positional thinking where sex is involved comes through clearly in the sexual taboo system. As mentioned earlier, stepping over a woman's legs, or even her bedroll or backpack cords, is symbolically equivalent to fornication with her. A man doing this has superposed himself immediately above her in the position of a lover; therefore he can be forced to pay compensation for adultery or seduction as appropriate. In some cases, merely talking about stepping over someone, because of its implications of sexual transgressions, becomes a curse and cause of serious quarrels.

CULTURAL AND NATURAL SPACE

Besides this sexually defined dualistic view of life, there is also for the Baegu a prime distinction between the world of nature and that of man or the cultural world. This nature/culture dualism expresses itself objectively in two ways: in the settlement pattern by a careful maintenance of borders, and through a taxonomic distinction between wild and tame things.

Hamlet clearings and gardens are artifacts of human settlement and activity. They are carefully and purposefully separated from the wild nature that in Malaita so overwhelmingly (almost oppressively) surrounds them. Hamlet clearings (*labata*) are usually square-cornered and have very obvious borders. Some groups reinforce these borders by fences or ditches to restrain pigs, or by planting a floral border of ornamental shrubs such as flowering hibiscus (*tatale*) or the croton plant (*'ala'ala*) with its many-colored leaves. The clearing itself is carefully maintained and tended. Pigs, chickens, cats, and dogs do some of the scavenging work. Hard-working Baegu women sweep their hamlet clearings daily, plucking out grass or weeds growing in unwanted spots. Everyone helps keep clearings free from garbage and trash. The forest outside the clearing is untended; it is useful as a source of wild raw materials and as a place for waste disposal.

This careful tending of settlement clearings has some direct functional value. By clearing away the brush, people lessen the danger from venomous snakes, centipedes, and scorpions. In earlier days the clearing provided a slight amount of early warning of enemy attack and offered a field of fire for the arrows and spears of the defenders. By disposing of trash and garbage outside the clearing, sanitation and presumably health are also improved. Proper disposal of this rubbish also protects against sorcery (*arua*) using contagious magic.

Gardens (*ole*) too, another product of human settlement, are clearly separated from wild, untended nature. Like hamlet clearings, garden plots are rectangular. One of the first acts of the Baegu gardener after clearing his land is to construct a fence around his plot. This fence is made of logs laid horizontally, or alternatively in a palisade of sticks set on end and called *biru* after their fancied resemblance to a necklace of porpoise teeth. People say fences prevent theft and raiding by pigs. If so, they must act magically, for such fences are by no means sturdy enough to deter either human or porcine raiders. Planting of the magical cordyline (*sango*) in the four corners of a garden suggests that magical techniques are indeed relied upon more than the physical efficacy of the barrier. The fence is a symbolic boundary between the garden as a cultural work of man and the wild nature of the surrounding forest.

Baegu habitually classify or describe things as tame or wild, part of human life or part of nature. Those things connected with human settlements are described by the adjective *fera,* that is (as a noun) the word for a hamlet or settlement site. Wild things of the forest are identified by the adjective *kwasi,* meaning untamed or not under control. Domesticated animals such as pigs or imported European housecats are *boso fera* or *fusi fera.* Feral animals are *boso kwasi* or *fusi kwasi.* A type of areca palm not planted around hamlets but harvested from the woods is *agero kwasi.* Ghosts not associated with a living human descent group or sacred shrine are *akalo kwasi.*

Thus one would deduce that, as the Baegu see things, it is important to recognize and maintain a distinction between natural and cultural space. In a region where nature is so rampant and where human efforts to control it require strenuous exertion, this would seem to be an altogether reasonable interpretation for an indigenous people.

SOCIAL AND PERSONAL SPACE

The Baegu are acutely aware of their own personal positions in space, of their spatial relations to one another, and of the information conveyed by physical position. Oliver's "spatial dimension" of interaction therefore becomes an apt one for approaching the holy grail of social structure through observation of routine social relationships (Oliver 1958:804-6).

As Hall (1966:12-14) and Birdwhistell (1964) have pointed out, the position of the body, both in itself and in relation to other people, can communicate. In its simplest form this can be merely the assertion or acknowledgment of membership in the group. This is Heddiger's "social distance," inside of which comes the feeling of belonging, of cooperation; outside is isolation and anxiety. His definition of "personal distance" is the "normal spacing of non-contact species" that Hall (1966:112-116) correlates with social position within the groups. Birdwhistell (1964) describes how human beings use posture, bodily attitudes, and movement to convey emotional states and value judgments. Seen in this way, "taking a position" on an issue is not a wholly fortuitous linguistic construction. Hall (1966:1-6) develops a more systematic concept he calls "proxemics," dealing with the way two or more actors communicate with one another in a largely informal manner, by their distance apart, bodily movements, and gestures. In our preoccupation with verbal communication, we generally tend to underestimate the importance of such paralinguistic communication systems.

The point of all this is that any culture has its own proxemic vocabulary and grammar, and that one of the ethnographer's problems is to learn and to translate this. This is no easy task, for, since we are largely unaware of it, we are probably more constrained or trapped by our own proxemic communication system than we are by our language.

In a way the Whorfian hypothesis may be more relevant here than it is for verbal speech.

Among the Baegu sex has far more relevance than it does in America. Hall points out that only lovers space themselves within "intimate distance" (less than one and a half feet), where interpersonal stimuli are overwhelming. "Personal distance" (between one and a half and four feet), where hands can touch and which is the normal limit of domination, is for close friends and is most appropriate for male and female. In America males and females take intimate-distance spacing when they embrace on meeting. This is naturally most appropriate for married couples, lovers, and close relatives; it is most appropriate when done privately, but may be done in public. Personal distance is quite acceptable for married couples and can be done by dating pairs publicly, but is forbidden a man and "other women." American males who encroach on the intimate or personal distance of another male do so only at the risk of being considered queer.

Baegu men and women simply do not get that close together publicly. Beyond childhood, only married couples and lovers assume intimate-distance spacing, and then only in private. Where males and females are concerned, even our "personal distance" becomes their "intimate distance" and is not proper in public. In crowds men and women do not stand together except in groups of relatives. Women form little knots with their menfolk around them. If men and women do come within "personal distance" of one another, most Baegu assume they are or at least want to be lovers. Superposition of male over female in particular is (as noted above) equated with sex or desire, and is simply not done casually.

Actually, this concept of relative position goes well beyond purely sexual roles. The position of people vis-à-vis one another also conveys information about relative social status. An upper position, as it does elsewhere in the world, implies social superiority. Juniors do not stand or sit above their betters. Seniors stand to address a seated crowd. Important men lead the way when traveling, enter a village first among a crowd of visitors, and speak from the head of the line of dancers at formal dance performances. Well-bred Baegu do not step over or stand above an important man. The senior is always "on top" both socially and spatially; this is much more explicit than it is in our own culture.

Important men in the northern Malaitan hill country take their personal dignity very seriously. Children may romp and tumble, but adults would not dream of doing so. Children may as a stunt descend a palm tree head first; an adult, never. The heads, in particular the teeth and hair, of important men are not to be taken lightly and are "out of bounds" to lesser folk. People, both boys and girls, learn early to carry themselves gracefully and modestly. A naked Baegu girl looks far more "proper" than a fully-clothed but awkward American teenager. Feminine comeliness is equated with grace, and clumsy girls become old maids. The bush people take great pride in walking gracefully; slipping and falling on muddy trails is clumsy and ill-bred. It embarrasses the fallen one and causes guffaws of laughter among the luckier onlookers. Although I was not particularly amused, my cross-country walking brought many little rays of sunshine into Baegu land.

Emphasis on physical grace, awareness of body position, and the general worry about one's dignity make the hill people slow moving, carefully restrained, and not exactly sparkling in new situations. Europeans and other Melanesians (even coastal Malaitan people) think Malaitan bush men like the Baegu or Kwaio are taciturn and dull, but their slowness and stubbornness is more apparent than real and disappears in the hills among friends. It stems not from hostility or dimwittedness, but from a resolve to do nothing embarrassing.

Baegu formal dancing reflects this awareness of position and dignity; carriage and movement are carefully controlled to express religious and aesthetic fervor. There is, to be sure, a certain amount of dancing for the pure fun of it. This is secular dancing, done at weddings or at all-night bull sessions during the full of the moon. Dance styles of this sort diffuse throughout the Solomons via plantation labor gangs and are greatly affected by the twist-frug-jerk tradition learned at the cinema in Honiara. Traditional dances are performed during the great ceremonies (*maoma*) honoring the dead. The formal dance (*agae*) features two files of male dancers (hill women do not dance in public), with a small cluster of panpipers in the middle of each line (Figure 13). Ideally each file will have eight leading dancers, eight panpipers, and eight following dancers. This perfect number rarely works out, however. In the good old days, I am told, there were more talented dancers, and two extra dance lines could be added, making the basic pattern cruciform. But since this pattern is not important in traditional Malaitan iconography, I suspect this may well be a Christian invention. All the dancers and panpipers are dressed in their finest ornaments and wear seedpod leg rattles. The dancers carry cordyline leaves (*sango*) and carved wooden dance paddles (*reba*) of stylized hornbill shape. The dance is relatively slow. The men have rapt, otherworldly expressions on their faces, move carefully and peacefully, and have a regular routine of hand and body movements. During the dance, the lines walk through a number of patterns said to be birds in flight, rivers in flood, or snakes gliding through the trees. Dancing is to some extent com-

Figure 13. Geometry of the Baegu Dance

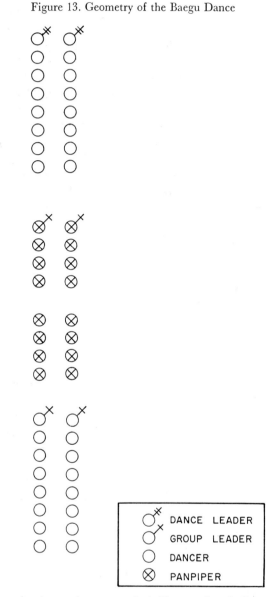

In modern dancing, only two vertical files are found. Some Baegu people say, however, that a "perfect" dance would also have two horizontal ranks, completing a cruciform pattern. Multiples of eight (*kwalu*) are significant in Baegu cosmology, numerology, mathematics, everyday reckoning, and as a figure of speech.

petitive, and men try to excel in the grace and emotion of their performances.

Interestingly enough, these formal dances provide simultaneously the climax of the road to fame through bodily control and aesthetics for most men, and the chance to make a fool of oneself for senior, important men, those who live with the most self-conscious dignity of all. At intervals during the dance the lines return to the basic pattern form and rest briefly. During those breaks important men march or run around the dancers, pausing at the head of the dance lines to address the crowd. Here they have literally the center of the stage, and some of them use it to become incredible hams. Leaders of impeccable social position, sages and judges, may lose their gravity and become clowns. They may cavort around the dancers, goosing people, talking nonsense, and making ribald insults. Not all are clowns, of course; some people always remain serious. The point is that the ceremony (the formal dance) is an ambiguous affair. Men can gain attention by playing it straight, *or* by reversing normal roles and being mummers.

OTHER ASPECTS OF PERSONAL SPACE

Baegu interpretations of spatial positioning and social seniority more or less make sense to us. Even the rigid male-female separation is understandable, albeit a trifle obsessive in our eyes. But as Hall describes for a number of non-Western societies, the spatial aspects of Baegu male-male interaction will almost drive an unwary Westerner to distraction.

Men and women do not go within personal, let alone intimate, distance of one another in public. Only married couples do, and then only in private. However, Baegu males get much closer to one another than Westerners can normally bear. Baegu men refer to male relatives and friends as brothers, and interaction within personal or even intimate distance is not only tolerated but sometimes preferred. Young males are especially intimate, holding hands and sitting or standing with arms across each other's shoulders. During the all-night singing or the gossip-cum-betel-chewing sessions at *maoma* times, men literally sit cheek to cheek and sleep side by side. Men seem to love to communicate by speaking softly directly into another's ear. All of this can be a bit difficult for middle-class white folk who subliminally associate male intimacy with homosexuality or bad breath.

The same rules apply to some extent to female-female interaction. Traders at markets along the seashore literally barter face to face.

"Public distance," on the other hand, does not differ significantly from our own concepts. A speaker at a public gathering or a native political leader addresses the crowd from a distance of twelve feet or more. Hall (1966:116-20) suggests that this quite possibly is a pan-human trait.

A SUMMARY OF BAEGU SPATIAL BEHAVIOR

It is of course wrong to oversimplify statements about Baegu classifications of or attitudes toward personal and social space. People are often ambivalent, groupings may be ambiguous, and things can vary from context to context. Nevertheless, it is possible to make some systematic generalizations.

First, opposite sexes do not interact closely in public. Men and women remain at a respectable impersonal distance. Women, perhaps because of their innate inferiority (perfectly obvious to a Baegu man), remain symbolically or physically downhill from men. On the other hand, men do not get *immediately* above women, because of the sexual imagery involved.

Second, spatial position should correlate directly with social position. Junior men should not sit or stand above the seniors, and an important man's head may be sacred.

Third, the Baegu can tolerate much more personal contact than we can when the actors are of the same sex. Women at the market and men in friendship interact routinely in extremely close positions that would disturb a European or an American.

Fourth, this preference for close interaction does not hold in all contexts. In much of daily life Baegu people seem to prefer privacy and more isolation than we normally want. The Baegu dislike and are unnerved by the crowded conditions of the island villages of the Lau Lagoon or at government or mission settlements, where people habitually live cheek by jowl. The traditional mountain settlement pattern is a dispersed one. Pagan families usually live in single-family farmsteads or in small hamlets of closely related families. Baegu talk explicitly of wanting to be alone and of disliking crowds. Hogbin noticed among the Toabaita further to the north, and I have seen among the Baegu, that people use their gardens as a tactful way of finding privacy. It seems almost as if these people can tolerate and enjoy stimulating interaction only if they are able to withdraw when they choose.

Fifth, the "normal" use of public distance suggests that, for larger public gatherings and less personal affairs, greater distances for interaction are more suitable, supporting if not really confirming the fourth conclusion.

All of us know that people need social stimulation, and most of us feel some need of intimacy. Doxiadis (1968:331) suggests that we also need space, even specifying how much per person and suggesting that we carry this need with us as we move about. So does Hall, dealing on a personal, more finite level. Although their perceptions of these needs may differ from ours, the Baegu are aware of their own desires both for social stimulation and for privacy or space. Habitual patterns of Baegu social relations and traditional settlement patterns are at least partially adaptations in response to these desires.

7. Baegu Kinship Ideology and Social Relations

Most technologically unsophisticated, non-Western, small-scale societies express their norms of social relations through the idiom of kinship. One unfortunate constraint in talking about kinship in a society is that kinship may well not exist in its usual anthropological manifestation. Real people may have an ideology about descent, customs governing recruitment to or filiation with corporate or noncorporate groups, rules controlling inheritance and succession, and traditional ways of arranging marriages and using the alliances thereby established. They have a rational set of terms covering the semantic field of human relationships, usually based logically upon some natural (genealogy, sex, age) and cultural (social, behavioral, residential) features of those relationships. Anthropologists, in talking of kinship ideologies and systems, are asserting that there is a systematic coherence to these things that may or may not exist in real life among the people who possess and use them. Nevertheless, a century of kinship studies in social anthropology has given us a useful vocabulary and conceptual framework for describing a wide range of human behavior.

Kinship terminology is not important to the Baegu. They use terms loosely, reinterpreting their meanings according to the nature of the situation, and do not worry about consistency or the logic of the system, which has some explicitly genealogical basis but admits social and behavioral modification. Kin terms are rarely used for address — usually only in those situations where the speaker hopes to remind his audience of their obligations toward him. The system is broadly "classificatory"; hence important men will have hundreds of "sons" and an aspiring politician will be almost everyone's "brother." On a day-to-day basis, most people address and refer to each other by personal names.

Baegu cousin terminology conforms to Murdock's Dakota-Iroquois type in that parallel cousins and siblings are classified together in the same category, while father's sister's children and mother's brother's children (cross cousins) are both called *dii* but are terminologically differentiated from parallel cousins and siblings (Murdock 1949:125). Kinship terminology is bifurcate merging according to Lowie's scheme, since in the first ascending generation there is one category for father and father's brother, a second for mother's brother (Murdock 1949: 118, 142). There is a single kinship category *kokoo*, consisting of grandparents, grandchildren, and mother's brother, that combines individuals (or kin types) of two generations in a manner analogous to Omaha kinship terminology which Buchler and Selby (1968:250) have called a Miwok system. Figure 14 presents some Baegu kin terms diagrammatically.

This diagram is simply an illustrative and mnemonic device, not an explanatory one. It is not intended to represent semantic space, or to serve as a basis for formal analysis. It is only a graphic way of saying that among the parental generation one's father and father's brothers (consanguineal paternal uncles) are called *maa*, one's mother and mother's sisters (consanguineal maternal aunts) are called *gaa*, a mother's brother (and his wife) are called *kokoo*, and a father's sister is called *aia* (her husband's label varies with social context). In one's own generation siblings and parallel cousins of the opposite sex are *waiwane*, while on another dimension older siblings and parallel cousins (regardless of sex) are *sauana* and younger ones are *sasina*.[1] Cross-cousins are *dii*. In ego's children's generation, his own children and the children of his siblings and parallel cousins of the same sex as himself are called simply "child" or *wela*. The children of ego's siblings and parallel cousins of the opposite sex and of his cross-cousins are known as *kokoo*. Consanguineal relatives in even older or younger generations (grandparents, grandchildren, great uncles/aunts, or great nephews/nieces of any degree, and all cousins beyond second cousins) are *kokoo*.

What does matter is that kinship ideology contains certain basic assumptions about human social relationships, concepts of descent and inheritance, and, derived from these, implicit or explicit norms governing interaction between individuals and establishing their rights and obligations toward one another.

---

[1] *-na* in the terms *sauana* and *sasina* is a third-person possessive pronominal suffix. "My brother" would be *sauaku* or *sasiku;* "your brother" would be *sauamu* or *sasimu.*

Figure 14. Schematic Diagram of Baegu Consanguineal Kin Terms

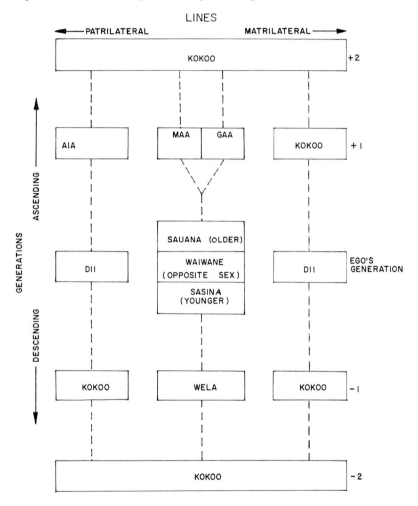

I have never cared to indulge in what may be sterile arguments about whether a given society is unilineal or cognatic, a mixture of both, or neither. People may have *ideas* about descent and kinship systems being unilineal or cognatic; *people* are not unilineal or cognatic. These labels may be in large measure artifacts of theoretical social anthropology. For example, regardless of how we describe them, all real people recognize that children have some sort of relationship with both their mothers' and their fathers' families. The genealogical or kinship models used to ascribe rights and obligations may vary in detail, but men everywhere know that reproduction and the human relationships deriving therefrom are bisexual.

Baegu beliefs about and attitudes toward kinship are no more uniform or disparate than those of other people. I sometimes feel that one could do equally well describing theirs as an agnatic system with some significant cognatic elements or as a cognatic system with a very strong agnatic bias. The point is that, like many societies, they have patrilineal clans and they recognize bilateral kin relationships. They themselves see no inherent contradictions. The Baegu seem to separate what we might call kinship into three different concepts. They spend a lot of time talking about genealogies (using a patrilineal model) and patrilineal descent groups (which hold land titles), and in this sense they use an agnatic system. They also use bilateral personal kindreds for a variety of social purposes, and they define most rights and obligations in terms of an ego-centered cognatic model (not in terms of relationships between a man's lineage and his mother's lineage). In this sense, they use a cognatic system. Finally, affinal relationships are something else again — not true kinship, but a relationship of sorts between groups of kinsmen created by marriage. Weddings are performed by kindreds, but the terminological system of affinal relationships assumes agnatic lineages.

These three kinds of kin relationships (descent groups, kindreds, and affinal alliances) exist simultaneously with no major interference or confusion apparent. Rather than try to reduce these to a single comprehensive system, I prefer to talk about them as if three discrete ideologies or concepts were involved: agnatic descent, cognatic relationship, and affinal relationship. This, albeit perhaps overly analytic, does more justice to Baegu kinship and social relations, and is certainly easier to handle in narrative format, than an attempt to treat Baegu society under a conventional anthropological rubric such as "agnatic" or "cognatic."

THE CONCEPT OF AGNATIC DESCENT

Given their premises of male superiority and female ritual impurity, it seems fairly logical that in an ideal arrangement people would stress male solidarity while downgrading or ignoring the contributions of women. Hence basic norms of Baegu social organization are that people *ought* to affiliate and cooperate with their patrilateral kinsmen, that patrilineal descent ought to be important, and that corporate groups ought to consist of agnatic relatives.

People assume that the closest relationship of all is the tie between father and son, and the social role of father is highly admired. According to the norms of family life, fathers feed, protect, and love their

children; sons in turn love, obey, and help their fathers. This relationship between fathers and sons serves as a prototype for social organization in other situations. The Baegu "gods," who provide the people
with sustenance and good health, are ancestral spirits and are both
theologically and literally fathers of the living. Baegu leaders are pro-
tective and generous, and are said to be as "fathers" to the many "sons"
who follow them.

Exact reckoning of patrilineal descent is important for establishing
connections with the ancestors and therefore with sources of supernatural power. The traditional oral genealogies (*talisibara*) may go
back to an original male ancestor thirty or more generations ago and
read very like the opening chapters of the Book of Matthew, a lengthy
series of begats broken occasionally by a brief side reference to a
peculiarity or noteworthy achievement of an ancestor. Priests must
know these genealogies, and laymen who do know them may gain a
certain amount of informal status as genealogical references.

The Baegu recognize named patrilineal descent groups called *'ae
bara,* meaning the base or the stem of the family. Membership in these
descent groups is almost without exception on the basis of patrilineal
descent (children automatically belong to their father's *'ae bara*) and
is unambiguous. Patrilineal descent groups are theologically custodians
of the land. Land is sacred to the ancestors (who are buried there),
and men are reverent toward the land because it gives them their living.
It is only fitting, as the Baegu see it, that those who are properly
descended (that is, agnatically) should have the stewardship of the
land and the responsibility for maintaining its fertility by honoring the
ancestors.

There is a particular district (*lolofaa*) associated with each descent
group. Usually most of the residents of that district are members of
that *'ae bara* and their ancestors are buried there in shrines associated
with sacred groves of primary forest. The local *'ae bara* is responsible
for the upkeep (minimal) of these shrines and for holding sacrifices in
honor of the ancestors buried there. Besides being a land-holding corporation, the descent group is therefore a church or a cult as well.

The descent group is not now exogamous and has little in practice
to do with marriage, although according to tradition *'ae bara* were once
exogamous. Descent groups are irrelevant to the definition of incest,
which is usually defined genealogically. Marriage is forbidden for first
cousins and disapproved for second cousins. Alternatively, people define
incest in terms of marriage exchange between two personal kindreds or
in terms of hamlet coresidence.

Unfortunately, *'ae bara* means different things in different contexts.
In some senses it is a maximal descent group containing all those who

claim descent from a distant apical ancestor and who are associated with a district. All of these claim to be descended patrilineally from a common male ancestor, but only important families can prove it by citing specific genealogies. The rest, and particularly marginal individuals, cannot really prove their agnatic rights to membership, but they may be accepted as such by the consensus of the descent group if they participate in group rituals. This would be a sib in Murdock's (1949:47) scheme, or a clan in Robin Fox's (1967:41-50) terminology. In other situations *'ae bara* refers to a minimal descent line within the descent group as a whole, who definitely can trace their descent patrilineally to an apical ancestor just a few generations back. Baegu *'ae bara* therefore branch and ramify like Evans-Pritchard's (1940:192-203) segmentary lineage model for Nuer social structure (Figure 15). These minimal descent lines would be true lineages according to Fox or Murdock. They are usually associated with a smaller tract of land within the district. Compounding the terminological confusion, the descent group

Figure 15. Segmentary Lineage Structure

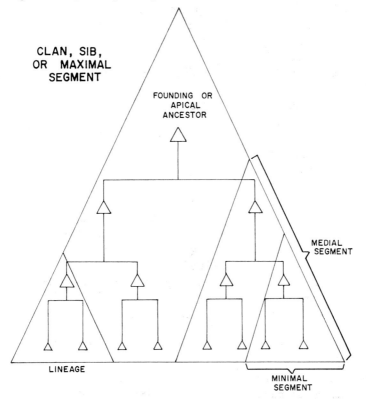

CLAN, SIB, OR MAXIMAL SEGMENT

FOUNDING OR APICAL ANCESTOR

MEDIAL SEGMENT

LINEAGE

MINIMAL SEGMENT

and the district have the same name, and the hearer must rely upon linguistic and social contexts to tell whether *Langane* is a patrilineage or several thousand acres of forest.

A woman's status in descent groups is particularly ambiguous. In her residence and daily life a married woman is obviously part of the community where she lives with her husband. Her activities in gardening, marketing, and care of pigs enhance the wealth and prestige of her husband's group. To a certain extent, though, she remains ritually a member of her father's *'ae bara,* since she returns to that group for the *maoma ni keni,* a special sacrificial feast for women following the more important male ceremonials, given in honor of her father's group's ancestors. If a woman wishes to offer a pig to the ancestral spirits, she does so through a male kinsman. If she has no grown sons, she offers the pig through her father or her brothers and the pig goes to her own ancestors. But if her father has died, she offers the pig through her own sons, and in effect the pig goes to her husband's ancestors.

Agnatic norms also establish hierarchical relationships, comparative statuses, and seniority within and between descent groups. The traditional head of the descent group (*wane initoo*) holds his status by virtue of primogeniture. He is not really a chief, but a hereditary landowner. His actual position is more nearly that of a chairman of the board of a land-holding corporation, with duties and powers somewhat like those of the Trukese *mwaaniici* described by Goodenough (1951: 42-45).

Within limits birth order establishes seniority within a descent line. Other things being equal, an elder son of a line descended from an elder brother will outrank his siblings and cousins. This is a ritual seniority and no material advantages result from it. In actual practice individual wealth, talent, and aggressiveness have more influence on status relationships.

There is also a genealogical charter establishing relationships between *'ae bara* as maximal lineages. Traditional origin myths tell how Baegu *'ae bara* descended from brothers and sons among the early settlers who moved into the various Baegu districts. Thus some descent groups are thought to be closely associated, while others remain outsiders.

Since the *'ae bara* functions as a group only in ritual contexts, and since land use and social interaction depend so much on other factors, it seems curious that patrilineal descent and agnatic groups should have such cognitive importance. In a way the "purpose" of the descent group is that it is an end in itself. Keesing (1965:192-201) explained how Kwaio descent groups in central Malaita seek to gain strength by recruiting members for the performance of important religious ceremonies. In like manner the only thing Baegu descent groups seem to "do" is to conduct religious festivals and sacrifices, and the Baegu insist that they must be maintained at maximum strength for that purpose. Pagan Baegu see the continuation of human well-being and world harmony as a result of cooperation between the living and the spirits of the dead ancestors. The ancestral ghosts control weather, productivity, and health. The role of the living is to seek such blessings by honoring the dead with prayers and sacrifices. Religious ceremonies honoring the dead are essential to public and private welfare. Descent groups carry out these ceremonies, which the Baegu themselves call "work." Therefore descent groups are essential and must be preserved.

In these religious activities, where men face directly the spirits of the ancestors who begat them, the relevance of agnatic descent is emphasized most strongly. Hence it is not surprising that the ideology of agnatic descent has acquired a mystique that tends to elevate it to a position of paramount importance in their hierarchy of social ideologies. Nor is it at all surprising that the Baegu use an "agnatic idiom to express group unity *vis-à-vis* other groups and to delimit 'proper' status within the group" (de Lepfervanche 1968:185). On the whole, the concept of agnatic descent is operative within limited but important contexts. It is essentially normative or ideological, belonging to the cosmological realm of ancestors and heroes and describing how in an ideal situation Baegu society ought to be organized. But this does not make agnatic descent any less important or influential, for as Scheffler pointed out for Choiseul Island, ideological statements are also part of social action (Scheffler 1965:294).

THE CONCEPT OF COGNATIC RELATIONSHIP

One kind of Baegu kinship (*futalanae*) refers to consanguineal cognatic relationships between people and their obligations to one another on the basis of real or assumed genetic relations. The Baegu, like most human societies, recognize that an individual has obligations to and can expect help from both his patrilateral (agnatic) and his matrilateral (uterine) kinsmen. Ivens, writing about the saltwater people of the Lau Lagoon, said that "the unit of culture is the bilateral family" (Ivens 1930:20). I am not sure exactly what he meant by this, but it is true that the Baegu explicitly recognize the bilateral ego-based kindred (Figure 16), and that these personal kindreds are the operational group in many important social (as opposed to primarily religious) situations.

The Baegu category *gule bara* includes all of a person's consanguineal relatives, both those joined by male linkages (*futa ana wane*) and female linkages (*futa ana keni*). Kinship terminology recognizes

Figure 16. The Bilateral Personal Kindred

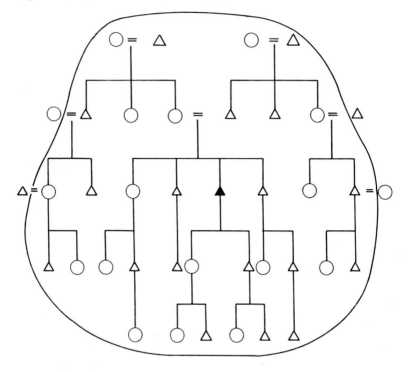

this. It is a coherent system including both patrilateral and matrilateral categories, and many terms override such a distinction specifically denoting kinsmen from both sides of the "family" — for examples, *dii* for cross-cousins, and the equating of siblings and parallel cousins. Norms and expectations about kinship reinforce this. A person needing help can claim it (and expect to get it) from either his father's or his mother's family. Conversely, he has a definite obligation to assist his siblings, his sons and daughters, and their children. Men have the privilege of offering sacrifices to any ancestor of either parent or of any of their grandparents, the rule being to any remembered ancestor to whom they can more or less prove relationship.

Since a personal kindred is ego-based (defined by reference to ego), its operation as a social or cultural group can best be seen in specific contexts where it is called upon to act. The limits of the Baegu kindred are elastic. Although an important man's kindred will be far larger than the typical person's, the practical limit — as defined by normal memory, by actual exchange of goods and services, and by incest rules — seems to be second cousins and their children.

One of the most obvious of contexts is at weddings. Weddings are an interaction for purposes of exchange between two cognatically defined *ad hoc* corporations literally called "sides." The man's side (*bali ni wane*) is the groom's kindred. They are obliged to a greater or lesser degree, depending on their wealth and the closeness of their relationship to the groom, to provide portions of the bride-price and the miscellaneous food donations and services accompanying the ceremonies. The woman's side (*bali ni keni*) are the bride's kindred, who are obliged to provide portions of the bride's group's contributions of food to wedding feasts, and all of whom (again, depending on the closeness of their relationship to the bride's sociological father) can claim portions of the bride-price paid for her.

Funerals, too, call for recognition of the kindred of the dead man. They perform the burial services (priests, however, because of their sanctity, are buried by nonkinsmen who are paid for the job), observe mourning procedures, and take part in the distribution of wealth following the death of a rich man.

Sacrifices of pigs to the ancestral spirits are more complex. The ancestors, being the founding fathers, are closely associated with the patrilineal descent groups, and as such they form an agnatic supernatural community. Nevertheless, sacrifices to the ancestral spirits are not restricted to agnatic lines. Any descendant, those born through female links as well as of male, is entitled to offer sacrifices to the ancestors. It is not too far off the mark to consider Baegu communal sacrifices as an exchange interaction between two corporations organized according to different principles of recruitment. The living, a cognatic stock or stem kindred rather than a personal kindred in this case (Davenport 1959:564), offer pigs and prayers to their joint ancestors, an agnatic supernatural corporation, in hopes that the latter will in return give them power, riches, and good health. Patrilineal descendants have an obligation to sacrifice to the ancestors; matrilineal descendants may do so. While one can interpret pig sacrifice in terms of cognatic kinship or complementary filiation (Fortes 1959:206), I am convinced that a worshiper's status depends upon inheritance rights accompanying a concept of cognatic or bilineal descent that operates simultaneously with agnatic ideology.

There are valid structural reasons for expecting some bilateral ties to be important even in strictly unilineal societies. Firth's analysis of mother's brother and father's sister relationships in Polynesian Tikopia shows how this can work (Figure 17). Close affective ties and gift exchange between a mother's brother and his sister's son help to continue links between exogamous partilineages over several generations. Simul-

Figure 17. MB-ZS-FZ-BS Kinship Configuration in Tikopia

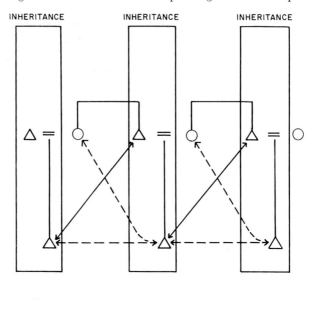

INHERITANCE   INHERITANCE   INHERITANCE

←———→   AFFECTION, GIFTS, SPECIAL SERVICES

←– – –→   RESTRAINT, FORMALITY, TABOO

taneously the restraint and respect characterizing the relationship between a man and his father's sister (extending to her children) controls
latent antagonism between a man's son (his natural heir under a system of patrilineal inheritance) and his sister's son who is receiving so
much of his affection and material presents (Firth 1936:186-213). This
function may or may not be relevant for the Baegu as well. Men habitually turn to their mother's brother for assistance in times of trouble, and
the mother's brother may play an important role in funerals. But if so,
it is by no means as formalized as in Tikopia. Baegu cognatic kinship
obligations seem to apply more generally as rights and duties between
consanguineal relatives of any type, and as rights to land through bilineal inheritance.

The coexistence of both agnatic and cognatic ideologies is characteristic of northern Malaita. Keesing reported it among the Kwaio, Hogbin among the Toabaita, and Ivens among the Lau. Keesing (1965)
rightly chose to emphasize cognatic kinship and descent among the
Kwaio, where descent groups are small, land holdings fragmented, and
shrines impermanent. Maranda and Maranda (n.d.) seem to empha-

size agnatic kinship among the Lau, where clans are large, population concentrated, and shrines long-lasting. They, too, are well justified in this. My impression, based on visits to the other areas and conversations with the ethnographers, is that the Baegu form a conservative mean between two local extremes. They pay more attention to agnatic ideals than the Kwaio, but are themselves less addicted to unilineal norms than are the Lau.

MARRIAGE AND AFFINAL RELATIONSHIPS

The marriage of a man and a women is a transaction between two kindreds. This transaction creates affinal relationships between the individuals involved and results in a semi-permanent alliance of the two groups. Marriage is the most spectacular secular happening in Baegu social life. (Ceremonies accompanying sacrifices to the ancestral spirits are sacred.) Although most people do marry, there is a surprising number of bachelors and spinsters. I knew of three divorces, but all couples had remarried. Divorce is rare and usually informal. Table 14 is a marital profile of the Baegu population.

TABLE 14. MARITAL STATUS OF THE BAEGU POPULATION

	Monog- amously married	Polyg- ynously married	Widow- ers	Widows	Bache- lors	Spin- sters	Depen- dent children	Totals
Sample area								
Pagans (traditional)	48	0	14	6	10	6	105	189
Pagans (Neo- Marching Rule)..	28	0	7	0	9	4	30	78
Anglicans........	58	3	2	8	6	5	69	151
Roman Catholics..	..	..	..	..	..	..	..	..
SSEC............	26	0	1	5	0	4	39	75
SDA............	12	0	1	1	2	1	13	30
Totals.......	172	3	25	20	27	20	256	523
Ataa area								
Pagans (traditional)	12	0	1	0	0	0	29	42
Pagans (Neo- Marching Rule)..	44	3	2	5	11	6	65	136
Anglicans........	12	0	2	1	0	0	24	39
Roman Catholics..	120	6	9	9	15	8	168	335
SSEC............	78	9	7	7	16	11	144	272
SDA............	6	0	0	0	0	0	7	13
Totals.......	272	18	21	22	42	25	437	837

Baegu marriage is both normatively and statistically monogamous. A wealthy man may marry polygynously, but he will get little or no financial help toward a bride-price for a second wife from his kinsmen. Plural wives do not have the economic value they do in some parts of Melanesia, since most competitive giving takes place in sacred contexts where women are not involved in production. According to popular belief, co-wives fight like cats and dogs. All told, it is rather difficult to see why a man would want more than one wife, and in fact less than 2 percent do marry polygynously. Seven men of a 1,360 population sample had plural wives; four more had lost a wife by death from a polygynous union. Known polygynists had only two wives. Two cases of three wives occur in recent genealogies. Apparently men do get a certain amount of prestige from being able to afford another wife, and, by keeping the peace in a polygamous household, they demonstrate social finesse and leadership ability.

The Baegu recognize a graded scale of marriages ranging from highly approved arranged marriages between sexually innocent young people from good families down to barely tolerated elopements involving promiscuous members of marginal families. Ivens (1930:188) reported Lau men married to women captured abroad in military raids, but this was more likely a form of rape followed by servitude. At any rate, it is not part of the present-day marital pattern. Status or prestige of the marriage depends upon the wealth and communal esteem of the principal families involved, the reputation and chastity of the bridal couple, and the faithfulness of observance of traditional forms and ceremonies. The amount of bride-price is more or less a linear function of these factors and is probably the best simple index of the prestige of the marriage. If it was a high one, married women are proud of the bride-price their husbands' families paid for them. Older women in particular enjoy this reckoning of their own youthful comeliness and reputation. No matter what we were talking about, these old girls let me know what bride-prices had once been paid for them.

Courting is accepted as preliminary to marriage, and young people do "date" (Keesing 1965:218). There should be a chaperone present, but evidence from folklore, informal gossip of youngsters, and the salacious reminiscences of old men make it clear that adolescent boys and girls take advantage of the system when they can. While I was there one young man beat his little sister severely because she served as a go-between for a secret rendezvous between two teenagers.

Bachelors (*alakwa* or *wane darai*) and girls (*saari*) have a great deal to say in choice of spouse, and I think that truly forced, approved marriages would be quite rare. Forced marriages after seduction or pregnancy are disapproved and are another story. Negotiations for the bride-price and the marriage ceremonies are family affairs.

All approved marriages begin with formal negotiations. The boy's father or his stand-in visits the girl's family; if the marriage appears feasible, he gives the girl's father (or his stand-in) one shell valuable (*tafuli'ae*) worth about $10.00 Australian as an earnest of their intentions, the transaction being known as "engaging (or marking) the girl" (*faafia saari*). Marriage is called *ade keni*.

Theoretically the girl's father can name the bride-price, and good form requires that the boy's family agree without haggling. The basic payment consists of ten shell valuables (*tafuli'ae*) worth about $100.00 Australian total and a necklace of 1,000 porpoise teeth (*lifoia*) worth about $50.00 Australian, but in practice this varies. Anglicans and Roman Catholics pay only five *tafuli'ae*, the Seventh Day Adventists forbid their adherents to pay any bride-price, and the South Seas Evangelical Church is not sure what position to take. The bride-price exchanged between families of low rank is substantially less, and marriages involving widows is lower. At the other extreme, highly approved marriages between important families involve exchange of small fortunes in ancillary goods such as teeth and shell ornaments, calico, and in some cases actual Australian currency. Both sides provide massive amounts of taro, sweet potatoes, and puddings for feasting, but no pigs are eaten since they are not for secular purposes.

On a prearranged date the groom's family or kindred (but not the groom) go to get the bride (*dao uri keni*). There is a mock fight between the two kindreds, and the groom's side presents the bride-price to the bride's side. The bride returns to the groom's father's hamlet, accompanied by some of her younger kin. There follows a period of feasting and celebrating, after which the girl works for a while for her new father-in-law.

After some time passes (said to be six months previously, but now usually shortened to a few weeks) the bride's family visit the groom's father's hamlet, bringing presents of food for the groom's family and the traditional married woman's insignia for their daughter. At this time, the newly married woman puts on the pubic apron (*masa*) and receives the belt of shell beads (*esu*) that certify her status as wife. This ceremony formally establishes the affinal relationship between the two kindreds and is called *faa'afe*, or "making the wife."

Remarriage of widows or widowers is approved, but the bride-price is much less and the sequence of events is shortened to negotiations and one quick ceremony. The levirate and sororate are correct but uncommon forms of remarriage. In my sample population 1 found two examples of the former, one of the latter.

Unapproved marriages begin with an elopement and are called *kwasilangae keni,* meaning literally "running off into the woods with a woman." Because of the scandal accompanying seduction, parental disapproval, or inability to provide the bride-price, the young couple flees and usually seeks refuge with spatially distant cognatic relatives of the boy. Honor may compel the girl's family to go to war, but usually, after tempers cool, some kinsmen of the boy will negotiate a settlement, pay the bride-price, and bring the runaways home. How much of this is serious and how much is an act to maintain proprieties is hard to say. This type of marriage is supposedly disapproved, but elder informants in particular discuss the custom with romantic glee. Cynical informants say that the eloping couple may let someone know where they are going, so that the girl's family will be able to chase them and bring them home. Keesing (1965:234) reports that such disapproved marriages in Kwaio may result in higher bride-prices. The Baegu custom is somewhat ambiguous. People say that the bride-price is reduced because the girl is no longer a virgin; but the boy's family usually has to pay two or three extra shell valuables to the girl's family as compensation because of the seduction and dishonor involved.

Taking shelter with the boy's uterine kinsmen, particularly his mother's brother, is a fortunate custom, for it automatically halves the forces arrayed against the runaway couple. The boy's uterine kinsmen are of course his patrilineage's affines (Figure 18). While there are prescribed, expensive ceremonies to expiate guilt accruing from wounding

Figure 18. Structural Reasons for Using Uterine Kin as Affines for Refuge

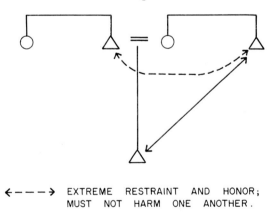

← — — →   EXTREME   RESTRAINT   AND   HONOR;
MUST   NOT   HARM   ONE   ANOTHER.

←————→   LOVE, HELP AND MUTUAL PROTECTION

or killing a consanguineal kinsman, it is unthinkable to kill an affine. Thus uterine kinsmen provide a ready haven for youngsters in the event of family quarrels.

Marriage does not really concern the patrilineal descent groups directly, although individuals are involved because of their relationship to one or the other of the bridal couple. Descent groups are not now exogamous, but traditions say that several generations ago they were. Collected genealogies partially support this, as Table 15 shows. There

TABLE 15. BAEGU TENDENCY TOWARD CLAN EXOGAMY

	Total marriages considered	Spouses from same clan	Spouses from different clans	% Exogamy
Generation				
+4 (1860)................	2	0	2	100
+3 (1880)................	9	1	8	89
+2 (1900)................	58	4	54	93
+1 (1920)................	121	25	96	79
0 (1940)................	145	50	95	66
−1 (1960)................	54	29	25	46

Numbers are derived from marriages recorded in genealogical notes from the sample population area. They include only marriages of living persons, and the marriages of parents of living persons. Generation "0" represents men 40-60 years old who are now influential in local affairs. There is no way to date marriages accurately, but dates in parentheses indicate approximately when that generation group would have been marrying. Note the decreasing frequency of exogamous marriage in recent times.

are no norms requiring reciprocal exchange between lineages or descent lines. Statistically, though, it may work out this way, because there is a marked tendency for people to feel that they ought to get their money back, expressed as, "We bought one of their girls; now they ought to buy one of ours." This may in effect result in a form of patrilateral cross-cousin marriage or delayed direct exchange (R. Fox 1967:206). In marriage women go one direction in one generation, and although there is no explicit prescriptive or preferential rule to reverse the direction of flow in the next generation, there is a slight statistical tendency to do so (Figure 19).

This can be seen by an analysis of mother-daughter comparisons. In families from my sample population where there were mature married daughters and where I had complete census and genealogical data,

Figure 19. Patrilineal Cross-Cousin Marriage

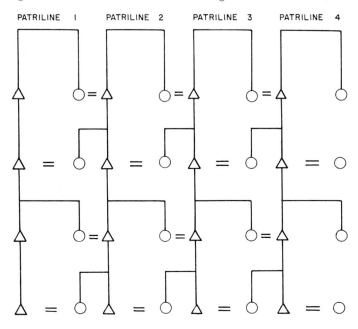

there was a marked tendency for at least one of the daughters to marry back into her mother's descent group. Thus if descent group X pays a bride-price to descent group Y for one of their girls, one of the daughters resulting from the union is apt to marry (in time) a young man of descent group Y, with the direction of bride-price payment in this second generation reversing, now going from group Y back to group X (Figure 20).

This reciprocation can occur in a single generation, with two groups exchanging girls (for bride-prices) at about the same time, or at least within the span of one generation. There is a tendency for a family (sibling group) to get a bride for one of their boys from the same descent group into which one of their girls has married; that is, men will have both wives and brothers-in-law (of two kinds) from the same descent group. Descent group X in this case pays a bride-price to descent group Y, receiving a bride from them. Within the same generation, descent group Y is very apt to pay a bride-price to descent group X for a sister of the boy who got the first bride (Figure 21). Table 16 reports this data. Keesing (1965) and Ogan (1966) also apply.

One practical definition of incest illustrates both the importance of the economic exchanges a marriage entails and the status of the kindred

Figure 20. Bride-Price Circulation: Mother-Daughter Comparisons

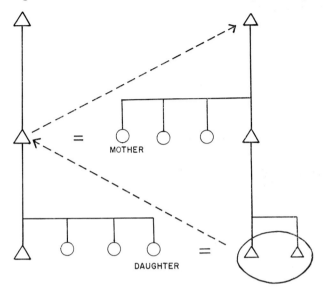

```
- - - -    BRIDE — PRICE   PAYMENT
```

Figure 21. Bride-Price Circulation: Brother-Sister Comparisons

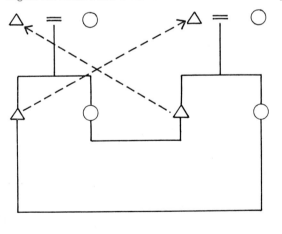

```
=   ⎫
    ⎬  MARRIAGE
⎿_⎿ ⎭

- - - - -  BRIDE — PRICE   PAYMENT
```

TABLE 16. BAEGU TENDENCIES TOWARD PATRILATERAL CROSS-COUSIN
MARRIAGE AND SYMMETRICAL MARRIAGE

	Total sets considered	Apparently random marriage	Reciprocal marital exchange	Frequency of marital exchange
Mother-daughter comparisons....... (Delayed reciprocal exchange in two adjacent generations)	108	70	38	35%
Sibling group comparisons.......... (Reciprocal exchange in one generation)	77	51	26	34%

Numbers are based on "sets" that in the first case were family groups with at least one married daughter, and in the second case were family groups with at least one married child of each sex.

as an exogamic category. An important old man of my district had eloped with his father's brother's daughter some thirty years ago. Normally marriage with second cousins or closer is disapproved. His relatives caused a terrible row, and apparently their loudest complaint was that, since the two were so closely related, it would be impossible to organize two "sides" for a proper wedding. He was wealthy, made the bride-price payment from his own resources, and sacrificed to the ancestors to ease their wrath; the two are still married and respected by the community.

Affinal kinship terminology is broadly classificatory. Affinal relatives are collectively *lumaa*. In general, affines of one's own generation are *baraa*, affines of ascending and descending generations are *fungo*, and spouses of spouse's consanguineal kinsmen are *saula*. In a bit of drollery based on the equation of siblings of the same sex, a man will call his wife's sister's husband *ruana nau* or "the other me."

Relationships between affines are restrained or, more precisely, respectful. Affines must not be physically injured, and it is forbidden to make war upon them. It is bad form to use obscene language or to engage in sexual joking in an affine's presence. Seduction of an affine is especially reprehensible, and if the seduced is married, the act is worse than simple adultery, itself once a capital crime. There are definite exchange duties. When a bride's first pregnancy is confirmed, the new husband delivers a gift (*lului wela*) of fish and a taro and canarium almond pudding (*kate*) to his wife's parents. Additionally, people are obliged to present their affines with presents (*falenga*) of fish or pudding whenever they visit each other.

RESIDENCE RULES

Traditional anthropological statements of residence rules are woefully inadequate, but since Baegu marriage by definition involves a change of residence for the woman (sex or marriage with a woman of the same hamlet is incest), this is a logical place to at least mention them. Ideally, a new bride moves to her husband's father's hamlet. For the first few months, the newly married couple lives with the husband's family, but they are expected to move into their own dwelling house by the time the first child is born. This new house may be in the same clearing, or they may start a new single-family farmstead of their own.

In Fischer's (1958:510) terms, using the hamlet as the frame of reference, residence for children is patrilocal; residence for males after marriage is at first patrilocal and then, perhaps, neolocal; and residence for married females is virilocal. Widows may after their husband's death continue living virilocally in the sense that they live with their late husband's close kinsmen, or they may choose to live patrilocally by returning to their own kinsmen's territory. Senile (*waaro*) old people live filiolocally with their children. Alternative residential norms permit some men for personal reasons to live uxorilocally with their wife's kin, or allow eloping couples to live avunculocally with the husband's uterine relatives, if familial feathers are so ruffled that they cannot go back.

Stated in terms of Goodenough's (1956b:29-30) rules for choice of residence, it is most accurate to say that the Baegu prefer to live in territory associated with the husband's descent group, and thus postmarital residence ought to be labeled patrilocal.

8. Baegu Land Tenure and Property Concepts

In the mind of Western Man, property must have an owner, and that ownership ought to be simple and clearly defined. Unfortunately for the ethnographer and colonial administrator, this is not self-evident to the Melanesians of northern Malaita, where many resources are only partially "owned" (if at all), and where what ownership there is tends to be collective, imprecise, stringently limited in some cases, and overlapping. Crocombe (1964), and in coauthorship with G. R. Hogbin (1963), has through seminal studies of land problems in the Cook Islands and New Guinea done much to clarify our understanding of Pacific land and property concepts. Explanation of Baegu property and land customs can add valuable comparative perspective.

There are cogent reasons for studying Baegu conceptions about the ownership of resources. First, as Goodenough (1951:29) points out, property is a convenient point of entry for the ethnographer. It is for the most part tangible, and inquiries about such problems "make sense" to most people. Second, the ownership of resources (of land in particular) is naturally germane and probably essential to any study of ecology and social organization.

As far as possible, I have tried to use Goodenough's (1951:30-42) terminology and definitions, not because they are necessarily superior but because they are convenient and useful. Goodenough's distinctions among various kinds of ownership are important. First, property can belong either to *individuals* or to *corporations*, groups of persons treated as an individual and having rights or liabilities distinct from the persons composing the group. *Full ownership* confers full title and carries with it the maximum number of obligations. *Divided ownership* divides title assymetrically between two or more parties, any of whom may be individuals or corporations. In assymetrical division of title, a *provisional title* holder gets physical possession and is responsible for maintenance of the property. A *residual title* holder has few if any responsibilities but retains some rights over the property. *Joint ownership* is conferred by membership in a property-owning corporation, as opposed to *individual property*. Since traditional Malaitan society is stateless, there is no real concept of *public property;* even large-scale joint property is still the private property of some segment of society. *Real property* refers to long-lasting capital goods that have productive value. Items of *personal property* are goods that do not last so long, and for the most part are consumer rather than capital goods.

Linguistic clues were not too useful, and it proved not feasible to do semantic or ethnoscientific analyses in the domain of land tenure. The innate complexity of local property concepts is aggravated by a general and highly imprecise use of terminology borrowed from Pidgin English. Translation itself is difficult, since in Baegu it is virtually impossible to ask who "owns" something or "to whom" a thing belongs, except by cumbersome circumlocutions. As a result, discussions in Baegu about property, particularly real property, turn into mare's nests requiring not just words but whole paragraphs of modifying clauses to clarify them. Semantic elegance is a lost cause.

LAND AND LAW

The legal status of title to land is at present the most pressing, and potentially the most disruptive, sociolegal problem facing the Protectorate's government in general and the Malaita District Administration most directly. For the Baegu, as for most subsistence agriculturalists, land is the paramount productive resource. Besides their labor as navvies or fieldhands in Honiara and on European-owned plantations in Guadalcanal or the Western Solomons, they have nothing to sell. Lacking direct access to the fishing grounds in the Lau Lagoon to the east and cut off from Indispensable Strait on the west by a string of settlements along the government road, the hill people have no means of earning a living except with the land they live on.

With a visceral folk wisdom they recognize the overwhelming economic importance of their land. Land is a prime emotional focus of the Baegu today. I have seen men of all ages, from otherwise smart-aleck adolescents to white-haired elders, get misty-eyed when they sing or hear the traditional epics about "our land." More prosaically, Allan's (1957) government report on land tenure cites the almost obsessive paranoia of Malaitans where their land is concerned (always fearful that the government is planning to take it away from them) and their general tendency toward overvaluation of land in the context of sale, leasing, or rental. Litigation over land title and usage is endemic in the native courts of Malaita. Quarrels about land disrupt native social relations and have generated the most serious misunderstandings between Malaitans and Europeans since Marching Rule days.

In mid-1968 the Baegu hills were in an uproar because of a simultaneous (but coincidental) government land-registration scheme seeking to research and establish title, and vigorous government mineral-prospecting activity following upon a Swedish aerial geophysical survey done in 1966. The hill people were convinced that the government was stealing their land. They swore noncooperation and even assembled armed parties to turn back government geological survey parties exploring river valleys to investigate geophysical anomalies indicated by the aerial survey. At the same time, some Lau Lagoon people were involved in court cases about land in the interior mountains, and again the Baegu were convinced that theft was imminent. Old men dutifully went to court sessions at Malu'u to testify on traditional lore and genealogical matters. When I returned to Baegu country after six months back in the United States, they met me with a lengthy catalogue of grievances. Little realizing the essential impotence of an American graduate student, they wanted me to go to court to protect their lands from the British and the Lau people.

OFFICIAL LAND LAW

Customary land tenure today exists within the framework of general Protectorate policy. The situation is becoming increasingly complex, both because of incipient population pressure and because of the imposition of superordinate, British-based title concepts upon customary Malaitan practices.

The British Crown assumes authority concerning Supreme Title to land within the Protectorate based on the Pacific Islanders Protection Acts of 1872 and 1875, the British Settlements Act of 1887, the Foreign Jurisdiction Act of 1890, the Pacific Order in Council of 1893, and proclamations made by Royal Navy captains in various island groups. The Western Pacific High Commission and the Protectorate and District Administration insist on maintaining a distinction between the statuses of colony and protectorate. Whereas in a colony the people and resources are used in the interest of the colonial power with im-

plicit loss of land interests, a protectorate is "a country under the protection of an alien, yet friendly and benevolent power, which protects
and administers the people in accordance with their own wishes and
interests." In the words of the Pacific Islanders Protection Act of 1875,
Her Majesty's Government as protecting power does not make "any
claim or title whatsoever to dominion or sovereignty over any such islands or places aforesaid or to derogate from the rights of the tribes or
people inhabiting such islands or places, or of chiefs or rulers thereof to
such sovereignty or dominion" (Allan 1957: 30-56). The administration
has really had no choice in reconciling conflicting claims of Melanesians,
long-resident Europeans, missions of various denominations, and the
government itself, but to try to sort them out in accordance with concepts of British justice that may or may not mesh neatly with traditional
Solomon Island ways. In doing so, the courts have evolved a practical
land law neither wholly British nor Melanesian.

Solomon Island land is legally either Alienated Land or Native Land.
Naturally enough, Alienated Land is land the title to which has permanently passed to an alien, while title to Native Land remains with a
native or natives. A "native" is legally defined by Protectorate law as
an indigenous inhabitant of Melanesian or mixed race. An "alien" is
any person, regardless of where he was born, who is required by law to
register as an alien. Operationally, this means all whites, Orientals, and
other Pacific Islanders (Allan 1957: 55-60).

Simplest title to Alienated Land is that in the category of *private
freehold,* that is, land that has been purchased outright by aliens from
original native owners. *Public land* is that held by the government
(usually for roads, airstrips, schools, hospitals, administration buildings,
etc.) and the Church of England (Melanesian Mission) as the established church. Although it has not yet done so, the Protectorate government reserves the right to claim appropriate areas as *national park land.*
There is also an archaic concept of *waste land,* dating from the era before Europeans understood that, in a bush-fallow economy, land was
in effect "in use" even though no gardens were on it at the time. According to earlier law, the Crown could assume certain title to such
putative "waste land," and some of these areas have passed to alien use
under *occupational licenses* previously approved by the government.

The vast majority of Native Land is *native freehold* under *customary
title,* meaning simply that the land belongs to the people who have
always lived there and are accepted as owners by the community. Title
to some tracts of waste land has also passed to natives through occupation licenses mentioned above, and the government has designated speci-

fied areas of public land as *native reserves,* mostly used for native housing near administrative settlements.

British law also recognizes *leasehold land,* although there is no such conception in customary land tenure. Either public land or native land can be leased for a specified time at a specified contractual rate, either to other natives or to non-natives. Residual title remains with the Crown or with the customary title-holders as appropriate. In recent years the government has granted *timber and mining leases* to overseas companies for exploitation of areas in Santa Isabel and the Western Solomons.

The land settlement project operating in Malaita in 1968-70 represents an attempt to clarify the situation by researching and registering title. Theoretically the courts have jurisdiction over land litigation. Wherever possible the government is attempting to finesse such issues in Malaita by leaving them to be heard in the native court system. The Magistrate's Court at district headquarters in Auki, where the District Commissioner becomes involved, and the High Court at Honiara on Guadalcanal serve as appellate courts.

It is becoming increasingly difficult for land to pass from native to alien ownership, and the status of title to previously alienated land is unclear. Table 17 shows the approximate distribution of Solomon Islands land as to class of ownership as of 1956 (Allan 1957:60). About 94 percent of the total land area is clearly held by native owners, with less than 1 percent of that being other than freehold. On the island of Malaita, the proportion of native freeholding is somewhat greater.

CUSTOMARY LAND TENURE

Ownership of land and rights to use land are conceptually different for the Baegu. An owner always has a right to use his land, but lack of ownership status does not necessarily mean that a person does not have a right to use the land.

The first basic fact to accept is that the Baegu (as well as other Malaitan people) use a model for land title that is structurally quite different from ours. To us, land is defined by borders. Dating from antiquity our mythical heroes have symbolically claimed land by walking around it; fencing is about the first order of business for homesteaders; New England poets tell us (as Robert Frost [1949] has) that "Good fences make good neighbors"; and border disputes loom large in the history of our wars and international law. Proper definition of areal extent and delineation of the periphery are fundamental to our concepts of real property ownership. But many Melanesians use a "focal land model" (Cochrane 1969:330). Basic to the Baegu concept

Table 17. Legal Status of Land Tenure in the British Solomon Islands Protectorate in 1956

	Number of titles	Acres
A. Solomon Islanders		
Customary................................	Inapplicable	6,922,800
Permits to occupy......................	13	3,300
Public leases............................	2	1
	15	6,926,101
B. Non-Natives		
Private land............................	190	146,430
Public leases............................	287	45,530
Native leases............................	84	6,170
Occupation licenses (or certificates of occupation)............................	4	160,080
	565	358,210
C. Public land		65,500
D. Waste land occupied by the Crown	At present vested in the Crown	11,500
		77,000

Thus, alienated land represents 6% of the total land in the Protectorate; unalienated land amounts to 65 acres per capita. It is estimated that land alienated represents 20% of the coastal land; of this proportion, probably 90% could be categorized as first-class coastal land.

of ownership are the sacred grove where the ancestors are buried or (of lesser import) the old hamlet site where one's trees still grow. These establish title, and rights to land focus around these central features (both geographically and ideologically). The strength of claims to ownership or usufruct diminishes with increasing distance from these foci, but a true boundary or outer limit does not exist.

Title to land is highly divided. Very little if any land is held in full, simple title; instead, ownership of most plots or tracts involves many people with many rights and claims. In nearly all cases, title is held by corporate groups of agnatically related kinsmen, not by individuals, and in the Baegu tongue it is almost always "our land," not "my land." When Baegu speak of owning land, they are usually referring to residual title. Land is at least partially inalienable. It once belonged to the ancestors, and no matter how many generations and transfers are involved, their heirs retain some claim to it. It is the concurrent operation of the principles of corporate or joint ownership and persisting residual rights despite time and transfers that makes land ownership in northern Malaita such a thorny problem. Since land is not divided among heirs, and since original owners always retain some interest in the land, title is inherently divided and subject to many degrees of overlapping claims.

Seen from this perspective the *'ae bara* (the patrilineage described earlier) is a title-holding or land-owning corporation. Mythology and traditional lore provide charters for claims to title. When the world was young the Culture Heroes, who were also the first ancestors, came to build their houses and gardens in the hills of northern Malaita. The founding ancestor of the Walelangi lineage, for example, was one of a pair of twins hatched in a primordial eagle's nest. From one egg came the ancestor of the eagles, and from the other the ancestor of the Walelangi lineage. The myth goes on to relate how he came to live on Marado ridge (the backbone of the island), and how he and his sons settled various parts of Baegu territory, claiming the virgin forest as their own land. As descendants of these mythical heroes the men of Walelangi claim the land — and, incidentally, maintain strict taboos against the killing of eagles. Other lineages have their own myths, and the whole body of folklore relates descent groups to particular territories.

The clans (*'ae bara*) are associated with and can be said to own (in the sense of holding residual title to) particular districts (*lolofaa*) of land. The districts have the same name as the proprietary descent groups leading to some terminological confusion. One or more sacred groves exist on the land where patrilineal ancestors of the descent group are buried. Lineages or lineage segments of the clan may own or be associated with smaller tracts of land within the district that may or may not be named. If there are several shrines nearby, it is almost impossible to tell except by reference to their genealogies and mythological charters whether they represent two coordinate districts, two coordinate neighborhoods within one district, or stand in a superordinate/subordinate relationship to one another. All Baegu land is divided into these districts associated with clans or lineages and ancestral shrines (Map 17).

The rules of descent assigning people to these land-owning corporate groups (*'ae bara*) are clearly stated and relatively inflexible. Descent and land inheritance are in theory strictly and in practice overwhelmingly patrilineal. Naturally, since the Baegu probably have no more moral rectitude than the rest of us, people do fiddle with the system. Seniority among siblings depends on birth order, and I noted in particular many disagreements about the relative seniority of siblings five to ten generations back. I suspect that an ambitious contemporary leader *prefers* to be descended from a senior sibling. Proof of member-

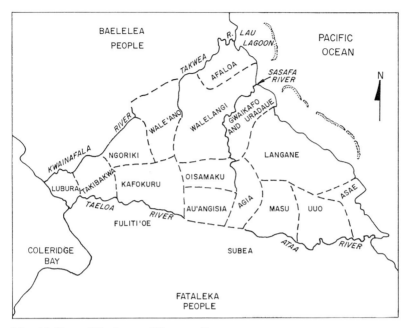

Map 17. Baegu Districts and Descent Groups

ship in the *'ae bara* — that is, proof of correct patrilineal descent — is twofold. Men must know their own genealogies, and they must be accepted as members of the rest of the lineage.

SUPERNATURAL BASIS FOR LAND CLAIMS

Baegu theology based upon ancestral spirits offers supernatural support for claims to land. Recall that ancestors, particularly powerful ones, can in death become *akalo,* spirits who are morally neutral, but who can at their whim send either good or evil to mankind. Pagan Baegu religion has rites to placate these spirits of the dead and to induce them to give their blessings (*mamanaa*) to their descendants. One of the blessings the *akalo* can give is productivity of the land.

People bury their dead in sacred groves (*beu aabu*) of virgin forest. The Baegu believe that the ghosts (*akalo*) continue to live in the groves, and most sacrifices and religious rites take place there. The crucial point is that the ancestors are buried in, and their ghosts continue to occupy, land that the lineage owns. The lineage is a ritual community. Priests are supposed to be descended from the ancestors buried at the particular sacred grove they serve, and they lead the worship honoring the ancestors buried there. Living members of the lineage placate the ancestral spirits by remembering them, by sacrificing to them, by observing sexual taboos, and by attending the communal religious ceremonies (*maoma*) honoring the dead. There is a division of religious labor in that each lineage is responsible for worshiping its own ancestral spirits. In a way, Baegu religion is a partnership between the living and the spirits of the dead to maintain the fertility of the land where the ancestors are buried and that the lineage owns. In Baegu territory, sacred places are of some antiquity and are of general knowledge; a priest cannot just create a sacred place anywhere he chooses.

Since in traditional society rights to land are inherited and validated by remembrance of and homage to the ancestors, problems may arise in the future. Christian Baegu today are first-generation converts and continue to use their traditional lineage lands, but it will be interesting to see how they will continue to exercise those rights as generations pass, since as Christians they cannot (or should not) sacrifice to the ancestral spirits.

RIGHTS OF LANDOWNERS

Theoretically all members of the lineage share in ownership of the land. In practice this means all male members. Whenever I asked questions about women owning land, my informants simply snickered. Women do talk about "our land," although landowner status (like the ritual and kinship status of women themselves) is ambiguous. For a woman, "our land" is sometimes her father's and sometimes her son's. However unresolved their status as proprietresses of the land may be, older women do testify in land litigation. Nonetheless Baegu ideology perceives the lineage as a group of brothers, and the men see themselves as the ones who make the decisions that really count. Membership rights in the landowning corporation (*'ae bara*) are essentially inalienable, and I do not think people can be lightly disinherited. If the lineage's land is inalienable, and if all members of a lineage are co-owners, it follows that members of the lineage are always owners. In practice emigrants are no longer participants in ownership, but even then people assume that such emigrants would be justified in reclaiming their ownership rights if they returned from living overseas.

Although the *'ae bara* owns its land jointly, naturally enough some individuals exert more influence within and upon the corporation. One in particular, the *wane initoo,* who succeeds to his position in the patrilineage through a rule of primogeniture, has a titularly preeminent status. People say that the land is "his." Despite this status he appears really to be a senior among largely equal peers. In this role he acts for the *'ae bara* but does not act independently. He can give plots or subdivisions of land as gifts, but he does so with the approval of the lineage as a whole. He cannot deny fellow *'ae bara* members their rights to use the land. Outsiders must ask the *wane initoo* for permission to make a garden on lineage land, but according to custom he should grant it. People must have gardens to live, and the community cannot conceive of a *wane initoo* too selfish as to deny this simple right. For granting this permission a *wane initoo* gets no rent or payment other than symbolic confirmation of his titular role. In a way all members of the lineage as a corporation have a veto power; the *wane initoo* cannot act alone. He is like a chairman of the board, having prestige but little real power.

DIVIDED OWNERSHIP

In districts where there are two or more *wane initoo,* the district may be divided into subdistricts owned by lineage segments of the superordinate lineage or clan. These subdistricts may be physically separate, with lineage segments of coordinate rank, or one larger lineage may be superordinate over lesser segments of the lineage. In this latter situation claims to land overlap, and title is obviously divided. Although the smaller group does own its plot of land, the superordinate larger lineage continues to hold to some degree residual title to the entire district, including the land of the smaller segment.

Provisional title and residual title in cases of divided ownership among the Baegu do not seem to entail precisely the sort of encumbrances, rights, and obligations that we assume to be inherent in divided ownership. There does not seem to be a native concept of lease or rental, or even sale of land. Under customary procedures, no first fruits or other rent is paid by one who gardens on another group's land. Solomon Islanders who rent or lease land from one another for planting coconuts pay in Australian currency and use the Pidgin term "interest land" for the transaction. Sales of land also involve cash payments, although Allan reports traditions from Malaita about purchases of land for baskets of customary shell valuables (Allan 1957:177).

It is significant that Baegu first-fruits offerings go via a priest to the ancestral spirits. The produce of a taro garden ought not to be used until an offering of its first fruits is ritually made by the owner to the gods. A priest blesses the offering with suitable prayers, thereby "opening" (*mole na*) the garden. Mason (1968:325-26) suggests that first-fruits offerings tend to go to the person symbolically associated with food production and ownership of the land; Baegu first-fruits offerings recognize symbolically the role of the ancestral spirits as ultimate owners.

Cases of divided ownership in a purely traditional setting seem mostly to result from gifts. In the customary Malaitan scheme of things, one good killing demands another. If a man were killed, his relatives would (and legitimately could) demand a life in revenge. In such instances a powerful lineage would ask for vengeance and propose a gift (*finisi*), often of land, to be offered as a bounty to the person who succeeded in avenging the first death. This gift of land would in effect pay for a hired assassin.

Gifts of land were also made to individuals or families who performed exceptional services during mortuary rites. Such rewards went to those who buried important priests, whose corpses were too sacred and thus too dangerous for their own kin to bury. Or in other circumstances the heirs of a powerful man might present land as a reciprocal gift to those whose contribution to the mortuary feast was significantly larger than normal.

Allan (1957:172-73) reports other events where gifts of land were appropriate:

1. In compensation for causing accidental death,
2. For services to important men,
3. To fugitives given protection,
4. As a reward for information leading to the killing of an assassin,
5. In payment for care in old age,
6. As grants to daughters who have brought a large bride-price (such a gift would, I think, be in the form of a trust for the expected grandchildren), and
7. In compensation for a customary offense or accidental injury.

People usually meet these obligations by giving shell valuables, and I suspect that gifts of land would occur only if the debtor were especially wealthy and ambitious for renown, or if the creditor were especially angry and dangerous. Allan (1957:173) also cites cases where title to land was seized by victors in war or in the aftermath of an assassination. My own impression is that this is simply theft made legitimate by the well-known principle of international law that might makes right.

Title to land given as a gift is divided. Once such a transfer is made, title to the plot ceded is held by a lineage corporation descended from the original recipient according to the same rules and usages as any other land; but people say that the original donor corporation still "owns" all of their land, including the plot given away. Land, as everyone knows, is inalienable.

Recipients of land gifts never pay rent or make a clear countergift: but along with every "gift," as Marcel Mauss (1954) has it, comes an obligation. In accepting land, recipients also accept an obligation to the donors that links them forever to those donors in a patron-client relationship, and it is this undischarged obligation that pays for the land. As in the Trukese *niffag* which Goodenough (1951:37) describes, there is no explicit repayment, but the recipients assume a perpetual debt to the donors. Since this obligation establishes long-term obligations of mutual cooperation and defense, it probably has more real value than an actual physical repayment. The donor corporation retains residual title; those who accept the land have provisional title, paying rent in the form of a continuing alliance with the givers.

In the long run provisional title proves to be as effective as residual title. Provisional title holders can in turn give plots to others, setting up a long claim of divided ownership where lineage corporations have residual title vis-à-vis later owners, but only provisional title vis-à-vis earlier owners, going back to the descendants of the ancestors who made the original gift (Figure 22).

In many ways gifts of land function as a kind of group adoption. In accepting the gift, the receiving lineage allies itself with the donor lineage. Land and descent are intimately linked in Baegu thought, and such a continuing alliance based on land ownership resembles Murdock's (1949:46) description of the relationship of lineages within a sib. In effect the receiving lineage is adopted into the sib of the donor lineage, even though it cannot always prove mutual descent from a common ancestor.

THE RIGHT TO USE THE LAND

Land usage rights are conceptually distinct from ownership, although in actuality they work out together. "Use" means for residence or for production. Building a house on a tract of land does not really imply any claim to ownership. When I arrived in the Baegu hills, I set about arranging to have a house and working space built. Thinking I was being very generous, I offered to buy both the house and the land where it stood. This greatly perturbed my Melanesian neighbors, and it cost me a week or so of wasted motion before I realized that both they and I would be happier if I paid for the house and forgot about the land. Nor does cultivation of a garden imply ownership of the land. The gardener owns the crops he has planted and the fence he has built, but the land itself remains the property of the proprietary lineage or segment thereof.

Owners (residual or provisional) have the right to use the land in any way they please (subject of course to the fact that land cannot be totally and permanently alienated), but non-owners can and do use the land. When men live uxorilocally with their wives, the wife's father's lineage permits them to build their houses there and nearly always gives

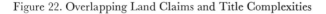

Figure 22. Overlapping Land Claims and Title Complexities

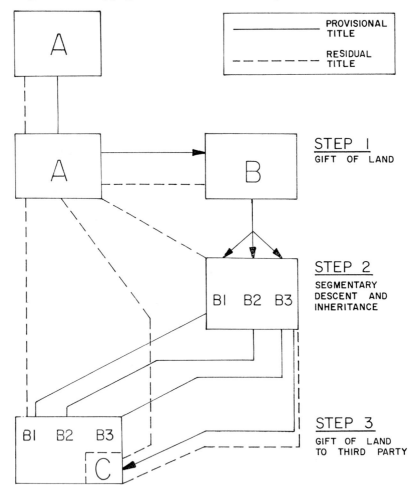

To begin with, A has full title singly to a plot of land. He gives it to B (Step #1), creating divided ownership wherein he transfers provisional title (right to occupy and use the land and to make further disposals) but retains residual title (Baegu land is by definition inalienable). Normal birth, death, and inheritance (Step #2) then result in joint ownership. Finally, if another gift is made to a third party C (Step #3), C receives provisional title with both B and A still retaining residual title.

the husband permission to garden on the lineage's land. This is seen as simple decency (after all, a man has to eat), but it is often phrased as "caring for our girl and grandchildren." Similarly, if men permit a refugee to live among them, tacitly agreeing to protect him, they will permit him to live and to garden on their land.

Cognatic kinsmen may come to live with their maternal relations, as refugees following an elopement or simply for political reasons (if the mother's brother or father is a significant power figure). These cognates or uterine kinsmen live and garden on the land of their hosts, but this is seen as a matter of right, not of tolerance. Cognatic rights to land usage are rarely explicitly stated but are almost universally accepted. There is a normative belief that men *ought* to give land to their children and to their children's children for houses and gardens. This applies to daughters as well as sons. The more general principle is that anyone descended from the original proprietary ancestors may *use* the land. Hence not only patrilineage members, but also their cognatic relatives, may and do use it.

SUPERNATURAL BASIS OF COGNATIC LAND RIGHTS

Although membership in lineages or clans and residual title to land depends upon patrilineal descent, the right to use land passes bilineally. A person may by right garden or live on land properly "belonging" to his cognatic or uterine kinsmen, the justification being that both parties share a common ancestor who was indeed of the patrilineage holding residual title. In practice this works out to mean that the criterion for claiming land usage rights is having a remembered ancestor buried in the sacred grove (*beu aabu*) associated with the land claimed. "Remembered" means remembered by the individual *and* accepted by the lineage. Men establish and validate their right to use the land by sacrificing pigs and first fruits to the *akalo* and by taking part in the great mortuary feasts (*maoma*). If a man wishes to live and garden in an area, he joins in worship at the local shrine. If the lineage group whose ancestors are buried at the shrine accept him as a communicant, they also accept his right to use the land.

Given the virtual panmixis that exists in northern Malaita, most Baegu men have ancestors buried everywhere. But men do not sacrifice randomly. Most men feel they must sacrifice to their paternal ancestors at their own patrilineage's shrine. If they do not live with their agnatic relatives, they will also sacrifice at the local shrines near where they live, and where they will somewhere along the genealogical line have a remembered ancestor. Occasionally men will try to keep alive interests in other areas by multiple sacrifices, but most do not.

THE NATURE OF COGNATIC LAND RIGHTS

In a way these cognatic land rights are like provisional title to the land. Keesing (1965:46-47), following Allan's and Hogbin's usage, talks of primary and secondary rights. Agnatic members of the patrilineal descent groups have primary rights and "own" the land. Cognatic relatives have secondary rights, can with permission use the land, and can (if the patrilineage dies out) assume primary rights over the land. But cognatic rights to land are more than that. Baegu thinkers, like Keesing's Kwaio, insist that those descended through female as well as male links do indeed have a right to use the land, and there is strong feeling that no one can deny them that right.

In summary, both agnatic and cognatic descendants have rights to use the land. Although Baegu kinship ideology has a strong patrilineal bias, ritual and residential communities end up being bilineal or ambilineal groups much like Keesing's (1965:43-48, 120) Kwaio "shrine descent categories." An agnatic core "owns" the land, inheriting residual title patrilineally from the founding ancestor, and has the responsibility for worshiping the ancestral spirits. Affiliated cognatic relatives have an inherited right to *use* the land and validate this right by worshiping their common ancestors at the sacred grove where they are buried.

Goodenough has suggested an ecological explanation for divided title situations like this. He argues (1955:81-83) that throughout much of the Malayo-Polynesian world land title is vested in non-unilinear groups derived from bilocal extended families, who had a need to restrict descent group limits in some way and have done so through land tenure definitions. Unilinear concepts (another way of limiting descent group membership) developed in Melanesia, where the tropical forest environment of large continental islands exploited swidden agriculture and promoted continuing movement and expansion. In his reply to Frake's (1956:173) criticism, he has refined this to say that although unilinear descent groups may insist jealously upon their title to land, they still may have a vested interest (in lush tropical forest regions) in seeing garden land *used* continuously so that it remains easily cleared secondary brush instead of reverting to hard-to-clear primary hardwoods (Goodenough 1956a:175-76).

The agnatic Baegu *'ae bara* are sensible in that they result in descent, inheritance, and residence that are unambiguous and compatible with the existential facts of male power and dominance (R. Fox 1967: 114-21). In ancient Malaita, when land was a free good, they could expand and grow unhindered. The clearly defined title of the *'ae bara* to the land reduced conflict, yet it was to the owner's advantage to let uterine kin or neighbors use the land in order to keep the forest under control (to let it regenerate, but not too far).

OWNERSHIP OF OTHER RESOURCES

Mountains and prominent ridges may be agriculturally unproductive, but they may be sacred places. As such, ownership of them is of considerable importance for Solomon Islanders. Marado ridge, the central spine of the northern Malaitan massif, is one of these. The Walelangi clan and other Baegu lineages claim that their first ancestors settled there, and they still claim the ridge jointly as a holy place.

Most land is at one time or another under cultivation, but there are some areas that are too steep, too stony, or too wet for gardening. These remain as bushlands, and the Baegu forage in them for game and forest products. The Baegu seem to have an intuitive knowledge of ecological succession, and they believe that all their lands were once stands of primary hardwood forest. Most of them agree that virgin forest game is unowned; that forest products and minerals are free goods, belonging to the one who collects them; and that initial clearance of virgin forest establishes a valid claim to the land. Today virgin hardwood timber still stands only in the sacred groves and on small parcels of land unsuitable for gardens. The rest is secondary forest, growing on potential garden land belonging to a lineage or a clan. Because of the ownership interests involved, people control access to and use of secondary forests more closely.

Although they do not guard the privilege jealously, the Baegu believe that the owners of the land also own the secondary forest and the game, bush products, and minerals found in it. As owners they have the right to hunt and gather in their forest, and (if they wish) to prevent others from doing so. Thus people should hunt and collect firewood, building material, and stones from their own land. If they wish to forage in someone else's bushland, they should ask permission and perhaps give a token share to the owners. In practice, no one insists upon this. There is little population pressure, and as long as collectors avoid settled and cultivated areas, taking only relatively small amounts of forest material, access remains more or less free to all.

WATER RIGHTS

Water rights similarly cause few problems. There is a spring or a brook near every settlement. The terrain is rugged and the brooks flow precipitously downhill, with many falls and rapids. Most hamlets have a watering place where the stream flows over a ledge, with a bamboo spigot for drinking and bathing. Residents of a hamlet are said to "own" the nearby spring or watering place they habitually use, but by custom travelers are free to drink if they are thirsty. With over 200 inches rainfall per year and virtually unlimited groundwater, water is a free good.

As in our own riparian law, it is bad form to pollute water that others living further downstream will use. Considering the fetid nature of our own streams, the Baegu probably take this responsibility more seriously than we do. Theoretically a person defecating or urinating in another's water supply can be made to pay shell money in compensation for his crime. Before the British stopped the practice, willful pollution of water supplies with excrement was justifiable cause for homicide.

Small streams are exploited according to the same principles as the land they flow through. If it is primary forest country, they are theoretically unowned and all are free to use them. Streams flowing through settled regions technically belong to the descent group owning the garden land or the secondary forest around them. In practice, people do usually limit their collecting to streams on their own lands.

Major rivers are often boundaries between clans or dialect groups. Either bank belongs to the landowning descent group bordering the river, but the channel itself is a no man's land with the people from both sides permitted to exploit it at will.

PUBLIC RIGHT OF WAY

Malaitan hill country "roads" are simply paths through the forest. Often little more than tunnels through a sea of green vegetation, the jungle crowds in closely from both sides and from overhead. The vines even seem to reach out to grab travelers. If traffic stops, the jungle soon reclaims the path. People make no concerted efforts to maintain trails, but passers-by will hack off with their bush knives particularly aggressive or uppity bits of plant life that encroach upon it. Wear (and care) are proportional to use.

There is no concept of public ownership or responsibility for trails, nor do most trails "belong" to any particular person or group. If no one has the responsibility to maintain the trails, no one has a right to forbid passage on them. Theoretically anyone who wants to can use a trail, if he can fight off the vegetable kingdom and if he trusts the people who live en route. Cross-country trails do not "belong" to the people whose lands they cross, but parties to a quarrel would not use a trail through enemy lands because of the danger of ambush.

Houses and gardens are usually set back some distance off the main trails. The Baegu like privacy and are almost pathologically afraid of theft. As far as gardens and pigs are concerned, they have good reason to be fearful, for the pilfering of crops and swine is routine. Individuals or families hack out their own paths and maintain them by repeated passage; they are the responsibility of the residents or gardeners involved.

People have a limited right to close off paths for private reasons. While I lived there, one man built a new garden astride a path down to the sea and insisted that travelers walk around. People complied but grumbled a bit about it. The consensus was that while he had a right to protect his crops by diverting the trail, it was bad taste to have done so. I made what I thought was a witty comment about him having "stolen the trail." This was passed along by the Baegu as being particularly apt and as an indication that maybe I was not as obtuse as I sometimes seemed.

People do feel that they should have free access to markets on or near the beach. Before pacification, market times were formal truce periods. Fighting was forbidden in the market's vicinity, and people could travel to and from the market in reasonable safety. Now the Baegu articulate this principle of free access in a different context. They complain bitterly that the saltwater people, by farming and settling along the coast, are trying to isolate them in the bush. Some even see the government's new coastal road, with its concomitant development of linear villages and coconut plantings, as a plot to close off their natural right-of-way to markets and beaches.

PRODUCTIVE PERSONAL PROPERTY

Land belongs to a lineage or clan while gardens belong to individuals, or are at most the joint property of a nuclear or (rarely) an extended family. Ownership of a garden does not imply ownership of the land where the garden is, for a person need not be of the title-holding descent group to plant his garden on the land. Cognatic relatives of the agnatic owners have a right to garden there, and even outsiders can do so with the owner's permission. There is good reason for gardens to be owned separately from the land. Land goes on forever, while gardens, given a bush-fallow agricultural technology, are transitory things.

The crops and the fence around the garden belong to the one who cleared the land, did the planting, and built the fence. Gardening is by and large an individual task, and husbands, wives, and older children usually will each have their own gardens. Yet in some ways it may be better to think of a set of these individual gardens as the joint property of a nuclear family. Family members, particularly husbands and wives, will work together on such heavy tasks as initial clearance of the land. Occasionally they exchange labor services for weeding or harvesting. Garden produce is pooled, with members of the family sharing the food. Finally, if a married person dies, his or her spouse inherits the deceased's garden. In a few cases, there is a similar arrangement for joint or extended families.

Some tree crops are also personal property or the joint property of a group of siblings. Since trees are mortal, inheritance rarely passes to broader descent groups. One can logically divide tree crops into three categories: those planted near residences, those planted in gardens, and those claimed in the forest (that may or may not be planted). Hill people have always planted coconuts (*malinge*), areca palms (*agero*), and certain magical or ornamental shrubs such as the cordyline (*sango*), croton (*'ala'ala*), or hibiscus (*tatale*) at their hamlets. Most gardens have groves of bananas or clumps of sugarcane, and people return to harvest these for a few years after they otherwise abandon the garden. The canarium almond (*ngali*) is the most valued forest tree. They are gigantic trees, long lived, and produce many bushels of nuts annually. Nutting season is August through November and is a time of considerable excitement. Hill people hire out as climbers to harvest nuts belonging to coastal people. Convivial groups gather to hull and smoke the nuts for storage. There is much singing and dancing (and, for young people, some flirtation in the forest). Smoked nuts are traded at the markets or hoarded for use throughout the year. *Ngali* nuts bring out the glutton in people. Some gossiped about one man who had a house full of them but refused to share with his children. (This was not entirely true; I did let them eat a few.) A few canarium trees are truly wild, but most have an owner. Some men plant a few nuts, but most owned trees are volunteers claimed as saplings. The local sago or ivory-nut palms (*sao*) are nearly always planted as seeds, and they usually have owners. Some other forest trees, the Pacific chestnut (*alite*), the Malay apple (*kabarai*), and the *Spondias dulcis* fruit called *inikori*, are owned but are rarely planted.

Owners give away trees as presents. When an owner dies, his child or children inherit his trees. He can make a testamentary (verbal) disposal, whereby inheritance is individual and separate. Otherwise his children inherit jointly. Ownership of a tree is not proof of land ownership, but in a way a man's tree holdings do indicate interests and rights in the land. Because trees outlive settlements, gardens, and people, individuals may own trees scattered in a number of places where their immediate ancestors once lived or farmed. Hence the overall pattern of a man's tree holdings is evidence of where the owner's hereditary land interests and usage rights are to be found.

Pigs, chickens, ducks, dogs, cats, and other pets or livestock are personal property. They can be given away at will, either as presents or in payment of debts. Adults often give young animals as pets or investment stakes to their younger relatives. Pigs in particular are valuable investments. Surviving children or siblings inherit a person's animals.

OTHER PERSONAL PROPERTY

Houses are a form of personal property, having a life expectancy of five or ten years. A men's house (*beu*) is said to belong to the senior resident male, who shares it with his brothers, sons, and grandsons. They probably helped him build it and have a recognized right to live in it. In view of this right to occupy, it is probably best to see the *beu* as the joint property of all coresident adult males, led by the senior male. Often when a senior male dies, particularly if he is still vigorous, people suspect sorcery or divine wrath, and they elect to move the entire hamlet. In this case, inheritance of the *beu* is irrelevant. It is shut up, abandoned, and allowed to decay. On other occasions, if the "owner" is senile and death seems natural, the men's house continues to be the joint property of the same male groups, but a younger brother or the eldest son of the dead man will succeed to his position of leadership. He may in fact already have been the leader.

The dwelling house (*luma*) belongs jointly to the nuclear family occupying it. People identify dwelling houses using the name of either husband or wife interchangeably according to context. When a husband dies, and if there is still a senior male left to be in charge of the hamlet, the widow and her children continue to live in their own *luma*. Otherwise she abandons the house to live with relatives. When a woman dies, there is less disruption, for her husband was spending much of his time in the men's house anyway. If the children are grown, the dwelling house is simply abandoned. Adolescents or older children (six to twelve years old) continue to live in the *luma* with their father, the eldest daughter taking over the mother's economic role. Small children and infants, if there are no older siblings, are usually fostered by relatives; in this case, too, the *luma* is abandoned.

Tools, household utensils, clothing, and miscellaneous impedimenta belong to the person who made them and are strictly personal property to be disposed of as the owner sees fit. If someone dies without making previous verbal testamentary disposal of his possessions in this category, his surviving spouse, siblings, and children divide them.

Plate 11. A characteristic Baegu hamlet with one men's house (*beu*) and three dwelling houses (*luma*).

Traditional valuables (shell money, beaded ornaments, turtle shell badges, porpoise teeth, weapons, and relics) are also personal property subject to this sort of inheritance, but traditional valuables arouse much more interest in their disposal and can lead to some ugly scenes. Individuals have custody of ancestral relics, but the entire lineage segment retains interests in them and would be outraged if the custodian refused to share the relics. The married woman's beaded belt (*esu*) always passes from mother to daughter or from aunt to niece, while the giant clam (with turtle-shell inlay) forehead badges (*dala*) are inherited along male lines, thereby creating channels of parallel inheritance.

There is a small amount of incorporeal property. Knowledge of traditional prayers, ritual lore, and genealogies are qualifications for the priesthood and are of value only within that context. They are not sold, traded, or inherited. Orthodox (in pagan terms) priests control garden and war magic. Curing magic and divination are learned by those with natural aptitudes (those who have a "call"). Technical skills are so generally shared that there is no concept of a right to exclusive possession of them. Only the skills and formulae for *arua,* a form of malevolent sorcery based on contagious magic, are sold to apprentices or passed along to heirs.

9. Baegu Residential Groups

To the air traveler, Malaita looks green. The jungle begins at the shore-line, climbs over the mountains, and drops to the sea on the other side, an apparently unbroken green wilderness. Only as he comes close enough to pick out individual trees, and as his eye begins to see patterns and variations in the overwhelming greenness, does he notice here and there at irregular and rather distant intervals small clearings with a few tiny buildings. These are the homes of the Malaitan bush people and the elementary residential units of Malaitan society.

These hamlets or, as the Baegu call them, *fera,* are the logical place to begin to describe Baegu settlement patterns. They are the socio-residential atoms that compose larger and more complex patterns. Although the hamlet is composed of individuals and of family house-holds, there is no need at this time to try to break the hamlet down into constituent elements. Nearly all socially relevant persons are affiliated with some sort of group; only the misfit, the criminal, or the fugitive lives alone. The nuclear-family household does exist and is important, but in the present context the hamlet is more important. Although they can pick out "households" within a village when asked to do so, there is no Baegu word for the concept, and memberships seem frustratingly variable. With the hamlet, one feels comfortable.

"Hamlet" is only an approximate translation of the Baegu *fera.* A *fera* is actually a named locality or parcel of land. If a man builds his house there, he applies the name of the land to his dwelling place. When he says, "Our *fera* is X," he is really saying, "Our house is built on locality X." But when used in the context of residence, everybody understands that *fera* means "dwelling place."

THE HAMLET

If the island's greenness is overwhelming from the air, it is appalling to the traveler on foot. Paths are narrow tunnels slashed through the dense secondary forest, and visibility is usually restricted to a few yards. I never arrived at a hamlet without feeling a brief surprise at stepping out of the jungle into the sunlight of a clearing. Hamlets are set in clearings (*labata*) hacked out of the bush. The clearing is usually rectangular and is in most cases kept fastidiously cleaned and well-brushed. Hamlet size varies so much that dimensions are almost meaningless. Small, single-family hamlets have clearings about twenty or twenty-five yards on a side, while a large, Neo-Marching Rule village may exceed one hundred yards in length. Structures within the clearing vary in size and elegance depending on the wealth and social pretensions of the inhabitants, although all conform to the same general pattern. The clearing itself is divided into a men's and a women's area. The men's area is sacred. The women's area contains public and profane zones.

WOMEN'S WORLD: THE PROFANE AND PUBLIC PARTS OF THE HAMLET

Family life centers about a family or dwelling house (*luma*). Women and children eat, sleep, and spend most of their leisure time there. Husbands enjoy their wives and children there, too. Nights in the Malaitan mountains are cold and wet, so the houses are built close to the ground with dirt floors and no windows. Since most people keep a fire going continually inside, the houses are as smoky and poorly ventilated as a leaf house can be.

The floor plan is rectangular. The structural members are four upright posts for the corners, triangular gables at each end, and longitudinal beams for the roof (Figure 23). Upright timbers set between the corner posts may help support the longitudinal members of the gable and the roof beams. To these structural members are attached a framework of sticks lashed together with vines. The roof is shingled with layers of neatly trimmed sago or ivory-palm leaves sewn onto six-foot lengths of bamboo splints, and the walls are a combination of palm leaves, bark, and bamboo. There is usually only one door.

When men first establish a new home, they build a single dwelling house. The interior of the house is divided conceptually if not physically into an "uphill side" (*kula i langi*), said to be the man's half (*kula ni wane*), and a "downhill side," said to belong to the woman (*kula ni keni*). The uphill or man's side is the eating and sitting area. The innermost, rear part of the house is the woman's sleeping quarters

Figure 23. Baegu House Construction

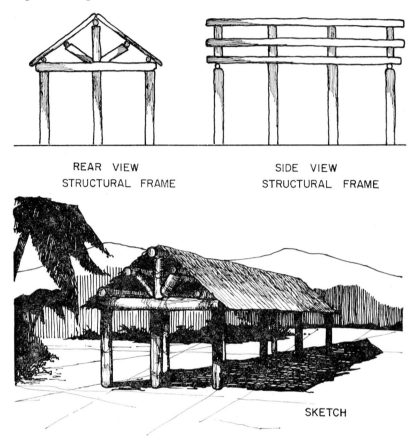

REAR VIEW
STRUCTURAL FRAME

SIDE VIEW
STRUCTURAL FRAME

SKETCH

(*lalo*). There may be a porch with a sloping roof attached to the front of the house for sitting, cooking, and gossiping (Figure 24), a common area not identified with either sex. After people have lived in a place for some time, they may build a second dwelling house, and the locus of family activity becomes a dwelling house pair functionally divided into a sleeping house (*luma tio*) and a cooking house (*luma nare*). The *lalo* or sleeping house is then forbidden to men other than the woman's husband. Men of great sanctity avoid women's quarters altogether, because of the danger of supernatural pollution (*sua*). In multiple-family hamlets there is usually a dwelling house (or a dwelling house pair) for every married woman.

These dwelling houses are in a public zone, shared by both men and women. Outside the clearing, but part of the hamlet, is a profane or ritually polluted (*sua*) zone for women only.

Figure 24. Dwelling House (*Luma*) Plan

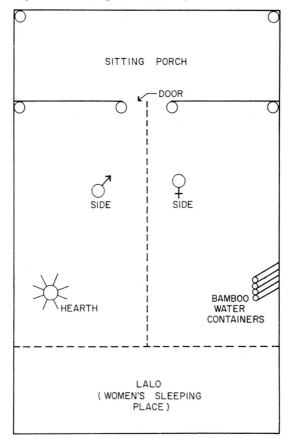

A few dozen yards outside the clearing, but screened from view by bushes and trees and always downhill from it, is the menstrual hut (*bisi*) where women must remain in isolation during their monthly periods. The *bisi* is built according to the same construction techniques as other houses, but is much smaller and looks like an old-fashioned outhouse. There is only one menstrual hut for each hamlet, shared by all the post-menarcheal females there. Menstrual isolation is not wholly burdensome. Men claim that lazy women sometimes fake a period to get out of work; postmenopausal women sometimes continue retreating to the *bisi* once a month, even though the theological reason for isolation no longer exists; and young people have assignations there. Although the Baegu believe that contact with menstrual blood is dangerous, this apparently applies only to fully adult (married with one child) men.

Old men glow with salacious delight when telling of their youthful flirtations in the *bisi* while the rest of the hamlet slept.

The birth hut (*bisi ni lafi*) is a small house isolated in the forest a considerable distance away from the hamlet where women go to give birth. Birth is the most defiling and polluting situation in Baegu cosmology. It is dangerous even for men to see the *bisi ni lafi,* and if a man does accidentally see the house, the woman must pay him compensation for damages. People say that if a pig goes near a birth house, the ancestral spirits will reject the pig as a sacrifice. To prevent these difficulties, women mark the path to their birth hut by breaking a sapling and folding it across the trail. A woman gives birth completely alone and without even a midwife. She does select one kinswoman or friend (*'ae oko*) to bring her food and water. If possible, the *bisi ni lafi* where the birth takes place should be abandoned and burned after ten to fifteen days. The mother then builds a second *bisi* where she stays for the remainder of her confinement, allowing the second birth house to decay after she leaves. A new mother spends a total of thirty-one days in isolation after a birth. On the last (thirty-first) night she sleeps in a temporary neo-natal isolation house (*suru*) on the outskirts of her husband's hamlet. Only then does she return to her own home and present the baby to its father and his kinsmen.

MEN'S WORLD: THE SACRED HALF OF THE HAMLET

Set somewhat apart from the family houses in an area reserved for the men of the settlement is the men's house (*beu*). The *beu* is a combination dormitory, clubhouse, and den, safely removed from contaminating and annoying association with women. If the settlement is large and there are several men, they may have both a sleeping house (*beu tio*) and another *beu* (with no particular name) for eating, betel-chewing, and miscellaneous socializing. If there are any unmarried males (*wane darai* or *alakwa*), they frequently build their own *beu* and sleep separately from the married men. In the area around the *beu* there are piles of stones used for ovens. The men may dedicate one of these to sacred purposes and call it the spirits' oven (*bii sa akalo*).

A priest will also have a sacred *beu* (*beu akalo* or *beu aabu*) a few dozen yards outside the clearing, always uphill from the rest of the hamlet and hidden from it by the forest. Here he stores his sacred paraphernalia (antique weapons or ornaments and relics of the ancestors) and keeps an oven for offerings to the spirits. All of these places are sacred (*aabu*) and are forbidden to females.

Men like to segregate themselves here, possibly because they enjoy the conviviality of the male peer-group, but also because it is an area relatively free from potentially dangerous contamination by women. The men eat many of their meals here, and a priest or a devoutly religious man will cook all of his own meals in the *beu* area, for he is forbidden to eat food prepared by women. Mountain hamlets lack the common space or plaza area found in Lau villages (Maranda and Maranda 1970:836), because dances or ceremonies take place in forest glades. It is proper, however, to see the men's houses (*beu*) as a sacred zone for men only, the dwelling houses (*luma*) as a public zone for more or less free sexual interaction, and the menstrual huts (*bisi*) as a profane or polluted zone for women only.

MISCELLANEOUS HAMLET FEATURES

Associated with the hamlet will be several logistic features. Among these are the structures for the care of pigs (*boso*), for the pig is absolutely essential as a religious sacrifice, and (as in many Melanesian societies) it is the most readily available means of capital accumulation. Many men build a timber pigpen (*sakale boso*) in the bush adjacent to the clearing to protect their investments. Others construct a small but sturdy elevated cage, patterned after the over-the-water pig cages of the saltwater people in the Lau Lagoon. Young pigs are allowed to run free, foraging in the clearing for refuse by day and sleeping in the dwelling houses at night. Unfortunately, however, many pigs escape, and pig-stealing is all too common. Good pig shelters reduce but do not completely prevent these troubles.

Some men build storehouses for foodstuffs (*babala kai,* literally "yam shelter"). Taro does not store well, yams are rare in the hills, and sweet potatoes are usually dug as needed, so these are not too important and are probably built in imitation of the saltwater practice.

Each hamlet has its own water source, usually a place where a small stream or spring falls over a rocky outcrop. People frequently improve the watering place by running a split tube of bamboo out from the rock, making bathing or bottling the water in bamboo tubes easier. Drinking water is very pure and is collected upstream from the bathing areas. If the geology of the area permits, there is one bathing area for men (*kafo wane ki*) and a second for women (*kafo keni ki*).

A gully or depression below the hamlet serves as a trash dump (*tafu*). There is not much refuse except for sweepings, since garbage is carefully collected and burned to prevent its being used for sorcery (*arua*).

On one side of the hamlet and below it is the women's latrine (*tale keni*), with the men's latrine (*tale wane*) on the other side of the clearing. These usually empty into a deep fissure, cleft, or sink hole in the soft limestone, although a deep hole may be dug if necessary. The women's latrine is especially malignant in terms of ritual pollution and men avoid the place like poison. One classic folktale relates how a raiding party attacked their enemies' village by doing the impossible: approaching through the women's latrine and so catching them completely by surprise.

In summary, certain features characterize the Baegu hamlet. There are one or more clearings cut from secondary growth. There is a dwelling house for each married woman in the hamlet, and these family houses are the loci that define (in spatial terms) the household group. There is one men's area (house, ovens, and trees) shared by the men of the hamlet but said to be owned by the hamlet's senior male. This *beu* area is the locus that defines (in spatial terms) the hamlet group. Symmetrically, there is also one menstrual isolation hut (*bisi*) shared by all the women of the hamlet; it defines the hamlet in terms of its female residents. Joint water source and sanitary facilities also help to define the hamlet.

HAMLET LOCATION

Hamlet location depends upon a number of factors. First, there is an economic basis for choice of hamlet site. Quite logically, people want to live within "reasonable" walking distance of good garden land. This usually means a twenty or thirty-minute walk, but at least one woman had her garden about one and a half hours from her hamlet. Also quite logically, hamlets are built on areas of hard, red soil, rather than on the more friable black soil that is preferred for gardens. All are on ridges or hillsides to avoid flooding. Then, too, hamlets have to be placed where adequate water supplies and facilities for sanitary disposal are available.

Second, there are social norms influencing choice of hamlet location. The senior adult male should have some sort of claim to the land on which the hamlet is built. He usually has a remembered ancestor who once occupied the area, making him a member of the ownership corporation (either through agnatic or cognatic linkage) and a member of the ritual community who worship at the shrine where that ancestor is buried.

Finally, hamlets are placed in particular sites for aesthetic reasons. Situated on hillsides or the brows of ridges, many have superb views of the Pacific or the forest in the valley below, and I am sure the Baegu appreciate this.

SOCIAL RELEVANCE OF THE HAMLET

The Baegu nuclear family does not differ greatly from others around the world. Baegu marriage is statistically monogamous, men and women have in theory (and usually in practice) exclusive rights over the spouse's sexual services, and adultery was once a capital crime. Hence a married couple forms an absolutely independent sexual team. Because of a sexual division of labor with men doing the more spectacular and women the more tedious work, and the requirements of first nursing and then feeding children, a nuclear family also forms a production and consumption unit in economic terms. Food produced is pooled, so that small children and invalids share in it. Mothers nurse and love their own children, and a youngster learns most of life's practical techniques from his father and mother. Despite the "classificatory" nature of the kinship terminology, the warmest emotional relationships (with the exception of foster children) exist between parents and their own biological offspring. Although most property is owned by other groups or individuals, a nuclear family does hold joint title to its dwelling or family house. Therefore I am not ignoring the nuclear family or household group because it does not exist (it does), but because a variety of cogent reasons convince me that as a residential unit the hamlet is sociologically more important.

The mere existence of the concept *"fera"* is prima facie evidence of its cultural importance. Men are identified by reference to their home hamlet. Linguistic evidence of a negative aspect is that it is rather difficult to talk in Baegu about a nuclear family. To do this, one has to use the circumlocution "So-and-so and his wife and their children" or the word *bara,* at best ambiguous since it means a group of any kind. One of the practical definitions of incest (the seduction or propositioning of an unmarried girl of the same *fera*) illustrates the importance of the hamlet. For the Baegu, as for Keesing's Kwaio, the young man, fostered by a kinsman or family friend, who seduces his protector's daughter is a symbol of basest ingratitude and moral degradation (Keesing 1965: 249).

Although arrangements of households into single, partially separated, and separated clearings exist among the Baegu, the hamlet remains the elementary residence unit. Keesing's socio-psychological explanation is quite adequate to explain the Baegu practice. Members of a Baegu hamlet who prefer relatively less frequent interaction will build their dwelling houses in partially or wholly separated clearings (Keesing 1965: 134).

There is some evidence from the settlement pattern itself that it is not necessary to subdivide and classify clearings, or to interpret a hamlet as a collection of household or nuclear family units. Instead, it is possible to make statements about the distribution of features in a hamlet (and this is the crux of the formal proof), regardless of whether the hamlet is the home of one nuclear family, several households, or a composite family.

> *Statement One:* There will be one dwelling house (*luma*) for every married woman in the hamlet. This is so for the wife in a nuclear family household, for widows affiliated with other families, for the several wives of a polygynous family, or for the wives of sons or brothers in extended-family settlements. The dwelling house may be divided into physically separated (but adjacent) structures for sleeping and cooking, but this does not spoil the generalization, since in these cases the pair functions as a single dwelling unit.

> *Statement Two:* There will be one men's house (*beu*), or more precisely, one men's area, shared by all the men of the settlement. There may well be separate sleeping arrangements for younger and for married men, and a priest will have a separate sacred *beu,* but these will be connected with a single physical location that serves as the locus of the ritual and social life of all the men of the hamlet.

> *Statement Three:* The entire hamlet will have a common water supply, trash dump, and separate sanitary facilities for men and for women.

The entire hamlet serves as the relevant unit for many child-care and socialization functions. Children's play groups include all the youngsters of the hamlet, and this informal peer group is the institution that inculcates values of cooperation and solidarity and (for boys) develops athletic and military skills. The hamlet also provides essential supervisory services. If parents choose to spend the day working in their gardens, or at the market, children are looked after, fed, and cared for by one of the hamlet's adults or older children, regardless of their biological parentage.

Even in economic activities the nuclear-family household unit surrenders some of its activities as a consumption unit to the hamlet or to individuals. Although the nuclear family does frequently eat together, men often (and priests always) maintain a separate communal table in the men's area of the hamlet. Children are inveterate scroungers, and norms of behavior oblige older kinsmen to give the little beggars a handout whenever they ask for one. Hence it is an open question whether a child gets a larger portion of his daily food intake from his parents or from some other hearth in the hamlet.

When Baegu informants replied to my queries about households within a hamlet, they apparently were referring to dwelling houses (*luma*) that as the cooking and sleeping place for a man, a woman, and their offspring are the nearest equivalent to the English category of "household." But in fact children are so mobile and so many of the unmarried (single, divorced, widows, widowers, and the very old) are dependent on relatives that I am simply unable to define "household" accurately.

BEYOND THE HAMLET

Baegu residential units larger than the hamlet are hard to find. Solomon Islands groups are, after all, traditionally atomistic and independent. But there are two such larger residential units: the neighborhood and the district. These two categories are so imprecise, so mixed, and so overlapping that they may cause more confusion than they resolve; for the first has much social but little cultural importance, while the latter has little social but immense cultural importance.

Neighborhoods consist of people who live near one another, who have common interests in the economic resources of their local area, and who accept the leadership of one or more important men (de facto leaders) who live among them. For these reasons the residents of a neighborhood tend to interact more frequently with one another than they do with outsiders.

Districts can be either geographic or socio-residential categories. As geographic categories, districts are the land residually owned by a clan (the largest named descent group). As socio-residential categories, they include the people living on such a named tract of land. Cognitively the district as a residential group is of great importance, for residential districts are supposed to be the physical embodiment of the ritual community; but unless the district is coterminous with (equivalent to) a single neighborhood, it does not nowadays approximate a social group in any routinely accepted sense.

It is almost impossible to sort out any regular distinction between neighborhood and district. In some instances neighborhoods simply do not exist. At other times a whole district is a single neighborhood, or one residential community with a common interest in the land. Other districts will have two or more discrete neighborhoods that may be secularly defined by physical separation plus internal cohesion, or they may be ritual groups associated with separate shrines. In some cases a neighborhood may overlap district boundaries, with people from different descent groups and districts sharing other common interests as neighbors (Figure 25). As Keesing (1965:138) pointed out, a neighborhood is the residential analog of the personal kindred, where relationships are based on residential rather than genealogical propinquity.

Figure 25. Overlapping Neighborhood and District Categories

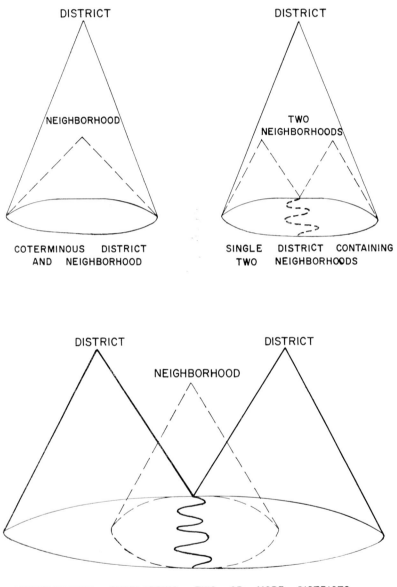

DISTRICT

NEIGHBORHOOD

COTERMINOUS   DISTRICT
AND   NEIGHBORHOOD

DISTRICT

TWO
NEIGHBORHOODS

SINGLE   DISTRICT   CONTAINING
TWO   NEIGHBORHOODS

DISTRICT   DISTRICT

NEIGHBORHOOD

NEIGHBORHOOD   OVERLAPPING   TWO   OR   MORE   DISTRICTS

NEIGHBORHOODS

The neighborhood is a collection of hamlets (loosely allied by ties of mutual obligation and sentiment) and their associated resources, usually geographically adjacent and focused about particular localities, characterized by occasional communal or joint action, and having for the most part a higher frequency of interaction among members of the neighborhood than between residents and outsiders. The cultural reality of the neighborhood is much harder to prove, since the Baegu language does not have a word for it.

Hamlets are on the average some fifteen to forty-five minutes walking time apart. (Melanesians can cover this distance somewhat faster than I could.) This spacing is not uniform throughout Baegu territory. In favorably endowed areas (such as around Beliga's hamlet of Fatakalie in Agia district, where there is plenty of water and good garden land), the hamlets are much closer to one another. Conversely, in the bamboo forests near the summit of Borofunga Mountain and in the interior of Langane District where surface water is painfully scarce, settlements are few and far between. This difference is due to ecological factors in some cases, but to social ones in others. There are clusters or networks of hamlets here and there, and perhaps (but not always) areas of less-frequent settlement between. Aerial photographs taken during cartographic surveys in the past two decades confirm this pattern (BSIP 1962).

Neighborhoods are in some senses created by the distribution of economic resources. Hamlets must have access to water supplies and to fertile garden land within reasonable walking distance. If these are lacking, people will be less apt to settle there, and hamlets will tend to cluster where such resources are. Gardens are usually not immediately adjacent to the hamlet. The rough Malaitan topography means that suitable plots are small and it is unlikely that good land for a new garden will adjoin the old garden plot. People do not abandon their hamlets as often as they abandon their gardens, and so, after a few years, most gardens are located at some distance from the hamlet. Quite often, the walk to a man's garden will take him past one or more neighboring hamlets. Economically useful long-lived trees are the other major productive resource causing a Baegu man's interests to be spread over a considerable area not restricted to the immediate vicinity of his present residence. Men plant coconuts and areca palms in the men's area of their hamlet, and their ownership of these trees does not cease after they build new houses at another *fera* and abandon the old site. Since people move every five to ten years, the dynamics of the shifting residence pattern mean that after a few decades a man will own coconuts and betel-nut palms growing at a number of sites in the area.

Thus there are cogent economic reasons for maintaining friendly ties with neighboring hamlets. For access to their scattered garden plots and tree holdings, and to avoid theft, men must maintain amicable relationships with residents of intervening settlements. To exercise rights in surrounding bushlands and streams for hunting, fishing, and foraging, men of hamlets in the same area must keep the peace. But economic factors are neither as useful criteria for defining neighborhoods nor as compelling proofs of the neighborhood's importance as social factors are.

Plate 12. A priest's sacred house (*beu*) for relics in the forest near Ao'ana hamlet (photograph by Kathryn P. Ross).

The most obvious social characteristic of a Baegu neighborhood is that it tends to concentrate about influential adult males. These men serve as foci of community feeling and mobilizers of community action; they might as well be called "focal males." The focal male may have a formal, specialized status, or he may be simply an informal leader in the classic Melanesian Big Man mode (Sahlins 1963). If there are several focal males in a neighborhood, they tend to be allied in a hierarchical relationship or to occupy specialists' roles. Baegu society recognizes a number of specialized leadership roles. Most neighborhood communities will have more than one of these, but rarely if ever will a single neighborhood have all. These leaders or focal males are called, literally, "big men" (*wane baita*). It is worth noting now that community action or decisions are nearly always the result of consensus; rarely are they caused by overt command of the Big Men.

One of the most noticeable of these important men is the *wane initoo* or hereditary landowner, titularly the senior member of a clan or lineage as a joint land-owning group. His position is an ascribed one, resulting from primogeniture in the course of patrilineal descent, but the position has very little innate power. However, because of genealogical position, their direct descent from the ancestors, and their titular role in granting permission for land use, *wane initoo* are inherently already in a strategically valuable focal position and can easily turn this favorable sociocentric status into a means of attaining economic and executive power that goes far beyond the direct perquisites of office. The Baegu recognize intuitively the dynamics of leadership and the status potential involved, and they sometimes by metaphor call other (nonhereditary) important men *wane initoo,* too. Hogbin (1944: 258) actually glosses the Toabaita title *wane inoto* as center man, reflecting the realization of his strategic position.

Probably the most important focal male in any neighborhood is the priest. The Baegu have two names for their priests: *fata aabu,* meaning "speak sacred things," a usage similar to that of the Fataleka people to the south; or, following the Lau custom and terminology, *wane ni foa,* meaning "man who prays." A Baegu priest is very much a priest and not a shaman or prophet. The priest is the representative of the community for dealings with the supernatural; only the priest can present sacrifices to the ancestral spirits, and only the priest can through prayer ask them to grant blessings (*mamanaa*) to their descendants. His office is socially created and validated. He is elected (by consensus of the ritual community) on the basis of his temperament and mastery of specific ritual knowledge. He must know detailed genealogies, the exact wording of all the relevant prayers, and the details of all sacrificial and ritual procedures. Most neighborhoods do have a resident priest, but it is possible for a community to use the services of a priest from another neighborhood. Conversely a single man can fill the role of priest in more than one neighborhood, since the critical factor is possession of the appropriate ritual knowledge for the particular shrine where the sacrifices are being made.

Although the priest's tasks are not particularly onerous, large ritual communities have assistant priests or curates (*wane anifoa* or *refoa*) to help the priest at major ceremonies. These men have only minimal ritual duties, primarily helping to cook and distribute pork at sacrificial feasts, but it is a good chance for them to learn the proper genealogies, prayers, and ritual techniques.

Hogbin (1939:106), writing about the Toabaita, says that the priest and the *wane inoto* roles were sometimes combined in the same person. My impression is that usually they are not; the Baegu priest (*fata aabu*) and wealthy man (*wane initoo*) are both subsumed under the category "important man" (*wane baita*). They do frequently say that the priest is "the same as" (*bobola*) the wealthy man, meaning usually that they are both important men in the community.

In the days before the British (chronic colonial spoilsports) put an end to institutionalized feuding, many neighborhood communities (but by no means all) had a war leader (*wane ramo*) who was also potentially a focal male. The actual role of the *ramo* is not too clear, since they have not been free to operate for over thirty years. It seems likely that their status in the society changed considerably after 1880, but they appear to have been combination military commanders–policemen–bounty hunters. *Ramo* were chosen (again by consensus) on the basis of their physical strength, aggressive temperament, and military skill. People living today who are said to be "most like *wane ramo*" tend to be nasty-tempered mesomorphs. In the traditional social setting they were useful as leaders of expeditions against external enemies, and — by way of threats or, if necessary, assassination — as a means of social control against troublemakers within the community. Baegu custom recognized and compensated them by a system of monetary rewards (*finisi*) offered for revenge killing of enemies. After traders introduced firearms in the late nineteenth century, assassination became relatively simple and safe. Successful *wane ramo* held large areas in terror, killing individuals from both parties to feuds and picking up a tidy profit along the way by collecting the reward or bounty from first one side and then the other. British District Officer Bell put an end to this lucrative practice in the 1920's by adopting for himself the role of "Super Ramo," dominating the Malaitan war leaders, and collecting their firearms. Bell himself was killed in a skirmish at Sinerango in 1927, but the subsequent punitive expedition against the Kwaio provided the great Götterdämmerung for the northern Malaitan *wane ramo*. Dozens of them volunteered to join the British-led expedition, and these Malaitans were probably the most relentless hatchet men in what turned out to be an extremely vicious retaliation against the Kwaio (Keesing 1965: 25-27). I met two old former *ramo* who had accompanied the expedition and who still recited, with obvious relish, tales of the Kwaio men, women, and children they had murdered. This put an end to the *ramo* system in northern Malaita, and since then the *ramo* have been only a memory and a source of epic tales.

Some neighborhoods have other specialists who are leaders of a lesser sort, but they are rather unlikely to be focal males unless they have some other claim to prestige as well. These include oracles through whom the ancestral spirits speak by possession, diviners who discover the will of the ancestors by ritually breaking leaves of the sacred cordyline plant, magical healers, and genealogical experts whose memories serve as data banks for important ritual knowledge. Among Neo-Marching Rule cultists, the status of genealogical expert has been formalized in the office of "Clerk," the functionary who travels around the hills collecting and recording genealogical data. Finally, there are men whose keen intelligence and managerial talents make them "big."

Regardless of the source of their original claim to prominence, important men are by definition the leaders of the residential community living around them. As organizers and leaders they are focal as far as the neighborhood is concerned. Their original status, their impetus toward greatness, may be ascribed or achieved, but in the process of becoming a bigger man, a *wane baita* accomplishes by virtue of his ability to use what he already has. Their influence expresses itself through arbitration of local disputes and through mobilization of communal action for joint labor and feasting in either secular or religious contexts. This influence comes about by means of their proven ability to accumulate wealth by hard work, skillful trading and investment, clever manipulation of allies, and timely cashing in of outstanding kinship ties and other obligations in order to provide the considerable sums of goods needed for the purchase of brides by younger kinsmen and neighbors, and to assemble the vast amounts of taro and pigs needed for major religious sacrifices.

It is important not to overemphasize the competitive behavior of these achieved-status, typically Melanesian-style Big Men in Baegu society. Although, as in New Guinea, there are formal friendships and gift-giving relationships between partners called *kwaimani,* who may exchange presents and obligations, true economic redistribution and competition occurs mostly in ritual contexts. For the Baegu, prestige and power are group attributes rather than individual ones. Men acquire renown through the demonstrated power and wealth of their groups, not by way of individual competition or potlatch-style giving; a leader's prestige derives from his group's prestige, wealth, and power. Achieved status comes in two steps. Within a group, a leader enhances cooperation, manipulating relationships to achieve group ends and demonstrating his own generosity through monetary, material, and labor contributions. Competition is between groups. Prestige comes to the leader of a successful group which gives the best feasts and dances.

Communal labor as a joint activity of the neighborhood community appears in several guises. Men prepare special gardens for the taro to be offered to the ancestral spirits at sacrifices. Most secular gardening is an individual task, but the more difficult labor of felling trees and clearing brush from new garden plots may be done communally. Recently (while I was in the field) Christian villagers and Neo-Marching Rule cultists have begun organizing "unions" that put such communal tasks as garden clearance on a cash payment basis. All residents of the neighborhood belong to the "union." For a small fee (about $2.00 Australian) the union will clear a man's new garden. Union members who do not show up to work are fined one shilling. Theoretically the money collected will go for community improvements such as water tanks, meeting houses, or more elegant religious structures, but as none have been built yet it remains to be seen if the ideas will work out in practice. House-building is also a joint activity and something of a holiday. Labor is theoretically recruited in terms of the kinship idiom, a man's classificatory brothers being obliged to help him build a new house. Because of the difficulties of travel it usually works out that a man's "brothers" help him only if they are living in or near the same neighborhood.

In days before the British pacified the island, the neighborhood could also be the basis for military organization. Bands of neighbors and kinsmen (either status could involve men in feuds) made up the war parties (fikua ome) for offensive operations, usually ambushes or dawn raids on unsuspecting settlements. During extended or particularly vicious periods of warfare, residents of a threatened neighborhood would sometimes retire to prepared defensive positions in the higher parts of the district. There they would live in fortified villages (labu) protected by defensive ditches and palisades until the emergency passed.

Although it is useful to know how a neighborhood behaves as a community in joint action, some sort of sociometric definition of the community may be more useful. Stated baldly, frequency of interaction within the neighborhood community is relatively higher than is interaction between neighborhoods.

This is particularly clear when one considers interaction between a focal male and his followers. For a variety of reasons people like to live close to a Big Man, and his hamlet will almost always be larger and more populous than others, containing more households and more affiliated single individuals. Being close to the source of power, it is easier to play political games and to get his help when needed; he has relatively more wealth to distribute; sorcery and physical assault are less likely in his vicinity; a certain amount of his prestige rubs off on his coresidents; and, since his status is to a certain extent acquired, Big Men (focal males) probably tend to have more pleasant social personalities. In sociometric terms, interaction between focal males and the individuals attracted to them is frequent. The important man informally influences the behavior of the neighborhood, people seek his advice and aid in times of personal crisis, and he in turn needs their help for his prestige and achievement. Big Men of one neighborhood deal with those of another neighborhood, but the common people usually do not; they tend to observe the chain of command. The influence of the focal male ends and the people cease to look to him for advice and leadership at the boundaries of the neighborhood.

Gossip and informal calls are also more frequent within neighborhoods than between them. Both men and women on their way to or from their gardens will casually drop in at hamlets en route to talk and chew betel. But they will not do so as frequently in hamlets outside their own neighborhood. Markets and dance performances associated with sacrifices are the notable exceptions. At both of these crowds gather from miles around, and they are great opportunities for exchanging gossip and for girl-watching. Hamlets lying along the trails from the interior to the twice-weekly marketplaces along the coast are sometimes besieged with visitors. (I still have not recovered from the strain of my strategic ethnographic location.)

Such joint activities as communal worship and cooperative labor ought also to be considered from a sociometric aspect. Kinsmen from nonadjacent or even distant neighborhoods do in fact help their relatives at house-building time and do contribute to and participate in sacrifices to the ancestral spirits in other neighborhoods. However, the crucial factor here is frequency. Individuals participate in communal activity in their own neighborhoods more than in the communal activities of other neighborhoods.

Neighborhoods do not always have a name, but if they do, they may take it from the shrine where most of the residents worship, from the name of the hamlet of a particularly important focal male, or from the descent group that is locally most important. Those who live in the Kafo Kekero Valley and who worship at Oisamaku shrine are "people of Oisamaku." People living near Beliga's hamlet of Fatakalie in Agia district are "people of Fatakalie" in some contexts, even if they do not live in the hamlet itself. The eastern slopes of Borofunga Mountain drain into either the Sasafa or the Takwea rivers. Most of the men living in both drainage areas claim to belong to the same maximal descent group, but those in the Sasafa drainage pattern are *Walelangi*, the senior branch of *Wale*, while people from the Takwea drainage are *Waleano*, the junior or cadet branch of *Wale*.

In summary, then, a neighborhood is a group of friendly or allied hamlets occupying a geographic area. They are spatially related to the distribution of economic resources and possibly to supernatural resources in the form of shrines or groves sacred to the ancestral spirits. Socially they are characterized by physical and social concentration around the settlement of focal males. Sociometrically they are a definite community with a high frequency of interaction between members of the neighborhood and a lower frequency of interaction with residents of other neighborhoods. An actual geographic separation may or may not accompany these social parameters.

RELIGION AND RESIDENCE

The most prominent man-made feature of the Baegu landscape and the physical focus of Baegu religious life is the shrine at a sacred grove (*beu aabu*). Stands of virgin hardwoods rising out of the green blanket of secondary growth like the superstructures of ships above surface mists at sea, the sacred groves are both temples and cemeteries. Their traditional importance is tremendous, since it is here that the ancestors are buried, and it is here that the greatest religious ceremonies take place. They are the clearly visible locus of communal religious activity and the interface between natural and supernatural worlds. Sacred places are of some antiquity and publicly acknowledged; a priest cannot create a shrine just anywhere he chooses.

Given this importance, it would seem likely that sacred groves would be a natural focus for neighborhoods. Unfortunately this idea does not work out in practice, and the congruence between ritual and residential communities is only vague at best. In a way this complexity may have a culturally integrative value, because the sacred groves are at once important to ancestral spirits (whose bodies are buried there), districts of land which they help identify, the descent groups who are obligated to worship there, cognatic kinsmen of a descent group's agnates who can by choice and permission worship there, crowds of folks who come for miles to see the dancing at ceremonies, and in some cases to residential neighborhoods that are associated with the grove itself.

There are situations where a shrine at a sacred grove can be the focus of neighborhood identity. Smaller districts may have only one sacred grove. If so, neighborhood and district are essentially identical. But in large districts there may be several sacred groves, and a neighborhood may (but not always) be defined as the hamlets that are associated with a particular sacred grove and that participate in religious ceremonies there. *Beu aabu* are named and, inasmuch as a neighborhood has a name, it is often the name of its sacred grove.

An entire shrine consists of a sacred grove, a sacred enclosure for ceremonies, and associated features for services and performances. The sacred grove is the most evident feature and the holiest part of the shrine complex. The grove is in a sense man-made, because it is a stand of virgin hardwoods that are never cut and that tower high above the surrounding secondary bush forest. The sacred dead are buried here, and the ghosts live in the grove. There are many sacred groves, but not all are actively used for ceremonies or worship during a single individual's lifetime. The groves persist because no one (even a modern Christian) is sacrilegious enough to put an axe to trees sacred to the ancestral dead. A priest can reactivate one of these latent groves and begin holding sacrifices there, if he learns through divination or inspiration that the ancestral spirits living there ought to be propitiated. No one ever enters an active sacred grove except with a priest or a burial party that has business there. People can enter a currently unused grove, but most hesitate to do so, behave quite reverently while there, and would not dream of using the grove for secular or profane purposes. The interiors of the groves are quite dark and still, dappled with little bits of sunlight filtering through the high branches, and surprisingly free of undergrowth. I was always deeply moved by the eerie stillness of the groves and, sensing their otherworldly ambience, was quite ready to believe that one could talk to the ancestors there.

At the edge of the sacred grove, people build a rectangular enclosure (*maa na beu*) delineated by earthen embankments or stone walls. It is here that the most sacred ceremonies, the sacrifices offered to the ancestral spirits, take place. Dead priests are buried here, and their successors build a palm-leaf shelter over the grave where worshipers sleep during the cycle of occasional ceremonies over the next few years. Mourners plant magical herbs on the grave and stick fern leaves used in funeral ceremonies into the roof of the shelter. At one edge of the courtyard is a rocky area where priests kill the pigs used in sacrifices, and at the other is the slit gong used to announce sacrifices to the ancestors. There are several piles of rocks used for cooking ovens at ceremonies and a wooden storage rack for keeping the cooked pork up off the ground out of the reach of ants and dogs. Just outside the sacred enclosure (women are forbidden to enter it), people build a leaf shelter for the women to sit in so they can hear the panpipe music and the epic chants while they are cleaning taro corms for the ceremonial ovens. In or near the enclosure one often finds a large rock or ancient tree stump called a *bibie* that they say is the dwelling place of the spirits and the source of heavenly "power" (*mamanaa*). These are used for oaths and ordeals, since men can speak only the truth when in the presence of the *bibie*. A short ways downhill from the enclosure is the dance ground, a cleared, level area. At the end of the sacred feasts, there are panpipe concerts and sacred dance performances here, attracting spectators from dozens of miles around.

Even where a sacred grove is not a focus for a neighborhood as ritual community, neighborhoods must still use a local sacred grove as a grave yard. Sacred groves are used for cemeteries as well as for ceremonies, and certain status distinctions are maintained even in death. Most communities have a separate cemetery for men, and another for women and children. Large neighborhoods have an entirely separate *beu aabu* for interment of important men only. Although many Malaitans practice secondary burial or skull retrieval, the Baegu do not. As one old man phrased it, "No, when we plant a crop, it stays there."

One of the most obvious of joint activities is communal worship. When a neighborhood is spatially focused upon a shrine or sacred grove where ceremonies (*maoma*) take place, and when it is at least partially socially focused about a priest as a focal male, it is to a large extent a ritual community. It is the ritual community living around a shrine that attend the ceremonies there, and who contribute the bulk of the taro and pigs for sacrifices to the ancestral spirits. Even where the ritual community conducting public worship at a sacred grove is not simply the neighborhood community, the grove will still be a focus of sorts. At times of public feasts all residents living nearby will attend. The men of the neighborhood, joining the actual contributing community, are the ones who eat the communal meal of taro and pork at the sacrificial ceremonies (distribution of portions follows residential lines), and the entire community gathers to watch the dancing and hear the panpipe concerts.

Plate 13. Sure'au, Fulaga, and Rimanu carrying pigs to be sacrificed (photograph by Kathryn P. Ross).

Plate 14. Women and boys making taro and coconut pudding (*lakeno*) for a feast (photograph by Kathryn P. Ross).

Plate 15. Men at a Masu clan mortuary feast (*maoma*) cooking taro in a stone and leaf oven (*bii*).

DISTRICTS AND LARGER RESIDENTIAL UNITS

Baegu territory is divided into a number of named territories or districts (*lolofaa*), each associated with a particular patrilineal descent group (*'ae bara*), most of whose members live within the district. District and descent groups share a common name (Map 17).

Most people think they know what their district is. Districts are identifiable parcels of land bounded by water courses, ridges, and imaginary lines joining large rocks or prominent trees. However, the land disputes among the Toabaita that Hogbin (1939:147) describes indicate that two persons or two groups may not agree on what these boundaries are. The physical features of all districts are roughly similar. Most are in the range of three to ten square miles. All have approximately the same economic resources: garden land and tracts of secondary growth, some rough inaccessible areas, and springs and streams. There are several sacred groves of primary forest that are the nuclei of, and truly define, the district. Districts are in fact focused upon shrines, not circumscribed by boundaries. Hamlets are grouped geographically into settlement clusters or arranged socially into neighborhood communities.

If the district is small and contains only one residential neighborhood, the neighborhood and district will be coterminous. However, some districts do contain more than one neighborhood. In this case, the relation-

Plate 16. Dancers performing a sacred *agae* at a Langane clan mortuary feast (*maoma*).

ships between the neighborhoods depend to a large extent upon the characteristics of the focal males, the Big Men and the priests, in the neighborhoods.

Since most Baegu worship consists of the communal offering of sacrifices by a social group directed by a socially approved leader (priest) according to prescribed forms and accompanied by the proper prayers to their common ancestral spirits, there is no theoretical reason why a priest could not conduct sacrifices to any of his ancestors, provided he knows the proper rituals and the group accepts his leadership. In the days before Christian missionaries disrupted the pagan religion, descent groups did indeed appoint chief priests (*gwau ni foa*), literally "head of prayers," who were said to be qualified to conduct sacrifices and offer prayers at any sacred grove or shrine (*beu aabu*) within their districts. Because most residents of a district are members of or related to the dominant descent group, and because members of the same descent group are assumed to be related at some point by a common apical ancestor, there were nearly always a few men who could claim an ancestor buried at each of the shrines. If a man had learned the genealogies and prayers associated with the ancestral spirits at the different shrines, he was eligible for selection as a priest; if he had enough sacred knowledge and enough political influence, he could be selected as a chief priest. Hence the machinery existed for communal worship on a large scale involving members of more than one neighborhood or descent segment.

Similarly, in the secular sphere the influence of an important man could extend beyond his own neighborhood, and he could become a focal male for an entire district. An aspirant to this sort of position would have to be quite aggressive, consistently successful, and very, very rich. Nowadays, no such men exist, but a generation or two ago many districts claimed an exceptionally important man (*wane taloa*), whose title means "man of prestige." The authority of the *wane taloa* extended throughout the entire district, and all the neighborhoods recognized his status. His official duties seem to have been to direct whatever district-wide activity might occur, to settle affairs involving men from different neighborhoods, and (most important) to initiate and provide the greater part of the material offered at sacrifices involving all the ritual communities of the district. The *wane taloa* was confirmed in office and given explicit recognition at a "dedication" ceremony conducted by a chief priest. The "man of prestige" offered a pig to the ancestors and ate some of the fat raw. The chief priest presented him to the ancestors, anointed his forehead with pork fat, and gave him as a badge of office a tropical flower called *filu*.

I was told that years ago people recognized the title of *wane saungia,* a man so powerful that his influence extended over more than one district, and who was said to have had the power of life and death over the people. Although the concept is similar to the offices of *aofia* and *taniota* reported among the Fataleka by Russell (1950:8), there is no way to tell if the *wane saungia* is myth or reality, for no one now living can personally recall those days.

Districts have great cognitive importance, since they are the category of the physical universe corresponding to the descent groups of the living and to their counterparts among the ancestral spirits who are buried there. However, districts are socially important today only if they are more or less congruent with a single descent group (*'ae bara*) as a ritual community or with a neighborhood as a residential community. Otherwise the district is largely a mental abstraction, of cultural but perhaps not social importance.

The district is the largest socio-residential unit. All larger, more inclusive, or superordinate categories are simply that: conceptualizations or generalizations made for convenience, a sort of mental shorthand. The Sasafa River does divide Baegu territory into two conceptual halves, "our side" and the "other side." There is some ambiguous justification for this in mythology, since most of the descent groups occupying the left bank claim descent from a place in the interior mountains called Marado, where the ancestors are supposed to have first settled after landing on the west coast of the island. Those south and east of the river, with the exception of Langane, do not; Agia came from Kwaio or 'Are'are, others from Kwara'ae, and still others from overseas, landing at a coastal site called Bina. But for the most part this is just prejudice on the part of individuals. People on my side of the river are more like me; they are potential allies, and the ghosts are more friendly. People on the other side are strangers; they are potential enemies, and the ghosts are dangerous. It seems likely that this is simply xenophobia expressed culturally, using the river as an index line.

There is no such thing as a Baegu state, for "Baegu" is a dialect, and "the Baegu" are the people who use that dialect. Certain descent groups are generally accepted as being "Baegu," and the districts they occupy are Baegu territory. I could not conceive of the Baegu acting as a unit, but Russell (1950:10) reports that the Fataleka (the next dialect group to the south) once did so, and recent revitalization cults talk of Baegu unity.

There is a certain validity in the traditional division of the northern Malaita population into "bush people" (*wane tolo*) and "saltwater people" (*wane asi*) that the people themselves recognize and accept.

The people realize that all of northern Malaita is linguistically and culturally similar. Values and norms are basically the same, marriage exchange takes place across dialect lines, and all use the same system of shell currency manufactured in the Langalanga Lagoon on the west coast. Although it did not exist in pre-European days, the concept of pan-Malaitan unity was an important part of Marching Rule ideology just after World War II and persists today among two classes that are rather unlikely bedfellows: the Western-educated elite committed to the British administration or to church hierarchies, and the present crop of cargo cultists.

10. The Social Composition
of Residential Groups

Previous chapters have considered Baegu social and residential groups in terms of what purposes they serve, or in terms of characteristics that define the group and make it a meaningful category within the framework of Baegu culture. But for several reasons these descriptions are incomplete. First, simply the size and range of variation of typical residential groups is important, since the dynamics of social interaction may vary with scale. Second, it is necessary to know something about the social roles that are found in these groups, and that may even be said to be essential to their existence. Third, groups of real people change, whereas most functional or structural explanations tend to have only limited time dimensions. Residential groups vary in time, largely because their memberships and the relations between members change. Both biological realities of age and the way culture interprets human developmental stages help determine whom a person will live with and what the quality of his social relationships will be.

SINGLE-FAMILY HAMLETS

Initially the most striking characteristic of Baegu hamlets is their small size. Unlike the Melanesian villages of coastal New Guinea, or even the nearby villages of the saltwater people in Malaita's Lau Lagoon, Baegu hamlets are tiny.

Table 18 analyzes census data in terms of average hamlet and household size. Numerical data are more accurate for my sample population area, essentially the Sasafa River drainage basin and the crests of the ridges around it, where I have some personal familiarity with everyone living in the area. "Household" is an imprecise, only marginally native, concept. Table 19 tells in terms of family social structure what the households as groups of people are. "Households," vaguely definable

TABLE 18. BAEGU HAMLET SIZE AND COMPOSITION

	Number of hamlets	People	Average hamlet size	Households (Baegu definition)	House- holds per hamlet	Average house- hold size
Sample area						
Pagans (traditional) . . .	14	189	13.5	48	3.4	3.9
Pagans (Neo-Marching						
Rule).	3	78	26.0	25	8.3	3.1
Anglicans	4	151	37.8	36	9.0	4.2
Roman Catholics.	. .	. .	. .	. .	. .	. .
SSEC.	4	75	18.8	18	4.5	4.2
SDA.	1	30	30.0	9	9.0	3.3
Totals	26	523	20.1	136	5.2	3.8
Ataa area*						
Pagans (traditional)	3	42	14.0	7	2.3	6.0
Pagans (Neo-Marching						
Rule).	5	136	27.2	31	6.2	4.4
Anglicans	1	39	39.0	9	9.0	4.3
Roman Catholics.	4	335	83.8	87	21.8	3.9
SSEC.	4	272	68.0	61	15.3	4.5
SDA.	1	13	13.0	3	3.0	4.3
Totals	18	837	46.5	198	11.0	4.2

* Ataa (southeastern Baegu area) data were collected by a Baegu schoolteacher, Joel Roboalasa, acting as my assistant.

TABLE 19. NATURE OF BAEGU HOUSEHOLDS IN THE SASAFA
RIVER BASIN SAMPLE POPULATION AREA

	Number of hamlets	Number of households	Intact nuclear families	Widowed persons with children	Not parent- child households	Persons living alone
Pagans (traditional). .	14	48	24	16	7	1
Pagans (Neo-						
Marching Rule). . .	3	25	14	7	4	0
Anglicans	4	36	30	4	1	1
SSEC.	4	18	13	3	2	0
SDA.	1	9	6	2	1	0
Totals	26	136	87	32	15	2

as people who tend to eat, work, and sleep together, may consist of an intact nuclear family (both parents still living and having children with them), or of partial families. These partial family households can be a widow or widower with her or his children; alternatively, they can be households not organized about a parent-child axis, such as a sibling group (with no parents), cooperative unisexual groups of two or more bachelors or spinsters, or old people with no children. Appendix B reproduces my census data for the sample area.

Using this classification of household types, it is possible to find out what kinds of households compose each hamlet and then to portray the frequency of hamlet types classified according to the number of nuclear families they contain. This is Table 20, revealing a frustratingly random nonpattern.

The sample population area contains several large villages that are plainly aberrant. Three pagan hamlets are centers of Neo-Marching Rule activity and ideology, a quiescent nativistic movement based on a concept of brotherhood that urges people to settle and live in large towns. Five Christian hamlets have churches or chapels attracting converts to settle there (as urged by mission officials) for the supernatural advantages coming from regular attendance at worship services. Removing these settlements (they have a combined population of 308 persons, 78 pagan and 230 Christian) from the computations produces Table 21, showing the frequency of occurrence of "natural" hamlets of various sizes in Baegu territory. These corrected data show most strikingly a mode at the two-nuclear-family level, independently supporting the contention of traditionally oriented Baegu themselves that it is "best" to live in a small hamlet with just a few relatives. Secondarily it shows that about 39 percent of Baegu *fera* are hamlets of less than two nuclear families. These single-family hamlets include a significant

TABLE 20. HAMLET TYPE DISTRIBUTION (SASAFA RIVER
BASIN SAMPLE POPULATION AREA)

Number of nuclear families	Number of hamlets	% of hamlets	People living thus	% of population
5 or more	6	23.1	260	49.7
4	2	7.7	46	8.8
3	1	3.8	22	4.2
2	10	38.5	141	27.0
1 + affiliated households	4	15.4	34	6.5
1	2	7.7	11	2.1
0	1	3.8	9	1.7
Totals	26	100	523	100

TABLE 21. "NATURAL" HAMLETS: DISTRIBUTION BY FREQUENCY OF OCCURRENCE

Number of nuclear families	Number of hamlets	% of hamlets	People living thus	% of population
5 or more..........................	0	0	0	0
4.................................	1	5.6	20	9.3
3.................................	1	5.6	22	10.2
2.................................	9	50.0	119	55.4
1 + affiliated households..............	4	22.2	34	15.8
1.................................	2	11.1	11	5.1
0.................................	1	5.6	9	4.2
Totals......................	18	100	215	100

Figures eliminate three Neo-Marching Rule villages with a combined population of 78, and five Christian villages (having churches or chapels) with a combined population of 230. These 308 people have congregated because of nontraditional ideologies, leaving 215 persons living in traditional small hamlets in the sample population area.

portion of the Baegu population (about 25 percent) and provide a convenient starting place for considering the social composition of Baegu residential groups, and how this typical composition comes to be.

FAMILY LIFE

Typically in such hamlets the most important or core members are a married couple and their children, either biological or adopted. In most cases marriage takes place relatively late. Although it is almost impossible to say exactly how old anyone is (they simply do not know), it is possible to estimate ages by relating personal developmental stages to significant events in recent Malaitan history such as World War I, the coming of local missionaries, the murder of District Officer Bell (1927), visits to northeastern Malaita by Fox, Ivens, and Hogbin, the Japanese and American invasions in World War II, Marching Rule, and Roger Keesing's fieldwork among the Kwaio. It appears that most girls marry for the first time at about age twenty to twenty-five, and most boys during their middle or late twenties.

Child-bearing occurs throughout the natural span of a woman's fertility, so there is usually a considerable age difference between the oldest and youngest siblings in a family. Family size is quite variable. Viewed synchronically, the average married couple in my intensive census sample had 2.7 living children. Analysis of genealogical information indicates that, in the past, about two or three children of each nuclear family would live to maturity (defined as having had children of their own). I have the distinct impression that younger families I actually observed have more living children than older families had in the past, but there is really no way to tell, since children who died in infancy or early childhood would be apt to be left out of genealogies. This is particularly true of saltwater families in the Lau Lagoon, and of Christian converts among the Baegu who are more apt to use the limited medical care provided. Pagan families in the interior highlands, who either fear or cannot find medical help, may be smaller. The British administration at any rate fears that they may have an incipient population explosion now underway (see Table 12).

Births are usually, but not invariably, spaced two or more years apart. There is no rigidly observed post-partum sex taboo, but there is a general feeling that it is improper to conceive another child before the next elder is able to walk. People covertly ridicule those whose children are born too close together, saying that a woman who nurses two children at once is like a dog, dirty and immoral. (Pigs have litters, too, but Baegu people admire pigs.) This community disapproval inhibits sexual activity severely enough so that most families are "properly" spaced. That it does not prevent improper spacing altogether is probably a result of the Baegu theory of conception. People believe that pregnancy results only from the accumulation of seminal fluid and that one night of dalliance is usually safe, a logical enough intepretation given the periodicity of female fertility. Although deterred from frequent cohabitation by fear of pregnancy and consequent community disapproval, most young couples probably feel safe in sneaking in a little love-making now and then. Thanks to biological probabilities they usually get away with it, but the inevitable exceptions result and "improper" spacing of childen occurs.

As in all human societies, there is some sexual division of labor. A man and wife each has his or her own garden; routine gardening is largely an independent task, although men usually help their wives with the heavier tasks of initial tree-felling and fence-building. In sacred taro gardens, dedicated for mortuary feasts, men do all the work except weeding. Wives are expected to care for their husband's and their sons' pigs as well as their own. This is no small task, since valuable pigs are given cooked and peeled sweet potatoes, and younger ones are fed premasticated ones. Men do most of the house-building and repair, although women may help. Women carry the heavy loads of firewood and garden produce, the rationale being that men must be free to use their clubs and spears in case of ambush along the trails. Either men or women make the large pandanus mats used as bedding and umbrellas, but most crafts, particularly the artistic woodcarving and manufacture of ornaments from shell beads, are left to the men. Care and feeding of infants is naturally done by women, but men and older children frequently care for children while the mother works in her garden. Women usually cook the morning and evening meals, but men and boys can and do prepare frequent snacks. The sexes usually eat separately. Marketing is a woman's task. Women carry produce to the semi-weekly markets along the coast and do the actual trading while the men go along to supervise. Ritual belongs to the men.

Analysis of roles in single-family hamlets is relatively straightforward. The husband or father as an adult male has both the major responsibility and the authority. He selects the hamlet site and builds the living quarters. He protects the residents against physical dangers and (as ritual leader) against supernatural ones, and he teaches his sons by example. Most important policy decisions are made by him. Wives or mothers are responsible for routine upkeep of the hamlet (cleaning and minor repairs) and for daily subsistence (water, firewood, food for meals, and marketing). Wives produce and nurture infants, and train and supervise daughters. Younger children lead the good life, but they are expected to obey and conform to rules for proper behavior. Older children gradually assume more and more routine household duties.

LIFE'S DEVELOPMENTAL STAGES

As Meyer Fortes (1958:1-13) among others has pointed out, social structures in some ways grow out of the human developmental process. Because physical requirements and cultural implications vary at different developmental stages, all individuals will occupy several social statuses (child, parent, old person, etc.) and will participate in different families (consanguineal or conjugal) during their lifetimes. For understanding Baegu residential behavior it is particularly important to know this, since whom a Baegu person lives with depends upon his developmental stage (constantly changing), and since composite family residence is largely based on familial relationships that obviously change with age.

The Baegu perceive life as a progression, not as a cycle. A baby is conceived (inheriting substance and soul jointly from both mother and father), progresses through life, and dies, at which time its soul joins the ancestral spirits, whose interest in the world of the living continues indefinitely.

Life, in a social sense, begins when the mother and the newborn return from their month's isolation in the birth hut in the forest. If the baby dies before this time, the mother disposes of the corpse, and the community never notes its existence. On the thirty-first night, mother and new child sleep in a temporary hut nearby but outside the hamlet and return to the community the following day. The mother gives a present of taro, fish, and a shell ornament (*galu*) to the woman who assisted her as a quasi-midwife. Some person whom the new parents wish to honor has the privilege of naming the baby. Names can be those of distinguished relatives, or references to heroic qualities they hope the child will possess or to significant events, or they can be metaphoric or even humorous. It all seems to depend on the whim of the name-giver. People also acquire other names as they grow older, a particularly perverted custom invented to confuse and embarrass social anthropologists.

At some time between this ceremonial entry into social life and the time when the child begins to show a personality (smiling, laughing, responsive to human beings) the child ceases to be a *wela aabu* (literally "sacred child") and becomes an infant (*wela tu'u*). Baegu divide infancy into stages defined by the accomplishments of the baby (smiles, sits up, crawls, etc.) and named after the characteristic behavior. Infancy ends at some vague time after the child has begun to walk. Infants are serviced whenever they cry, and they enjoy almost constant day and night physical contact. Adults and older children pass a baby around during the day so that it is held or carried most of the time, and the mother sleeps with it in her arms at night.

At some time during infancy, parents take the baby to pay a formal call on the mother's parents. There is no ceremony associated with this visit, but people say that the child's father will make sure that the gift normally given by men when they call on their affines is more elaborate than usual. This is particularly so for the first child of a marriage. Keesing (1965:233) reports that Kwaio fathers offer gifts to their wives' parents when their first children are born as a final installment of the marriage payment. In the Baegu variant of this Malaitan custom, the payment (*lului wela*) is a futurity stake paid when the wife first becomes pregnant, rather than upon delivery. Baegu say this is done because by conceiving the bride has proved her fertility. If she miscarries, or if the baby has some birth defect, the fault is not hers, but lies with the husband's ancestral spirits.

For baby boys the transition from infancy to childhood is marked by a religious ceremony called *faaramoelae*, "strengthening" or "making him strong." After the baby has begun to walk, but before he is talking, the father takes him for the first official time into the men's house (*beu*) and introduces him formally to the ancestral spirits. The father, if he knows the formulae, or a kinsman who is a priest, prays to the ancestral spirits, introduces the baby boy to them, and asks them to assist the child. The men feed the boy taro puddings and fish (the first time he will have eaten these, since they are taboo for infants and are assumed to cause a fatal illness), give him his first taste of betel quid, and show him the sacred relics of their ancestors (usually weapons or locks of hair saved for generations).

Otherwise, childhood comes on gradually for both sexes. Children slowly become more independent of parental care and assume more self-responsibilities. As they become more mobile, they join informal children's play groups and spend most of their time with other children away from immediate supervision by adults. Boys' play groups are more important, take up more of a boy's time, and last longer than the girls' groups. Girls start to carry bamboo water tubes, sticks of firewood, and parcels of garden produce almost as soon as they walk, and by the time they are adolescents they are expected to spend almost all of their time looking after younger children and working with their mothers. The Baegu girls who carried water and did housework for me while I was in the field put my own two-and-a-half-year-old daughter to work hauling water tubes with them when they went to the spring.

During childhood, children of both sexes begin accompanying their parents to gardens and markets. At first, the child simply plays, but he or she progressively comes to take more part in the actual work. As they approach adolescence, children spend relatively more time with their parent of the same sex, learning skills and behavior proper for their sex. Much of the activity in children's play groups seems random. Particularly among the small boys there is much running, scuffling, tree-climbing, swimming, and rock or spear-throwing. But there is a certain amount of playing at work. This begins with stealing food from adults' gardens, but older children (above eight years) will clear tiny plots and plant little gardens from cuttings given them by older relatives. Boys will build rickety little houses to play in, and occasionally mixed-sex play groups will "play house." Children spend a lot of time foraging for food in the bushland and streams. When a group of boys spends hours damming and diverting a stream to gather prawns and eels from the old stream bed, it is hard to say where play ends and work begins.

At some point during childhood, people say that a child can or does *saitamana,* meaning that it has acquired cultural competence, that it knows right from wrong, and that one can hold it responsible for "proper" Baegu behavior.

There are no real puberty rituals, and the transition to adolescence is a gradual one. Adolescent boys (*wane darai* or *alakwa*) are expected to work hard, but most people suppose them to be somewhat vain and

lazy. They are presumed to be self-reliant, capable of feeding themselves
(from garden-planting to dinner table) by this time. Youths will normally build themselves a separate house, usually a very neat one with
a raised floor. They say they do not like to live with their parents because older people's houses are too dirty and smoky. They spend much
of their time going to markets and traveling about to visit relatives,
frequently living for months with uncles or cousins away from their
home clearings. This is the courting period and old men grumble that
the boys "borrow" or steal their father's most prized weapons and ornaments in order to impress the girls.

At menarche, girls begin to retire to the menstrual hut (*bisi*) during
their monthly periods, but there is no particular ceremony associated
with first menstruation. Traditionally, children of both sexes wear no
clothes, but a post-menarcheal girl (*saari*) will wear a belt of red-dyed
cane (*oko obi*) as a badge of her pubescent status.

Boys and girls begin courting (*gwalulae*) during adolescence (see
Keesing 1965). Young people are supposed to refrain from sexual contact and to amuse each other with pleasant but "nice" conversation.
Their behavior ought to be polite and formal; adults think double or
triple-dating is better than single-couple liaisons, and most grown-ups
feel they should provide chaperonage. Adults state emphatically that
sexual play or petting should not, and among "decent" young people
does not, take place. Nevertheless nearly all grown-ups seem to assume
the worst and become outraged if they find a young couple together
without explicit approval. In fact, young men do try to take advantage
of the system (and the girl) whenever they can.

There is predictably a certain amount of conflict between generations
about sex. In one folk tale, a mother cursed her daughter as a result of
such a quarrel. The mother discovered the girl in conversation with a
boy near a spring and berated her for loose conduct, warning her that
she would get pregnant if she did not behave herself. The daughter,
who was of course chaste and innocent, shouted back, "You say that
because you fornicated with all the boys when you were young." And
the quarrel was on. Although parents nag their children about the
need to remain pure, old men of the grandparental generation have
no such pretensions and love to brag about the salacious adventures of
their own youth.

Although the transition from adolescence to maturity is gradual
(really established by marriage), in traditional times boys of important
families might ceremonially establish their ritual maturity. Even young
male children are permitted to eat the pork, taro, and puddings at the
sacred mortuary feasts (*maoma*), but they are not contributing participants. A young man could earn his right to contribute by planting

and growing his own sacred taro garden. He supposedly did not bathe, cut his hair, or talk during the growing period. When the crop was ready, it was dedicated to the ancestral spirits (*akalo*), and the boy's father gave a feast in his honor.

Although girls remain at home until marriage, the British Empire and Commonwealth have added a new stage to the male life cycle. Over 95 percent of all adult males have spent at least a year as wage laborers on coconut plantations on Guadalcanal, in the Russell Islands, or in the New Georgia group. They do this not to obtain the bride-price, since this must be paid in traditional shell money, but to accumulate a cash reserve for tobacco or kerosene and to pay the District Council's head tax.

Nowadays, marriage itself is the entrée to full adult status, validated by the birth of the first child. In approved marriages, the young couple initially resides in the boy's family's clearing. The bride will sleep in a family dwelling house (*luma*) belonging to her new husband's father and mother or to his brother and sister-in-law. In unapproved marriages, the couple will most likely take refuge in a hamlet belonging to one of the boy's maternal kinsmen. In either case, the groom sleeps in the local men's house (*beu*). The bride is expected to obey and to work for her husband's older relatives, and many women complain that they are unduly exploited during this period of service. After a few months (this usually coincides approximately with the bride's first pregnancy), the young husband builds a new dwelling house (*luma*) that will belong exclusively to his wife and himself. This may be in the same clearing, or the boy may start a new clearing elsewhere, or (in a few cases where political ambitions are involved or where the boy's parents disapprove of the bride) the couple may return to live with the girl's family. Usually after the girl moves to her new house, and definitely after she bears her first child, her affines excuse her from service and leave her to her own work.

Since Baegu society does perpetuate itself, it is obvious that most people do marry and procreate. But despite the pressures toward marriage and the puritanical attitudes toward sex outside marriage, there are significant numbers of spinsters and bachelors, many of whom will never marry. Table 14 illustrates the marital status of the Baegu population.

Social maturity really comes with the birth of one's first child, both for men and for women. People are frequently amused at young fathers who begin to put on airs about this time, self-consciously carrying more elegant betel-chewing apparatus and adopting the mannerisms of the important men.

Fosterage is fairly common and occurs in at least three ways. Because the population is somewhat inbred, and because kinship ties are widely ramified, orphans are more or less automatically taken in by relatives who "need" or can adequately care for children of a particular age and sex. If a man is childless, one of his patrilateral kinsmen who has several offspring gives away one of his own to be raised by the childless couple. Finally, people try to establish semipermanent alliances with important men by placing one of their children in that man's home. The foster child (*wela sarea* or *wela saungia*) has a more prosperous life, the parents are allied with power, and the Big Man has another "servant" for labor and military purposes.

Marriage is relatively stable. Among some 1,360 people involving nearly 300 marriages I knew of only three divorces, although there was one other old couple who, while not divorced, no longer bothered to live together. Two of the divorces were due to adultery; in one the husband was lusting after younger women, and in the other the wife had an illegitimate child while the husband was away working on a European plantation. In the third, the husband ended the marriage and forfeited the bride-price because he thought his wife was dirty, lazy, and stupid. (She was.) At the time I was there, all divorcees had remarried.

Either husband or wife, as an injured party, can take the initiative in divorce; women by simply returning to their parents' hamlet, and men by ordering the offending wife to leave. Usually the kindred of a guilty husband forfeit their bride-price, and the kindred of a guilty wife must repay it. If one or more children have been born and the wife is the guilty one, only part of the bride-price may actually be refunded. Theoretically, the husband owns the children no matter whose the guilt, but when he has been flagrantly misbehaving and if his kindred are embarrassed about it, the children may stay with their mother. The ultimate and most irrevocable act of divorce is for the wife to take off her pubic apron (*lafua masa*), but I have not known this to occur in real life.

When death takes one of a married couple, the ideology of agnatic descent asserts itself most strongly. When a woman dies, her husband raises their children himself. For a nursing infant he must find a female kinsman or wife of a kinsman to feed the baby, but the baby is supposed to return to the father once it is weaned. If a woman dies before producing children, most of the bride-price should be refunded. If she has had one child, only a token refund is paid; after bearing two or more offspring, no refund need be made. If a man dies, and if children are involved, his widow is expected to remain with her husband's kin. Baegu norms state that leviratic marriage is "good" for widows, but

I noted only two instances of this. If a widow wishes to return to her own kinsmen, people expect her to leave her children with her husband's relatives; this does happen. Exceptions to this practice occur if the widow's family is significantly more important and more powerful than the dead husband's. Both widows and widowers can and do re-

Plate 17. Koloedia holding her daughter, Rosa, while she smokes her pipe.

marry after the mourning period, but they are expected to marry others who have also been widowed. The bride-price for widows is usually 20-50 percent of the original bride-price paid for the woman at her first marriage and is divided between the girl's own kindred and her dead husband's.

The transition to old age is indistinct. Status and prestige increase with age and, as long as old people remain alert and competent, others choose to ignore their increasing infirmity and really do seem to like them. Even octogenarians continue to plant small gardens and spend an hour or so almost every day puttering in them. Old people are served first at meals, they get the best positions at songs and dances, and people nearly always defer to their wishes. Because of their great age and experience, old men are extremely important as expert witnesses in land litigation and seniority disputes. When failing strength, vision, and mental faculties finally reach senility, old people simply sit around the hamlet and wait for death. Younger relatives feed and still profess to respect these senile old people (*wane waaro*), but they no longer really listen to them or make any serious efforts to treat their illnesses. Some old men, preferring to avoid such an ignoble end, will declare themselves sacred; they go to live by themselves in the sacred grove (*beu aabu*) or, as they say, to live among the ghosts of their ancestors. There they are fed by their kinsmen, who bring them puddings and soups. One old man in Masu district has been awaiting death in this way for several years.

At death, kinsmen bury the corpse in a sacred grove within a few hours. Mourning customs are more stringently observed and last longer if the deceased was an important male still vigorous at the time of death. Major feasts and redistribution of wealth follow the death of important men; after the death of a priest, his successor begins the lengthy cycle of rituals in his honor. Thus his soul joins the ancestors but retains his ties with those kinsmen still living. As a spirit he is more powerful, for good or evil, than he was in life.

HAMLETS WITH AFFILIATES

Hamlets where more than one nuclear family live result from decisions based on kinship ideology and from unique events in various life stages. Hamlets grow more complex (than a single nuclear family) in several ways. While it is important to remember that the nuclear family is not of fundamental ("emic") importance to the Baegu, it remains nevertheless a useful analytic concept and a more than convenient starting place for descriptions. This is so because for the Baegu a satisfactory adjustment to life requires that each settlement or hamlet have an adult male and an adult female: the man for leadership, sacred responsibilities, and house-building; the woman for child care, ritually or physically unclean tasks, tedious (yet necessary) drudgery, and routine chores such as the hauling of water and firewood. An intact nuclear family almost by definition automatically fills these roles. Individuals or households that are not intact nuclear families must neglect one of them, force its members into cross-sex role-playing, or affiliate with and rely upon a nuclear family that is intact. Thus, while it is structurally negligible, the nuclear family is functionally valuable. Empirically only one Baegu hamlet lacks an intact nuclear family, maintaining functional integrity by means of cooperation between a widowed brother (with his children) and his widowed sister (with her children). In some ways, then, the classification of hamlets according to number of nuclear families within them (as in Tables 20 and 21) is not completely arbitrary. Nuclear-family households can stand alone; households of less than one nuclear family cannot.

The simplest of the more complex forms of hamlet organization is a single intact nuclear family with one or more outsiders adhering to it. These *affiliated individuals* stand more or less in a client status vis-à-vis the senior male (father) and can be adopted or foster children, bachelors, spinsters, or very old dependent (supposedly honored) parents. Alternatively, several persons in one of these classes can join to form a *partial household* that is not an intact nuclear family, but that for functional reasons will affiliate with one as part of a more complex hamlet. These partial households can be widowed persons (male or female) with their children, in effect a nuclear family minus one parent and thus lacking one sex role. In other cases orphaned but semi-mature sibling groups, childless old people or older folk whose children have grown and left, or two or more bachelors (or spinsters) can form a household. But these households are still partial, since they affiliate with intact nuclear families (or occasionally with other partials) to secure the functional services of a married, still vigorous adult of each sex. One should note in passing that outside individuals may affiliate with partial as well as with intact nuclear-family households. Table 22 identifies the kinds and indicates their relative frequency of occurrence for the Baegu population (sample area).

Affiliation of individuals with nuclear families not their own may happen in several ways, but nearly all result from particular events in the normally orderly development of a human life. Foster children are usually treated like one's own children, and so it may be more accurate to consider them as members of the family rather than as clients. How-

TABLE 22. PARTIAL HOUSEHOLDS AND AFFILIATED INDIVIDUALS

	Households composed of widowed persons with children		Not parent-child family households				
	Widow-ers	Widows	Bach-elors (2 or more)	Spin-sters (2 or more)	Sibling groups	Depen-dent old people	Foster children
Partial family house-holds..............	21	11	6	4	2	3	..
Affiliated persons (living with other households)	..	..	3	2	..	3	8
Solitary persons (living in a hamlet but not a household).........	..	..	1	..	..	1	..

The table is designed to show Baegu alternatives to life in an intact nuclear family household, with both parents still alive. Data come from the sample population area. Affiliated individuals eat and sleep with a household other than their own nuclear family. Partial households behave economically like nuclear families, but they lack one or both "parents." They affiliate with intact nuclear families, with the exception of Rue, where three partial households compose the entire hamlet.

ever, the Cinderella concept does exist, so the status of foster children seems somewhat ambiguous. Fosterage as noted above results from more than one cause: adoption of orphans, loaning of children to barren relatives, or placing of one's own child as protegé in the household of an important man. During adolescence and courtship, adolescent boys may become more or less permanent residents in the hamlet of an uncle or older cousin. There they act as clients of the senior male and serve to amplify his economic and military power. Such bachelors, if they do not marry, may continue in this leader-follower relationship well into adulthood. Perpetual spinsters also affiliate with a household. Widows with or without their children also join (or remain affiliated with) another nuclear family, for it is inconceivable to the Baegu that a woman could live without male supervision. Statistically, most widows with immature children live with their dead husband's father or brother; only about 25 percent return to their own parents' hamlet. If they did so, public opinion (or at least a good part of it) would try to influence them to leave their children with the dead husband's kinsmen. Young widows with no children usually return to their parents or to a brother and eventually remarry, while old women with grown children live with a son or daughter. Thus a widow and her children will always be a subunit dependent upon and subordinate to a male, and they will live in his hamlet. Senile old people will be largely if not totally dependent upon the household of a child, grandchild, or nephew (niece) and will of course live with them. Such an old man will sleep in the men's house (*beu*) that is said to be "his" whether or not he actually built it. Old women may or may not have dwelling houses (*luma*) of their own. If a senile woman's (*keni waaro*) house

TABLE 23. RESIDENTIAL BEHAVIOR OF WIDOWS

	Stay with dead husband's hamlet	Go home to own consanguineal kinsmen's hamlet	
		Give up children	Take children with her
Widows with children....................	9	2	1
Old widows (no dependent children)........	9	..	..
Totals............................	18	2	1

Numbers refer only to current widows living in the sample population area who have not remarried. Note the marked tendency for the father's group to retain custody of children, thereby maintaining the integrity of the patrilineage and assuring that most children grow up with an agnatic kin group.

deteriorates, her kinsmen will not build her a new one, but expect her to move in with one of the younger women.

MULTI-FAMILY HAMLETS

Besides these single-nuclear-family-plus-affiliate hamlets, there are multi-family hamlets composed of more than one nuclear-family house-hold. Table 21 in fact shows a striking mode (50 percent) at the two-nuclear-family level, tending to indicate that in some respects the two-nuclear-family settlement may be the ideal or the most "natural" way for the Baegu hill people to live. According to those figures, 55.4 percent of the population live in a small hamlet based upon coresidence by two nuclear families, making this the most typical form of Baegu residence.

Such two-nuclear-family residential systems (or patterns approaching the same structure) can come about variously. While polygyny is permitted by Baegu marital norms, it is statistically rare and is considered a foolish thing for a man to do. They say that a man may marry two wives, not that he ought to do so. I knew personally only two living men with plural wives, and one old man who had had two wives but the first of whom was now dead. Occurrence of polygyny in genealogies covering the last five generations was only slightly more common. In the murky past ancestral figures are supposed to have had eight or ten wives apiece, but this is part of their heroic stature. Indeed, co-wives are assumed to be harridans and bitter enemies, and it is a measure of a man's leadership ability that he can keep the peace in a polygynous household. One of my aged informants liked to boast that his household was so well-controlled that he could even sleep with both wives in the same bed. But most men would not dream of doing such a thing, so each wife of a polygynous marriage nearly always has her own dwelling house (*luma*) for herself and her children. The husband, if he has good sense, tries to divide his time about equally between the two dwelling houses (*luma*); or better still, he spends most of his time in his men's house (*beu*).

Because of the normative pattern of virilocal (followed by neolocal) residence for newly married couples, nearly all Baegu spend at least a short time living in a patrilineal extended family residential unit. Many such father-son axis settlements divide after a couple of years, with the young couple moving off into the bush, cutting a clearing, and building their own dwelling house. Depending on the personalities involved, this trial period (when a new bride works for the groom's parents) does seem to create friction, and the Baegu explicitly say that the young couple moves so that the husband's family will leave the bride alone and let her do her own work. It seems reasonable that the shift to neolocal residence (either in a totally separate hamlet, a separate but related clearing nearby, or at least in a separate dwelling house within the extended family clearing) does serve to maintain family (lineage) solidarity by reducing the chances for squabbling started by affines, in this case the bride and the man's kinsmen. The concept of a stem family (with at least one son remaining with the parents and inheriting their property) does not apply to Baegu society, since settlements are abandoned every few years, land is owned jointly by all members of a patrilineage, and land-use rights are cognatically defined and essentially free.

Most hamlets containing more than one nuclear family are organized about an agnatic axis. Patrilineal extended families with sons continuing to live in or adjacent to their father's clearing result from two situations. First, because of the virilocal initial residence norm, young men may continue to live in or adjacent to their father's clearing after marriage and share his men's house (*beu*). They do not always move to a new site later. Second, feeble old people usually live with their children, since they cannot adequately care for themselves. Other multi-family hamlets are fraternal joint families with two or more brothers sharing the site. Whether this fraternal joint family is structurally different from a patrilineal extended family or merely is the latter with the father dead or otherwise absent is a moot point.

Multi-family hamlets organized around other than agnatic axes are not that common. Nativistic cult (Neo-Marching Rule) villages and Christian mission villages do contain aggregations of agnatic, cognatic,

TABLE 24. FAMILIAL LINKAGES IN MULTI-NUCLEAR FAMILY HAMLETS

Father-son	Siblings	Uterine kinsmen
4	3	3
Agnatic uncle-nephew	Agnastic cousins	Affines
1	5	4

Data are from so-called natural hamlets in the sample population area, excluding Christian villages with churches and Neo-Marching Rule pagan settlements. Familial linkage refers to the relationship of male heads of nuclear family households to one another. Categories are arranged in columns that connote structural similarity.

TABLE 25. FAMILIAL LINKAGES OF AFFILIATED PARTIAL OR NON-NUCLEAR FAMILY HOUSEHOLDS

Father-son	Siblings	Uterine kinsmen
5	3	4
Agnatic uncle-nephew	Agnatic cousins	Affines
2	9	1
		Non-Kin
		1

In most cases linkage is simply the genealogical relationship of the head of household with the acknowledged head of the hamlet. For partial households headed by widows who have remained with their dead husband's people, it refers to the relationship between dead husband and the hamlet head. The "siblings" category includes one brother-sister link (others are brother-brother) where a widow has returned to live with her brother.

near, distant and non-kin, but these result from nontraditional forces and ideologies. Even in traditional settings, men do occasionally elect to reside with their maternal kin, thereby creating a multi-family hamlet based on a cognatic kin axis. This occurs as a result of an unapproved marriage where the eloping couple take refuge with the boy's mother's kinsmen, usually the mother's brother (*kokoo*), to avoid the anger of both families. Second, ambitious but poor young men may choose to attach themselves to a maternal kinsman who is an extremely important man (*wane baita*), for obvious political reasons. Occasionally a young man will disregard the viri-neolocal residence norms altogether and simply move in with his wife's family. But this is not common, and the Baegu themselves consider it somewhat eccentric. A young couple might, however, live uxorilocally if the girl's family's status is markedly higher than the boy's, or if the boy's parents are particularly unhappy about the match. For example, Gere, an orphan, lives with his wife in her father Lediomea's clearing. Lediomea is an influential cargo cult leader among the Agia people. All along the coastal region, Baegu are to some extent "acculturating" to the Lau Lagoon people, who are rich and powerful compared to the bush populations, and there is a whole series of villages along the beach that are neither truly saltwater nor bush. They see themselves as Lau, but they are not always accepted by the lagoon folk as such. When Baegu men marry one of these girls, the girl often refuses to move up into the bush with what she perceives as a ragged mob of hillbillies, so the groom settles on the beach with his in-laws. In the hills proper parental acceptance also matters. Robo brought his new wife home to his parents, and about four months after the marriage she gave birth to a baby boy. This is not unusual, but for some reason Robo's parents refused to ignore the situation and gossiped incessantly about "the whore our son married." The girl finally refused to take any more of this, and the couple now lives with her parents in another district.

ROLES IN MULTI-FAMILY HAMLETS

Naturally, the intrafamily roles of husband-father, wife-mother, child, younger and older siblings are found here just as they are in single-nuclear-family hamlets; but in addition there are certain distinctive new roles. The senior male is the man who "owns" the hamlet and is its acknowledged head. He is usually the father in patrilineally extended families, the elder brother in fraternal joint families (or elder cousin if they are not biologically brothers), the mother's brother in cognatic groups, or the wife's father. Even feeble old men are still said to own the hamlet, but their physical condition may prevent them from effec-

TABLE 26. GENEALOGICAL POSITIONS OF ACKNOWLEDGED HEADS OF HAMLETS

Father	Elder brother	Uterine kinsman	Cargo cult leader
6	2	3	2

Agnatic uncle	Agnatic cousin	Affine	Church elder
1	5	1	6

Baegu people tend to explain a focal male's position in terms of his genealogical position. Unfortunately this can be ambiguous, because it is oversimplified. It considers only his relationship to his more important coresidents, and it neglects the fact that in a tiny, relatively inbred society most people can actually establish more than one genealogical link between themselves. Nevertheless, "reasons" for leadership are as explained by other residents and presumably as seen by them.

tively exercising authority. The senior male literally owns the men's house and cares for the weapons and sacred relics (if any) in it. Most individuals garden or go to the market whenever they wish, and the senior male's only command authority seems to be where decisions to repair, rebuild, or move the hamlet are concerned. He also divides the food for communal (ritual) meals among the members of the hamlet. In pre-British days he probably had some power regarding defense of the hamlet during wartime. In return, the women or the younger men do his cooking. And all residents theoretically (and usually in fact do) defer to his wishes.

Lesser adult males who are also married share the men's house with him. Of course, they have their own husband-father roles in their own families of procreation. As far as the whole hamlet is concerned, they assist the senior male in construction or repair projects, and they have the privilege of joining with him in important tasks such as discussing genealogies or carrying out ritual activities (singing, magic, cooking festival meals, etc.). Each married woman has her own dwelling house (*luma*), where she cares for her children and husband. On the whole women, children, and unmarried males are to an extent nonpersons. They are in a patron-client relationship with the senior male, helping and deferring to him in secular matters, and having only a marginal role if any in sacred affairs.

NEIGHBORHOOD COMMUNITIES

Although they do not have a word for them, the Baegu tend to cluster in "neighborhoods" or areas where the residents interact more frequently with each other than they do with outsiders. In a sense neighborhoods are a relative concept, since their social reality lies in a sociometric definition, and since they are socially important only in that they are focused about a Big Man's (*wane baita*) hamlet. These neighborhoods usually consist of geographically contiguous hamlets. This is not literally true, of course, since considerable tracts of garden land and secondary bush forests usually separate hamlets, but the Baegu perceive them as adjacent.

In a way the neighborhood community, as an actual residential group, is a basic unit of social relations. These are the people who grew up together; who play, gossip, and work together; and who have common interests in use of the land and in the ancestral spirits associated with the land. However, it must be stressed that the Baegu themselves speak of, and hence presumably think of, such neighborhood communities as if they were kinship or descent groups. Although neighborhoods may be important at a practical, day-to-day social level, they have little theological, metaphysical, or ideological importance. Since the Baegu have no word for the category, identification of neighborhoods is a subjective act.

It is not easy to tell precisely, but it appears that the neighborhood may well be the most relevant exogamic category. According to older informants (supported by traditional genealogical material), the patrilineal clans (*'ae bara*) were formerly exogamous. For the last two or three generations they have not been so, but it is my impression that when men do marry women from the same *'ae bara,* they usually come from different neighborhoods. This is not true for Christian villages that are larger, that frequently contain members of several lineages, and that are urged by mission officials to practice cult endogamy. Finally, incest prohibitions apply both to genealogically closely related consanguineal kin and to coresidents. Courtship and marriage are more apt to be approved if the prospective partners are members of different lineages or residents of different neighborhoods. Stated crudely, the probability of copulation is directly proportional to the distance apart — which is anthropologically proper, even if anatomically inconvenient.

THE AGNATIC CORE

In keeping with anthropology's traditional patrilateral bias, social analysis of neighborhoods means studying the men who live there, not the women. This is not so arbitrary as it may at first seem, because for the Baegu (as for many Melanesian peoples) women are irrelevant, at least as far as descent ideology is concerned.

In every neighborhood community the most important people are a group of agnatically or patrilaterally related males. Agnatic ideology is dominant; indeed, operation of residential norms (wherein most men bring their wives to live with or near the husband's father or brother) does create local communities of men who are patrilaterally related to one another. Sons remain with their fathers, brothers remain together, and children grow up among patrilateral uncles and parallel cousins. Even fosterage tends to support the integrity of these agnatic core groups. Widows are expected to continue to live among their dead husband's kin, or to leave their children there if they do not. Paternal grandparents or paternal uncles always have first claim on orphans; in some cases where the parents are thought to be irresponsible, the paternal grandparents' claim may take precedence over the biological parents. Most cases of voluntary adoption (on both sides) involve the giving of a child to a childless brother or patrilateral parallel cousin.

"OUTSIDERS" IN THE NEIGHBORHOOD

The percentage of agnatically related males in the community is nearly always large enough to approximate the ideal patrilaterally related group that people believe it to be. Nevertheless, some "outsiders" are almost always present. These situations result from application of residence rules, or more precisely from exceptions to them, and from acts of claiming land ownership or usage rights. Normally a boy grows up in his father's household, with his agnatic relatives living nearby, on land owned by his patrilineage. He himself makes his garden there and, when the time comes, establishes his own new conjugal family there. However, not all follow this ideal pattern; some men do not live with agnatic relatives when they marry, and some widows do not continue to live with their dead husband's kin.

When a man for personal, social status, or political reasons lives uxorilocally with his wife's relatives, his children grow up among their uterine or maternal kinsmen. The man himself is permitted to make his garden there, but it is a case of sufferance and not of right. His children do have a right to use the land, since the Baegu explicitly recognize claims based on cognatic relationship to the ancestral spirits associated with the land. That is, anyone who has a remembered ancestor, either patrilateral or matrilateral, buried there has a right to use the land.

If a man elopes in a disapproved marriage, he usually seeks refuge with his mother's brother or some other maternal kinsman. In this case he himself has a right to use the land on the basis of a relationship with the local ancestral spirits through his mother. If he and they continue to live there, his children will be able to use the land because it is their father's mother's.

A widow, like a wife, as long as she continues to live with her husband's kinsmen will be permitted (if she wishes) to make her garden on their land — although a woman can garden on her father's or brother's group's land, if it is within reasonable distance. If she returns to her own family, she makes her garden on their land. When they mature, her children may cultivate this land. They have a right to do so, because through their mother they are related to the proper ancestral spirits; alternatively, they may claim the right to use their father's group's land.

Because they recognize and accept bilineal descent where land-usage rights are concerned, men may claim these rights wherever any remembered ancestor is buried. Since the range of Baegu society is so small, and since in pre-European times patrilineages tended to be exogamous, this means that most men could (if they wished) exercise any one of a number of possible claims. Hence there is no pressing jural reason for a man to live in one district or neighborhood rather than another. Even though men grow up in neighborhoods where they are not members of the agnatic core, they still have some right in nearly every case to use the land there. Inevitably, as a result of the human developmental process, principles of land ownership and usage rights, and residence rules plus permissible exceptions, communities develop that include both an agnatic core and affiliated nonagnatic relatives.

FUNCTIONAL SUMMARY OF NEIGHBORHOOD COMMUNITIES

The agnatic core is both numerically and ideologically the most important portion of the community. Since agnatic kinship and virilocal initial residence are statistical as well as jural norms, most neighborhood residents are agnatically related; but there are always nonagnates affiliated with the core group. Naturally, given the incest prohibition, wives will tend not to be members of this core. The group's own daughters and sisters are usually proscribed for genealogical or residential (or both) reasons.

Of the affiliated male residents, most are cognatically related to the core group, either as refugees or because they grew up in an abnormal situation. But regardless of how coresidence came about, they do have the right to use the land, and they are fully participating members of the community.

Theoretically, men living uxorilocally or as refugees may be related only affinally with the agnatic core. In such a case, they might be permitted to use local land, since they are permitted after all to live there, but they could not claim the right to do so. But in actuality Baegu society is so small, and they are all so genealogically aware, that these "outsiders" seem always able to invoke some sort of genealogical claim (in fact usually several), so that an individual usually has the option of choosing the relationship he wishes to recognize.

Within these neighborhood communities the most important role is that of focal male, who directs communal activities. If a neighborhood is coterminous with the district belonging to the descent group, or if a plot of land has been given to someone there, there will be a hereditary landowner (*wane initoo*). Since neighborhoods sometimes focus about a shrine or sacred grove (*beu aabu*), there may be a priest (*fata aabu*) to officiate at ceremonies there. But there is always at least one Big Man (*wane baita*) who is the focal male, and who because of his genealogical position or achieved wealth and demonstrable leadership ability will be the community leader. Other specialists having varying degrees of prestige and esteem — war leaders, builders, genealogists, musicians, dancers, magicians, oracles, or healers — may or may not be present. "Specialist," by the way, is a relative concept, since all men are basically subsistence farmers.

It is very difficult if not impossible to define the statuses of agnatic core member and affiliated coresident. This is partly because of simultaneous acceptance of principles of patrilineal descent and cognatic land use rights, and partly because like all human conditions Baegu practice is not precisely congruent with Baegu theory. Agnates are expected to cooperate with and help one another, but so are coresidents. Relatives of senior generations have prestige and deserve respect, but so does any elder, kinsman or not. For the most part, rights and obligations of agnatic core members and nonagnates are essentially the same.

Most of the important men of a neighborhood will be of the agnatic core, but then most of the men in general are. Legally, hereditary landowners (*wane initoo*) must be, because land ownership is inherited patrilineally; and priests should be, since they ought to be members of the same lineage as the ancestral spirits. Most (but by no means all) of the other focal males and initiators of action are agnatic core members, too. The hamlet Ngalikwao consists of two brothers, Kafa and Laugwaro, and their sister Olina. Olina's husband, Osikona, lives with them, is the most dynamic of the group, and is the informal but accepted leader. Osikona's maternal grandmother was the sister of Kafa and Laugwaro's paternal grandfather, and the two lines merge at the fifth ascending generation; but as far as the Ngalikwao residential group and minimal lineage segment are concerned, Osikona is not of the agnatic core (Figure 26).

Keesing (1965:137) attributes to Raulet the suggestion that bilateral kinship groupings in Melanesia may be an adaptation insuring a communal labor supply for taro gardening. On the other hand, Hogbin has described the Toabaita (northern Malaita) love of privacy and their use of gardening as an excuse for getting it. The Baegu, too, connect gardens with privacy. Men may seek help for three or four days for the heavy work of clearing a new garden. After that, they choose to work alone. Most Baegu like solitude, and most activities (except for markets, religious festivals, and gathering to stare at an ethnographer) involve very small groups. Unlike the coastal or saltwater people nearby, they dislike crowds and tend to respect each other's desire for privacy. A man's garden is his personal place, and he goes there when he wants to be alone. Most Baegu understand and would not dream of intruding. Where communal labor does occur, it is usually justified in terms of obligations between agnatic kinsmen. Since an agnatic core is the majority in most neighborhoods, this is usually literally correct. But joint projects usually end up involving all coresident males, agnates or not, since few men care to get a reputation for laziness by sitting idly while everyone else works.

DISTRICTS

Baegu territory is divided into districts (*lolofaa*) that "belong" to one patrilineal clan (*'ae bara*). The first ancestors settled on the land, and genealogies connect these epic figures with living descendants still associated with the same land. In small lineages, everyone can prove his membership in this way, but in the large clans many unimportant or socially peripheral families do not know their own genealogies beyond four or five ascending generations. People accept them as relatives and assume their descent from the apical founding ancestor, but they cannot prove any specific path of descent that relates them to the more central families of the clan.

Each recognized district will have one or more neighborhood communities. Over half of the districts have only one neighborhood: that is, the district and neighborhood are congruent. Where there are several neighborhoods, the district does not act as a unit in a social sense. Folk tales, older informants, and Russell (1950:8-10) writing of the Fataleka do say that "once upon a time" there were men so powerful and so talented that whole districts would obey them. Such men were in Fataleka called *wane taniota,* and the Baegu have a tradition of

Figure 26. Genealogy of Ngalikwao Hamlet Residents

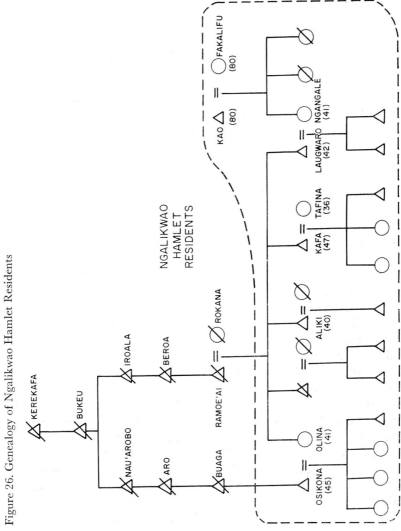

wane saungia, who could organize feasts on a district-wide basis. The chief priests (*gwau ni foa*) no longer exist, but since they were descended from the apical ancestor, since they were related to ancestors at each major shrine (*beu aabu*), and since they knew all the proper genealogies and prayers, they could sacrifice and conduct ceremonies at any neighborhood sacred grove within their district. That is, they could theoretically serve as ritual leader for the entire district, acting for that context as a single, superordinate ritual community. Influential Big Men (*wane baita*) could also conceivably become so powerful that by manipulating personal influence, economic leverage, and kinship connections they could extend their power beyond their own neighborhood to nearby ones. Theoretically it should be easier to extend one's influence into other neighborhoods within the same district, working within the agnatic kinship network, rather than working across it into other districts. Unfortunately, no data are available to test this hypothesis.

As things are today, districts are more conceptual than social. Residents of different neighborhoods may participate in ceremonies at each other's sacred groves, but so do kinsmen from other districts. However, in at least one context neighborhoods within the same district do share negative attributes distinguishing them from those in other districts. If a man quarrels seriously with his agnatic kinsmen, he will choose to live not just in another neighborhood, but in a neighborhood in another district.

District identity is mental and theological, not social, and thus tends to be relatively stable and little affected by shifts of personnel. This ideology marries the people to the land. To members of the lineage, the land of the district is "our" land and they are emotionally dedicated to it. The ancestors first claimed the land, and lineage members are responsible for maintaining the shrines and remembering the ancestors buried there — always remembering that any descendant of those ancestors can use the land if he sacrifices to them. In a very real way, the ancestral spirits and their living descendants are united in a partnership to maintain the fertility of the land. Since men are associated with districts of land via descent ideology, and since land-usage rights depend upon religious participation and obligations, it is sensible to look at the relationship between men and the land they use for residence and gardening, between clans and districts, in terms of religious behavior and ritual communities.

Patrilineages (*'ae bara*) are responsible for conducting the great mortuary festivals (*maoma*) to please their ancestral spirits. These are organized by a priest in the name of his patrilineage and are dedicated to the lineage ancestors. But it is through sacrificing to an ancestor and participating in these ceremonies that men establish their claims to rights to use the land. Thus all coresidents, and by implication all people who dwell upon or garden in the land associated with a sacred grove (*beu aabu*) where the ancestors are buried and where their spirits (*akalo*) live, participate in the same ceremonies. In this way both the agnatic core and affiliated non-agnates (who in a small society are usually cognatic relatives) prove their right to use the land and establish themselves as a community vis-à-vis the ancestral spirits. It is this ritual community that does the work for a *maoma*. Under the direction of a priest (*fata aabu*) belonging to the agnatic core and led by their Big Men, they plant the sacred taro garden, build the sacred structure at the sacred grove, and contribute pigs, taro, and puddings for the feast. And it is in the distribution of pork and puddings at the communal meal that the most explicit recognition of the neighborhood as a corporate group occurs. The priest and his helpers divide the food into portions that are allotted to focal males, and these focal males in turn divide the portions among all their coresident males. The *maoma* therefore is common to a variety of ideologies. Agnatic members of patrilineal descent groups satisfy their obligations to the familial ancestral spirits by participating; non-agnatic kinsmen and coresidents claim and validate their rights to use the land by contributing to the sacrifices; and neighborhood groups living around the shrines join the festivities as discrete units.

It remains to see how closely descent and residential groups coincide at the district level by comparing residential groups (users) with ideal descent groups (titular owners) as in Table 27. Theoretically, districts (*lolofaa*) are owned by patrilineal clans (*'ae bara*), the two homologous categories having the same name. Ideally, the male members of an *'ae bara* plus their wives (including widows), dependent children, and spinster daughters should be the ones using the district land for residence sites and garden land. But in fact not all people who are living and gardening on a particular parcel of land have an agnatically valid right to be there and to be using that land. Their claims depend upon recognition of cognatically determined rights in order to be valid. As a result, the descent-defined owning community and the empirically noted using community of coresidents may not be precisely the same. Table 27 indicates at least tentatively how closely practice conforms to ideology by presenting the proportions of agnatic claimants against cognatic claimants and other "outsiders" using the land belonging to a given *'ae bara*. One should not forget that these "outsiders" may well be there by right, not by sufferance, and are therefore (by the ideology of cognatic relationships) certainly not merely pretenders to community membership.

TABLE 27. DESCENT IDEOLOGY AND RESIDENCE AT THE DISTRICT LEVEL

Districts	Agnatic claimants	Non-agnatic users	Total residents	% of agnates
Agia	392	69	461	85.0
Asai	35	6	41	85.4
Au'angisia	13	0	13	100.0
Gwaikafo	29	10	39	74.4
Kafokuru	22	0	22	100.0
Langane	34	5	39	87.2
Masu	55	9	64	85.9
Oisamaku	28	0	28	100.0
Uradaue	47	15	62	75.8
Uuo	254	42	296	85.8
Walelangi	265	30	295	89.8
Totals	1,174	186	1,360	86.3

District residents are classified according to the basis of their claims to rights to use the land for residence and gardening. "Agnatic claims" are exercised by male members of the clan titularly "owning" the district, their wives (including widows), and their children. "Non-agnatic use" of the land is made by uterine kinsmen, affines, and non-kin of clan members living and gardening in the district.

11. A Structural Interpretation of Inconsistencies in Baegu Ideology and Practice

One of the most puzzling features of Baegu ethnography (and one I have never really resolved to my own satisfaction) is why my Baegu informants would invariably insist that they were behaving in accordance with agnatic or patrilineal norms when quite obviously they were in fact acting on the basis of cognatic or bilateral ones. Marriages are rather straightforward exchanges between two bilateral kindreds: bilateral relatives of the groom assemble a proper bride-price and give it to the bride's father for distribution among the bride's kindred. Yet without exception informants describe this process as a transaction between two patrilineages (*'ae bara*). Since the Baegu are (as we presume ourselves to be) essentially rational people, I ultimately deduced that there must be some compelling reason why they must see things in this way: that agnatic ideology must in some very basic way "override" other ideologies. As I see it now, the fundamental structure of Baegu cosmology (their world-view at a cognitive level) demands that agnatic ideology be emphasized, for it is part of a pattern common to several fields. Putting this into currently popular anthropological jargon, a single basic mental pattern may be expressed in several substantively different taxonomic or classificatory schemes (Figure 27). To develop this concept, one must consider how agnatic ideology is wedded with and expressed through religious belief and practice, particularly through the great integrative mortuary ceremonies, the *maoma*.

KINSHIP AND THE SUPERNATURAL

Religious beliefs *are* a part of kinship ideology, and vice versa. The essence of Baegu religion is the postulated continuity of relationship

Figure 27. A Basic Mental Pattern Reflected in Several Classificatory Schemes

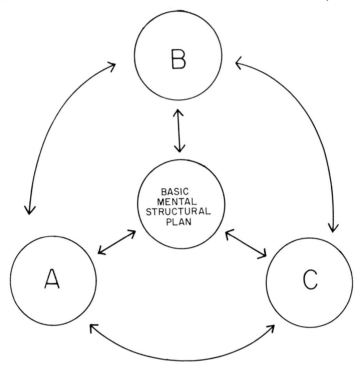

between the spirits of the ancestors and their living descendants. The role of the ancestral spirits is to provide their "children" with power, luck, health, and material well-being; religious practice is intended to insure that they do so.

As noted previously, a man has several souls: the *mango*, a vital spirit exemplified by the breath that simply ceases or disappears at death; the *ano*, a shade or spiritual personality that leaves the body during dreams and that eventually goes to a Hades called Ano Gwou or Ramos Island after death (there may be more than one *ano*); and finally the *akalo*, a disembodied but powerful vital personality or spirit of a great man that remains in the area after death and continues to be active in human affairs. The last-named can be either a good or an evil force. It might be more accurate to say that the *akalo* are a good force mainly in a negative way; they usually send good fortune by *not* causing misfortunes.

Success, riches, and good health depend on a supernatural concept called *mamanaa*. Although men do not have access to this directly, the *akalo* do and, if they choose to do so, can provide its blessings for their descendants. Religious practices are designed to induce the ancestral spirits (*akalo*) to grant this *mamanaa* to their living kinsmen. *Mamanaa* is fairly obviously a form of the common Oceanic concept of *mana*. This has been widely rendered as "supernatural power" and has been the source of much speculation about the origin of religion. But as Firth (1940:505-8) discovered in Tikopia, that translation is an over-simplification of a complex idea. As the Baegu use the word, it can refer to an innate property of holy things, to the blessings (luck or good fortune) granted by the gods, or to truth either as an abstract quality or in adjectival form. Confusion results because *mamanaa* is used grammatically as a noun, adjective, or adverb; structurally it has both subjective and objective word-class qualities. In the sense that spells and actions that lead to good fortune work and are thus true, *mamanaa* might also be translated as efficacy or power. There is no single good or correct translation. According to context, *mamanaa* refers to some aspect of the (to us) unusual constellation of meanings "holy, blessing, good fortune, true, effective, power."

Ancestors are buried in sacred groves on the land they occupied and farmed while living. Their spirits remain with the groves as *akalo,* and they are assumed to have a continuing interest in the affairs of their descendants and the use of the land. The sacred groves become shrines (*beu aabu*) where the living come to worship the ancestral spirits. Men are therefore greatly constrained in their choice of sites for shrines. A priest or group of men cannot arbitrarily create a shrine. Men can erect *ad hoc* altars for small-scale offerings and private worship, but a real shrine must be on sacred ground consecrated by the burial of the ancestors. These shrines, being in sacred groves of primary hardwood forest, are clearly visible, widely known, serve large parishes, and last for generations — as long as people remember that the ancestors are buried there.

The greatest of all Baegu religious ceremonies is the feast in honor of the dead, the *maoma*. It is the focus of ritual life and the single most prominent communal activity. A sequence of *maoma* extending over a period of several years takes place following the death of an important man. Ideally there will be four or eight memorial *maoma,* one held approximately every two years by the deceased's descent group. Each *maoma* requires elaborate preparations. Men plant and cultivate a ritual taro garden. They may build an artistically decorated sacred house, also called a *beu aabu*. Depending on their ambition and skill they create beautifully executed utensils and accouterments for the ceremony, such as food bowls and dance paddles. Dancers and singers rehearse their parts and plan beautiful costumes. Pigs are carefully fed and reared as sacrifices. The culmination of ritual activity takes place at a sacred grove, the shrine for the descent group whose ancestors are buried there, and consists of the sacrifice (accompanied by prayers) of numerous pigs to the ancestors, a communal meal of pork and taro cooked in leaf ovens, and the singing of traditional oral literature. Its climax is a panpipe concert and dance recital. Priests selected for their ritual knowledge plan and direct the proceedings. The descent group (*'ae bara*) claiming descent patrilineally from the ancestors being honored is responsible for the ceremony, and their Big Men make the largest donations and offerings. All living descendants of the ancestral spirits may contribute.

Maoma can be expensive affairs. Pigs (costing as much as $40.00 Australian) must be donated as sacrifices. Thousands of taro are cooked, and taro and coconut cream are mashed into a sacred pudding called *lakeno*. In addition, dancers, singers, and panpipers must be paid. Men acquire renown by the generosity of their contributions to these *maoma;* these are therefore a good setting for the acquisition of prestige through generous but at least partially competitive giving. Besides propitiating the ancestral spirits, pleasing them with the food, music, and dancing, and invoking their power in behalf of their descendants by prayers, the feasts also demonstrate the solidarity and power of the living members of the descent group (plus their contributing cognatic relatives).

Minor religious practices involve personal (but socially approved) sacrifices to the ancestors to keep them happy or to invoke special favors. People will make first-fruits offerings from their yam or taro gardens to the ancestors via the priests, sick people will offer a pig to the *akalo* in hopes of recovery, killers will offer a pig after a homicide, and violators of taboos will make a sacrifice to mollify the ancestral spirits.

The taboo system consists of supernatural sanctions against socially inappropriate or supernaturally dangerous behavior. Forbidden actions are those that offend the ancestors, causing them to withhold *mamanaa*, or to send disease, storms, crop blights, or agents of danger (*baekwa*) such as sharks, crocodiles, or venomous snakes. Such behavior results in illness, failure, accidents, or loss of luck. Behavior that offends the ancestors includes failure to make offerings or to be properly reverent, social crimes such as incest or killing a kinsman, and committing acts resulting in ritual pollution (*sua*), usually involving execretory or sexual functions or curses referring to these. Sex and sexual relations are foci for much of the taboo system. Violation of any of the customary observances of execretory practices, bodily position, physical intimacy,

menstrual and birth isolation, or sexual cohabitation angers the ancestral spirits.

Men are responsible not only for their own sins, but for the sins of
their minor offspring and other irresponsible members of their families
and households (such as women). Hence taboo observances and ritual
atonements follow traditional kinship lines and networks.

Regardless of the transgression, the ancestral spirits' anger must
not be taken lightly, for in Baegu eyes this is the ultimate or final cause
of ill fortune and disaster. Those responsible for taboo violations or
ritual pollution must offer a pig (or lesser but still suitable sacrifice)
to the ancestors to mollify them.

The most intriguing problem in this field of kinship and religion is
the question of why unilineal descent groups should be so important
in ritual contexts. A reasonable answer would seem to be that they
satisfy formal requirements in a way that is intellectually and emotionally satisfying to the people.

In an ancestral ghost cult, dieties are potentially limitless. One priest
or one group cannot remember and honor them all. But unilineal
descent groups can remember their own apical ancestors, and the simplicity of unilineal descent structure insures that the relevant ancestors
along the chain of descent connecting them with the present living will
not be forgotten. By assigning unilineal descent groups (the Baegu *'ae
bara*) the responsibility of worshiping their own ancestral spirits, a
society manages to touch all supernatural bases with a minimum of
worry about continued efficient operation of the religious system. There
is in effect a division of ritual labor according to wise managerial practices that assure all required tasks are assigned to someone, while no
single unit is overburdened with more tasks than it can handle.

The basis for this hypothesis is equivalent to the scheme for totemism
proposed by Levi-Strauss (1962b). The totality of the Baegu universe
is divided and classified according to one basic plan; several cultural
domains reflect the same basic mental pattern or structure. The physical
(land districts), the social (patrilineal descent groups), and the supernatural (ancestral spirits) domains follow isomorphic taxonomic patterns, are essentially congruent, and have more or less directly corresponding categories (Figure 28). The Baegu social universe is composed
of named descent groups (*'ae bara*). These own named districts of
land (*lolofaa*), which together comprise a set that is the Baegu physical or geographical universe. The supernatural universe is divided into
ghostly descent groups, the ancestors of the living *'ae bara*. All of these
universes thus exhibit a common classificatory pattern or structure.
Common to all universes and serving as reference points for compari-

Figure 28. The Baegu Mental Universe

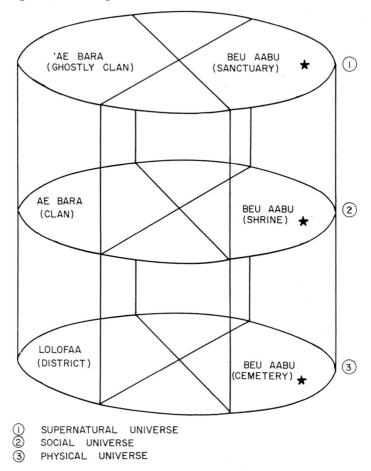

'AE BARA
(GHOSTLY CLAN)

BEU AABU
(SANCTUARY)   ★   ①

AE BARA
(CLAN)

BEU AABU
(SHRINE) ★   ②

LOLOFAA
(DISTRICT)

BEU AABU
(CEMETERY) ★   ③

① SUPERNATURAL UNIVERSE
② SOCIAL UNIVERSE
③ PHYSICAL UNIVERSE

sons are the sacred groves (*beu aabu*). In the physical universe they are stands of virgin hardwood timber, landmarks, that are used as cemeteries for the dead. For the living, *beu aabu* are shrines for the worship of ancestral deities, belonging to the clans (*'ae bara*) that are the constituent units of the social universe. Within the supernatural universe they are holy sanctuaries where the ghostly spirits of a clan's ancestors reside.

Linking the units of the social universe into a single system of relationships and tying the various worlds (supernatural, social, and physical) together is a huge network of exchange (communication) involving the cultural exchange of natural products. A secular network of markets and connubia provide channels for human communication by means of exchange among the various social groups on a horizontal (spatial, temporal, and formal) plane. Fish and vegetables circulate via the native barter market system, passing through nodal points along the coast area; valuable artifacts made of sea shells and great quantities of food circulate in connection with marriages allying personal kindreds and to a degree linking descent lines by a modified form of patrilateral cross-cousin marriage among classificatory kin. At the same time there is a sacred network of exchanges uniting physical, social, and super-natural worlds in a figuratively vertical direction (Figure 29). The land yields food to the men of the social groups who farm it; men offer sacrifices of pigs and taro to the ancestors; and the ancestors complete the cycle by granting their blessings to their descendants via the land in the form of productivity and wealth. The units taking part in this communication are the districts of land, the patrilineal descent groups (augmented by cognatic contributors), and the ancestral spirits also in agnatic corporate groups but (because they are dead) of a different order from the corporate groups of the living.

Each descent group is associated with a district of land bearing the same name as itself on the one hand, and with a group of its ancestors on the other hand. The ancestors are associated with the same district because they are buried there, and their souls (ano) remain in the sacred grove there. All land is covered, all ancestors remembered, and presumably the formal requirements for social and cognitive satisfaction are fulfilled. Again, this conforms to elementary managerial theory by assigning one unit definite responsibility for one discrete task. Here the task is the worship of ancestral spirits. Unilineal organization of descent groups, who have the ritual responsibility, is in accord with that managerial principle and assures that all relevant ancestors will be remembered. In a cognatic descent group, a ramage system, or some other form of less rigidly and arbitrarily restricted descent group per-mitting more flexibility and perhaps personal option in filiation, some ancestors could easily be forgotten. Their wrath could be disastrous. The simplicity and regularity of unilineal descent structure and seg-mentation helps to prevent this, for there is no question of a descendant choosing to remember and honor some patrilineal ancestors, neglecting others who may still be powerful and potentially dangerous.

There is some actual evidence that some Baegu have an intuitive feeling for the necessity of doing the whole task, of satisfying the formal requirements carefully. Maefasia of Uradaue has assumed the priesthood of the last remnants of Uradaue (nine people) who remain pagan although the rest of the 'ae bara, including his mother and elder brother, have become Anglicans. He says he remains faithful to the pagan religion to "remember the ancestors." His Christian relatives understand and respect his position and make no attempt to proselytize him. In the same vein, in 1966 an Anglican parish priest was found guilty by the High Court sitting in Auki of desecrating a Lau Lagoon pagan shrine whose erstwhile communicants had converted. Pagan plaintiffs argued successfully that shrines sacred to the ancestors retain their sanctity despite religious changes, and that it is in the public interest to maintain old shrines.

Figure 29. Metaphysical Communication and Exchange in the Baegu Universe

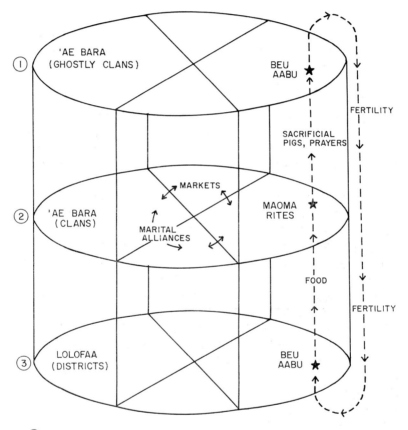

① SUPERNATURAL UNIVERSE
② SOCIAL UNIVERSE
③ PHYSICAL UNIVERSE

The obvious threat that a patrilineal segment will become extinct through failure to produce sons in some generation does not cause too much trouble. If a descent line does in fact die out from lack of male progeny, people assume that those ancestors have lost interest in the affairs of their descendants anyway. Being no longer interested, and demonstrably ineffective, they can be ignored. Besides, Baegu priests hedge a bit by making use of divination in times of crisis to discover what ancestors are angry, and by throwing into their prayers an honorific supplication or two to the forgotten spirits.

In a sense unilineal descent theory (in its agnatic form), because it is imbedded in Baegu religious belief, is a unifying principle or theme helping to make sense of the totality of the Baegu conceptual universe. According to Baegu religious ideas, it is absolutely essential to maintain continuous communication within the land-men-ancestors-land cycle. Their culture does this in two ways. First the physical, social, and supernatural aspects of their world are ordered according to the same basic mental plan and have roughly equivalent categories: land districts on the physical plane, discrete social groups (descent groups) on the social plane, and discrete groups of ancestors (buried in one place) on the supernatural plane. Human social groups are the middle term and the executive agency keeping the communication channels open from land to ancestral shrine by means of farming and sacrifices, and asking (by prayers and offerings) the ancestors to keep the cycle going, blessing the people indirectly through productivity, good health, and good weather. A simply and regularly restricted unilineal social group, directly descended from the ancestors and directly associated with a specific ancestral shrine and a specific land district, is the simplest way to match land-men-ancestors, to assure that no land or no ancestral spirits are inadvertently left out of the pattern, and to keep the exchange cycle going over several generations.

Given this metaphysical vested interest in unilineal descent groups and agnatic ideology, it is not surprising that the Baegu express marriage and land use in an agnatic idiom, even though operating rules are essentially bilateral. If unilineal groups are essential in the land-men-shrine connection, and if human social relationships depend on exchange and communication, then the social network among men on the social plane ought to involve communication and exchange among those same groups. Thus the interaction and exchange of goods and women between two personal kindreds at a wedding is described by them as an exchange between two unilineal descent lines, even though in fact matrilateral kin of groom and bride contribute to and share in the bride-wealth. People talk and think in terms of *'ae bara,* because, cognitively, they have to.

Just why this is so, no one really knows. The imagery of lines looms large in Melanesian minds, as those anthropologists who have worked in this part of the world know well. Many Melanesian societies are culturally preoccupied with genealogies, usually expressed or illustrated in linear terms. A typical genealogical format is the "begat" sequence linking names of genitor and son. This concept of lines establishing connections between living men and their quasi-mythical ancestors is a model whose users seem to find it highly satisfying. Perhaps this is nothing more than a form imposed by the exigencies of oral literature; "lines" are a handy mnemonic device for people without written records of vital statistics. Perhaps it has some phallic significance, as the common Melanesian preoccupation with masculine sexuality and the occasional appearance of male genital emphasis (such as the penis sheath of the New Guinea highlands) might suggest. My own feeling is that it is part of a fundamental, widespread, and probably very old ideology common to this part of the world. It is the Melanesian expression of some ill-defined concept of male superiority and a concomitant high valuation of male solidarity and continuity through time, traces of which appear throughout Oceania, Southeast Asia, and the Far East. Whether you see it as a culture stratum in the old *Kulturkreise* mode or a deep structure in the contemporary mental structuralist fashion does not matter. Male superiority, solidarity, and continuity are fundamental. In China it becomes filial piety; in Melanesia, linear genealogies; and in Malaita, Baegu *'ae bara* giving mortuary feasts (*maoma*).

As a result, the unilineal ideal, because of its moral and metaphysically imperative nature, is in a sense more "real" in Baegu life than is the bilateral empirical reality. It provides a scheme that makes human life and the universe meaningful, and it provides an idiom for a continuing harmonious communication system integrating physical, social, and supernatural aspects of the Malaitan world.

12. Residential Behavior: Settlement Patterns, Residence Rules, and Spacing Mechanisms

There are many ways to interpret and describe human behavior. One is by means of mechanical models composed of norms and suppositions about how norms influence actual behavior. Another is by means of statistical models phrased in statements about what most people do. The potential variety is probably infinite, but ethnographic descriptions have traditionally tended toward these two expressive modes.

Proof of validity is hard to offer in ethnography. Logical consistency is a test of sorts for mechanical models, but elegance is no guarantee of accuracy. Besides, explicit rules rarely exist; it is part of the ethnographer's job to discover and state them. For statistical models there is a whole battery of techniques for assessing significance, and the further possibility of cross-cultural comparative methods, but probability judgments are inherently ambiguous. Replicability, the classic test of the physical sciences, has not proved feasible so far.

In my own work I have tried to be pragmatic and eclectic, using both norms and statistics where I have needed them. What really existed were people, houses, and garden plots; but the patterns I found resulted from human decisions made according to certain criteria. Therefore I have tried to develop descriptions of aspects of Baegu behavior, based upon the way people make decisions. For this type of description, proof lies in predictability and the ability to generate appropriate behavior. I am correct if, based upon my descriptions, a reader could make a response or decision that Baegu people would approve; that behavior would approximate what Keesing (1970b:441), elaborating upon Chomsky, Frake, Goodenough, and Kay, calls "competence."

Residential behavior covers a wide range of situations and problems, but certain pattern variables occur throughout all phases. Actual residential patterns, as one sees them on the ground among the Baegu of northern Malaita, vary along three major axes. Each axis relates to the process of decision-making in one of three fields: a rights and property domain concerned with the basic relationship of people to the land, the problem of stability versus mobility, and the problem of social cohesion versus fragmentation.

THE RIGHTS AND PROPERTY AXIS

The rights and property axis has fixed geographic referents, and the individual must simply decide where on the landscape he is going to live, work, and worship. In a way the choices of where to live and where to work are one choice, because the underlying problem in both cases is the right to use the land (in one instance, the right to build a house on it; in the second, the right to make a garden on it). Neither house-building nor gardening convey title to land. Most people live and garden on the same land ("same" meaning owned by the same corporate group), although the house and garden sites may be a mile or so apart. For both house sites and gardens the elements of the problem are the same. The crucial factors are the right to use the land and the decision to assert or exercise that right.

The normal pattern (meaning both correct and usual) is for a man to live on his own land. This means on land belonging to the lineage or clan (*'ae bara*) of which he is a member by patrilineal descent. Since it is his land, he has an inalienable right to use the land for his house and his garden. But alternative patterns are permitted and do exist. Some men choose to live on the land of their maternal or uterine kinsmen. They have a perfect right to use this land, because of their cognatic descent from common ancestors associated with the land. Other men live uxorilocally on the land of their wives' paternal lineages. In this case they must have explicit permission to do so, usually granted because the Baegu are humane people and realize that a man must have land to support his wife and children (who are consanguineal kin of the landowners). Finally, fugitives may live among benefactors to whom they may be only distantly related. Reasons for such alternative residence vary. Quarrels resulting from disapproved marriage, rivalries, and personal animosities may cause men to avoid their own agnatic kinsmen. Or in other cases, the non-agnatic group may offer significant political or economic advantages. Hogbin (1939:25-30), for example, explains that among the Toabaita secondary owners (cognatic relatives) may choose to exercise their rights when it becomes apparent that the line of primary owners (agnates) is about to die out.

Worship takes place at sacred groves (*beu aabu*) where the ancestors are buried, and it is at these shrines that the great sacrifices are made. Sacrifices at these shrines establish rights to use the land. On a supernatural level, the individual pays homage to his ancestral spirits (*akalo*), pleasing them and supplicating their blessing. On a social level, such contributions to a sacrifice imply that the community accepts the individual's claims and his right to participate.

There is some degree of choice as to where an individual will make his offerings. He is more or less obliged to sacrifice to his own agnatic ancestors, for men have a duty to remember their lineage ancestors who first settled the land and who owned it in the past. Sacrificial rituals are organized and led by lineage priests, and lineage members are primary participants in what is called "their *maoma*." If men consistently refuse to participate, they effectively cease to be members of the ritual community, although people still insist that their land rights are inalienable. But men may also contribute offerings and be secondary participants in ceremonies (*maoma*) belonging to and organized by other lineages to whom they are cognatically related. They have a right (although not a duty) to honor their common ancestors in this way. Such contributions, publicly made, validate an individual's right to use the land where he has cognatic rights if he chooses to do so. There is, therefore, an element of strategy involved. A man will out of a sense of duty sacrifice at his own agnatic shrines, and he may also sacrifice at shrines to cognatic ancestors if he wishes to keep those ties active and their concomitant options open.

Shrines seem to be the crucial elements in the relationship of men to the land. They are prominent, widely recognized landmarks sacred to great numbers of people. People shift their gardens continuously and move their hamlets occasionally, but the sacred groves are fixed. The ancestors are literally anchored to the shrines, for they are buried there, and their spirits inhabit the grove. Living men are also tied to these groves to a lesser extent, for they have a duty to sacrifice there and have a sentimental attachment to the land where their ancestors are buried.

THE STABILITY-MOBILITY AXIS

For the stability-mobility axis of settlement patterns, the question (for the Baegu man) is whether to move to a new site or stay in the old one. This question is never asked, nor the decision made, in a logically "pure" situation. Multiple factors and ramifications are involved, but for ease of analysis and explication it is best to consider only possible moves involving physical removal of an entire hamlet from one location to another. The critical element is whether an old site or a new one is preferable.

Moves of this sort may or may not be related to shifting cultivation based on slash-and-burn horticultural technology. Traditionally the assumption has been that such farming practices permit leaching or mechanical erosion to accelerate soil depletion, forcing the people to move to a new village site where still fertile soil is more readily available. Freeman's (1955:132-41) study of shifting cultivation in tropical Borneo, addressing the intuitive assumption by British colonial officialdom that such horticultural practices are wasteful and hence inferior, rejects this simplistic conclusion. Considering the same problem in South America, Carneiro (1960:230-34) has argued that garden plots are often abandoned before their fertility is depleted, and villages usually moved while there is still plenty of uncleared land nearby. Writing about the South Pacific, Goodenough (1956a:174-75) points out that slash-and-burn gardeners in island Melanesia find it much easier to clear secondary growth than primary forest, suggesting that frequent shifts or migrations might actually (from a technological viewpoint) be disadvantageous since this would force farmers to move their operations to new areas where they must clear new primary-forest plots. There is no necessary logical connection between shifting garden plots and shifting village sites. It is entirely reasonable to live continually in one site and rotate garden sites, to shift to a new village site while continuing to cultivate the same garden plot, or to move to a new area where one would both build a new village and clear new garden plots.

The Baegu are no more energetic than any of the rest of us, and they do not relish making unnecessary work for themselves. They recognize cogent reasons for continuing to live at an old, familiar place. Since hamlet populations are small, and since a family needs only a few acres of garden at a time, there is usually sufficient land available in the vicinity. A move is not usually ecologically mandatory.

A hamlet site requires a constellation of certain natural features that, while not rare, are not always easy to combine into an optimum pattern. Although water is usually plentiful, people like to live near a brook with a cascade or fall where they can insert a bamboo conduit to facilitate drinking and bathing, and having a small pool below it where they can wash vegetables. Efficient disposal of wastes requires a fissure or deep crevice. Finally, people employ both utilitarian and aesthetic judgment about hamlet sites. They prefer a place that has a good breeze yet is sheltered from storms, and they like to live in a hamlet with a pleasant appearance and a good view. As a result, chances are that it will take an energetic search to find a new site matching or surpassing the known amenities of the old.

Long residence in one location creates vested interests leading to residential conservatism. Tree crops (coconuts and areca palms) associated with hamlets are long-lived and people hate to leave them; they prefer to live nearby to prevent pilferage. Even thatched houses require work to build, and people logically expect to get maximum use from one structure before they elect to construct another. There are also intangible factors that one should not underestimate. An old site is familiar territory whose natural features, trails, and spirits are known and trusted.

There are, conversely, equally valid reasons for moving. Houses do wear out and have to be rebuilt eventually. After a period of time the closest land gets used, and people have to hike to reach new garden land with desirable slope and pedological characteristics. Most important, the known spirits are not always benevolent. If angered, the ancestral spirits (*akalo*) can send disease and death, cause crop failures, and spoil a person's luck in general; the longer people remain in one place, the more apt they are to suffer from the spirits' disapproval. Supernatural consequences of long residence in one spot come in two ways. Over a long period of time, human frailty inevitably results in taboo violations. Improper sex, careless disposal of human wastes, and disregard of menstrual regulations anger the ancestral spirits, and human misfortunes result. A second consequence is a form of sorcery called *arua*, based on the principle of contagious magic. Malevolent persons who have learned the *arua* techniques can use old personal property, fragments of table scraps, or nail and hair trimmings to cause the enchantment, illness, or even death of the person who discarded or lost them. People take great pains to avoid losing things and to dispose of garbage and wastes safely, but slip-ups inevitably occur. Clearly the longer people live at one place, the greater the threat from *arua* becomes. Being a white man, I was too obtuse to understand and was invariably careless about such things. The Baegu eventually gave up on me, but they continued to watch my children like hawks, following them about and carefully picking up after them to protect them from *arua* sorcery. As Keesing (1965:129-31) argues, long residence in one spot leads to the accumulation of both taboo violations and of unhygienic rubbish and wastes. Eventually supernatural anger or deteriorating sanitary conditions result in sickness or death. Divination may reveal the cause; people abandon the site and build a new hamlet elsewhere in a locale spiritually or materially unpolluted. Such movements serve a public

health function, but they are made according to theological or supernatural tenets.

Movement of people to a new hamlet site, the stability-mobility axis,
can be described by a potential energy model (Figure 30) analogous
to the electrical models constructed by the mana theorists of primitive
religion, which is probably no more misleading than other such theories.
That is, it is "etically" descriptive and makes no claim to "emic" explanatory power. In this model life is a capacitor; the hamlet is the
load. Good, resulting from moral behavior pleasing to the spirits, has
a positive charge; evil, resulting from lapses angering the spirits, bears a
negative one. When an excess of negative charge builds up, a capacitor
discharges; negative current flows in the circuit, capable of doing work.
In non-electrical Baegu life the accumulation of "wrong-doing" builds
up the evil potential, bad luck is discharged into the hamlet group, and
this flow of misfortune is the motive power influencing people to move
to a new site.

Empirical evidence for this sort of reasoning is scant and irregular.
People are for the most part vague about their reasons for moving; the
usual answer is that they "felt like moving." Older men remember living
in six to nine sites during their lifetimes, an average duration of five to
twelve years for a settlement, but again, this is highly irregular. There

Figure 30. Potential Energy Model for Hamlet Location Shifts

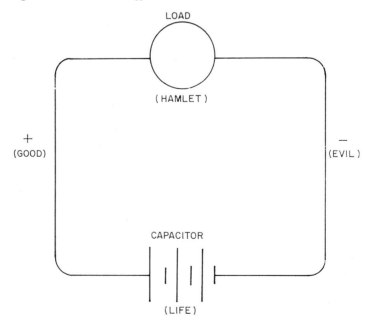

are half a dozen abandoned house sites in various stages of decay along the trail from the sea to Fatakalie in Agia, the hamlet of an old man named Beliga, yet Beliga's hamlet itself has stood where it is since Marching Rule days in the late 1940's. Such irregularity argues against any simplistic ecological explanation, but for an explanation incorporating the chance or "luck" element. People will stay put as long as they have good luck and will move when their luck turns bad. Big or important men (like Beliga) will tend to be more stable because by definition they, with wealth and influence, are lucky. Lesser men with less luck will be more apt to feel a need to move.

THE FUSION-FISSION AXIS

Another factor in population mobility is the choice of coresidents, creating variability along a fusion-fission axis. This results from decisions made by an individual about the relative merit of continuing to live with a given group, or of splitting off from a settlement to create a new, smaller one.

Centripetal tendencies result from the fact that there are obvious advantages to living in large groups. Before pacification, larger settlements meant better defense against hostile raiding parties. In larger hamlets it is easier to organize communal labor groups for garden clearance, house-building, and food preparation at feast times. With more people it is easier to share the load. The division of labor is potentially more equitable, and those with incipient special talents can efficiently practice their skills. A sick man or woman can be relieved to rest and recover while others temporarily assume his duties. With a larger number of coresidents, babysitting and geriatric care cease to be such burdens. There is also psychological relief from quarrels, since an individual can maintain normal human interactions with others during a cooling-off period and can avoid his opponent tactfully. In terms of political relations, a number of followers amplify the power of important men, and conversely clients find security in close association with powerful figures. Finally, there are kinship obligations to consider. Coresidence reinforces such bonds by keeping relatives together and facilitating mutual cooperation. With coresidence, norms and practice are congruent. All these factors to some degree tend to influence people toward living together in larger groups.

On the other hand, there are centrifugal tendencies or equally obvious advantages to splitting up into smaller groups. A settlement pattern with more, smaller residential units relieves pressure on available garden land, permitting people to live closer to the plots they are cultivating.

Smaller units also require less extensive water sources and sanitary facilities. Although kinship provides allies and mutual support, too many
or too persistent relations can be onerous. Father or elder brother is
boss, and some ambitious younger men dislike being constantly reminded
of their subordinate status. Kinship involves mutual services and sharing of possessions that can become a burden. Young wives in particular
complain that the husband's kin are too bossy and too demanding. And
if a bridegroom lives uxorilocally, he must for obvious practical reasons
disregard his obligation to present gifts to his affines when meeting
them. On the supernatural level, when there are numerous people
there are also numerous chances to violate taboos, thereby increasing the
probability of displeasing the spirits. When more people are around,
there are also more opportunities for disruptive personal quarrels.
Finally, regardless of how such a taste originated, the Baegu value privacy. They dislike the crowded conditions of coastal or offshore island
villages and compare the cosmopolitan Lau existence unfavorably with
Baegu village life on its smaller scale. These factors make smaller settlements more attractive.

As this works out in practice, there is a balance of centripetal and
centrifugal tendencies, with a definite strain toward smaller units. This
appears in three manifestations: first, in postmarital residence when a
young couple moves out of the parental household to build their own
dwelling house; second, in the tendency of pagan villages to split up
into partially separated or totally separated clearings although still in
the same neighborhood; and third, in the previously cited pattern
wherein Christian Baegu or Neo-Marching Rule settlements divide into
smaller units of typical traditional size.

Since science still lacks an adequate unified field theory, an atomic
nuclear model (representing persons, groups, and social distances) offers
one plausible way to describe Baegu settlement pattern variations along
the fusion-fission axis (Figure 31). People are the nuclear particles
and, like protons, they have contradictory electrostatic charges and
binding energy values. In normal, easily observed macrocosmic situations people, with their sense of independence and love of privacy,
repel each other like two protons (bearing similar positive electrostatic
charges). Thus they like to separate into small hamlets and clearings.
But on a more intimate microcosmic or intranuclear level, close-range
binding energy forces keep protons together in nuclei and people together in hamlets. The elements nearer the middle of the periodic table
have maximum binding energy with more stable nuclei and more potential nuclear energy, and Baegu hamlets seem to have an optimum
moderate size. As heavier nuclei at the upper end of the periodic table
are often unstable, so larger Baegu settlements are trouble-prone and

unstable. When repulsive electrostatic forces overcome binding energy, nuclear fission or radioactive decay releases energy, creating stable fission products of moderate atomic weight. Baegu villages, too, divide into stable hamlets of moderate size, presumably discharging some sort of social energy in the process of splitting. At the other end of the scale, tiny nuclear families are weak and ineffective; but their fusion into multifamily hamlets generates social power, a process analogous to the thermonuclear transformation of lighter isotopes into nuclei of heavier (and more stable) elements.

Figure 31. Nuclear Model for Stable Hamlet Size

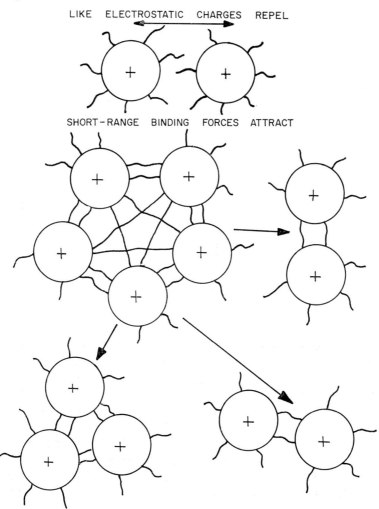

Figure 32. Central Tendencies of Population of "Natural Hamlets" in the Sample Area

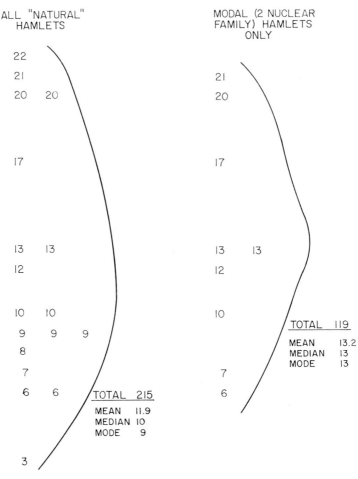

ALL "NATURAL" HAMLETS

MODAL (2 NUCLEAR FAMILY) HAMLETS ONLY

TOTAL 215
MEAN   11.9
MEDIAN 10
MODE   9

TOTAL 119
MEAN   13.2
MEDIAN 13
MODE   13

To pursue further the inference from this model that Baegu hamlets tend to approach an optimum size, Figure 32 conveys the central tendencies of population distribution in "natural" hamlets (as defined in Chapter 10). There is no guarantee that mean, median, or mode approximate an optimum size, but theoretically they should, for they are derived from empirical measurement of hamlets that are the end result of fusion-fission processes. It is better to think of optimum size as a range rather than as a central tendency, because Baegu hamlets form and break up by the association and splitting off of family and household groups rather than of individuals. Table 28 shows the optimum

TABLE 28. OPTIMUM POPULATION RANGE FOR BAEGU HAMLETS

	Number of hamlets	Number of house-holds	House-holds per hamlet	Persons living this way	Hamlet average	Persons per house-hold	Average persons for 2 nuclear family hamlet	Optimum hamlet population range Min.	Max.
Intact nuclear families:								7	10
Averages .	18	31	1.7	136	7.6	4.4	8.8		
Modes...	9	18	2	..	..	4.7	9.4		
Partial house-holds......	18	25	1.4	72	4.0	2.9	5.8	2	6
Affiliated individuals..	18	..	..	7	0.4	..	0.4	0	1
Totals...				215	12.0		13.8-15.6	9	17

Calculations are based on a two nuclear family mode for "natural" hamlets in the sample area.

size range that might result from the combination of family or household groups.

For a beginning, 136 persons living in 18 so-called natural hamlets would mean an average of 7.6 statistical persons living as part of intact nuclear families within the average natural hamlet. Going at it another way, with 31 intact nuclear-family households, there are 4.4 statistical persons for each such household or 8.8 in the modal hamlet of two of them. In view of the striking mode (50 percent) at the two-nuclear-family level (Table 21), we can assume that the typical natural hamlet will contain two intact nuclear families. In still a third approach, starting with the assumption of a modal two-nuclear-family hamlet and using the Table 11 figure of 2.7 children per marriage (4.7 people for an intact nuclear family), one would find 9.4 statistical persons in a two-nuclear-family combination. Extrapolating from these figures, since real people are inconveniently indivisible, one deduces that there should be a range of from seven to ten persons living as part of intact nuclear families in a typical Baegu two-family hamlet, given these central tendencies.

There are twenty-five partial households in the eighteen natural hamlets of the sample area, meaning that there are one or two partial households (average of 1.4) in each such hamlet. These twenty-five partial households contain a total of seventy-two persons, so there are 2.9 persons per partial household. These possibilities would result in a range of from two to six such persons living in the modal natural Baegu hamlet with one or two affiliated partial households. There are seven individuals living alone or affiliated with other households in the eighteen natural hamlets of the sample area, implying that there would be 0.4 such affiliated persons per hamlet — in commonsense terms, possibly one.

All told these mental gymnastics yield a range of from nine to seventeen persons for optimum-sized Baegu hamlets composed of two intact nuclear families plus affiliated partial households and individuals. "Optimum" hamlet size is, however, in some ways an ineffective descriptive vehicle. Since it requires knowledge of what the Baegu themselves have to say about hamlet size, it is not even truly descriptive in a statistical sense. For some purposes it is much better to rely upon standard measures of central tendency and range of variation. Since Professor Albert Damon (1969) of the Peabody Museum at Harvard was kind enough to make the calculations for me, and since he expresses his results far more lucidly than I could do, I think it best to let him report the facts in his own words.

In his summary comments he states, "I would treat this matter statistically and avoid notions of optimum. For 'natural' hamlets, I calculate a mean of 11.94 persons per hamlet, with a standard deviation of 5.765. The very large coefficient of variation:

$$\frac{100 \times S.D.}{Mean} = \frac{576.5}{11.94} = 48.4$$

shows a highly variable measure. The C.V. for (human) height is about 4; for (human body) weight (highly variable as we all know) about 15. This means that any single measure of central tendency is misleading, since it has very wide confidence limits. Specifically, the standard error of the mean is 1.36. Taking the customary limits of plus or minus 3 S.E., we get:

$$11.94 + 4.08 = 16.02 \text{ and}$$
$$11.94 - 4.08 = 7.86,$$

for the typical 'natural' hamlet, or a range of 8 to 16 persons.

"You may note that this corresponds closely with the actual number of persons calculated from . . . other tables. But this figure is a statistical abstraction, not necessarily the best possible arrangement."

RESIDENTIAL DECISIONS

Settlement patterns do exist, but residence rules are a mental shorthand created by ethnographers. An ethnographer describes how settlements are distributed across the landscape and infers principles that he thinks govern decisions about where people live. A few cultures may actually have explicit rules, but these are only one of the factors in residential decisions and may (if improperly used) be misleading, for there are always exceptions. Patterns and rules result from decisions in real-life situations made by actual people. Analytic emphasis should be on the *process* of decision-making, not on its results.

One of the first points to settle is, who makes the decision? Among the Baegu, men do; women and children follow. This is to greater or lesser degree probably a pan-human trait. Robin Fox (1967:31) assumes as an existential theorem that men are the decision-makers and "run" society, even in matrilineal groups. Anthropologists have intuitively accepted this bias. Classical approaches to kinship and residence, even as late as Murdock's (1949), state residence rules in a framework that is valid only for males. Fischer (1958:510) took special note of this, insisting that residence rules specifically state to whom they applied. But for the Baegu residential decisions are a male prerogative, although I am sure female nagging is as effective there as it is anywhere.

Baegu men must make at least three decisions that affect residence rules and settlement patterns. These are (1) what land to claim, (2) where to build the settlement, and (3) with whom to live. They are inextricably combined in real life. There are certain standard factors, criteria, or inputs affecting these decisions. Although a bit procrustean, a minimum list would include economic factors (not necessarily first in importance), social factors, personal or psychological factors, and supernatural factors. Again, in real life these are not distinctly separable.

DECISION: WHAT LAND TO CLAIM?

Decisions about what land to claim, or more precisely what options to exercise, result in observable variations along what I have defined as a "Rights and Property Axis" (matrix being perhaps the better term).

There are several economic considerations relevant here. First is the question of pressure on the land, or how much land is available. This is usually not critical, for land is almost a free good, and ownership by large clans makes competition diffuse. But members of populous groups may choose to stress their rights in other lineages/districts that have fewer people but more land. A second economic consideration is the cost of sacrifices. Sacrifices to the ancestral spirits or contributions to religious feasts are the means whereby men establish their rights to use ancestral land. Pigs, the "proper" sacrifices, cost as much as $40 Australian. Other things being equal, men prefer to minimize such expenses. If they wish to live and garden on land "owned" by their cognatic relatives, they must offer pigs to their common, cognatic ancestors. Yet these men are still obliged by custom and filial piety to sacrifice to their own patrilineal ancestors. Obviously the most economical way out is to use land belonging to your own patrilineage established by your own patrilineal ancestors. In this case one sacrifice both fulfills your filial obligations and establishes your right to live and garden on this land. Although multiple sacrifices create a severe economic strain, wealthy and ambitious men may use them to their own advantage. By contributing pigs or taro to many sacrifices and feasts, they ramify their political networks and keep alive many alternative rights and claims to land usage.

The overwhelming social factor is the obligation to cooperate with one's agnatic relatives for defense or raiding parties, in cooperative labor (house-building or garden clearance), in cultivating ritual taro gardens in preparation for mortuary feasts, and in sharing material goods. These obligations are easier to carry out if a person lives among his agnates — that is, if he lives in the same neighborhood or district and near their joint ancestral shrine.

Personal or psychological factors offer a pair of alternatives. If one is on good terms with his agnatic relatives, he will most likely wish to live among them. Alternatively, if he quarrels with them, he will probably want to live elsewhere. Physical violence between agnatic relatives often leads to the flight of one (usually the instigator) to seek refuge, for it is a great sin to harm an agnate and public opinion will not tolerate such misbehavior. Similarly, incest or seduction of an agnate's wife will result in the exile of the guilty person. Participants in illicit sexual affairs or disapproved marriages may live with more distant (frequently uterine) kinsmen until the heat is off, for their agnates will be shamed by their behavior. Sometimes a man's wife and his blood kin simply cannot stand one another, and a peaceful man may seek to avoid trouble by moving away. As in all human groups personal rivalries exist, and in some cases the bush is simply "not big enough for both." The easiest way out is for one of the competitors to move to a different location, leaving the field to his rival. Finally, there is another personal factor, that of habit. Most of us become attached to "home" and are more content among familiar scenes and people. Since the Baegu live virilocally after marriage and grow up among agnatic relatives, there may be a built-in tendency to continue living with them on land that is well known.

There are also supernatural factors affecting an individual's decisions about land use options. Your own ancestral spirits are to a degree prejudiced in your favor, since they are still in a sense part of the lineage. In some ways known ghosts are preferable to unknown ones; one is, after all, sacrificing to them to assure their good will. Sorcery also is less likely among close friends and relatives. These cultural assumptions enhance the desirability of living on familiar ancestral land. On the other hand, if the spirits manifest ill will toward a person, it is probably best to avoid them by living elsewhere.

One convenient way to represent "Rights and Property" decision-making is by means of an algebraic model (Figure 33), with each factor

Figure 33. Factors Affecting Rights and Property Decisions

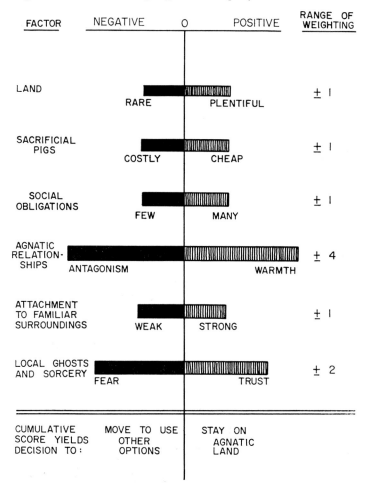

having an approximate numerical weighting. The question implicit in this decision is whether or not a man should live and garden on his own patrilineally inherited land. In such an either/or situation each factor has a plus or minus value. Plus means "yes, stay here"; minus means "no, move." When added algebraically, a cumulative positive score would indicate a decision to stay and use the land of the agnatic corporation; a negative score would represent a decision to move elsewhere and use other options. Unfortunately, the relative weighting of various factors is not obvious, so for illustrative purposes I have arbitrarily assigned values that I viscerally feel are appropriate. One could push this line of thought a bit further, arguing that a person may select which particular option (from among those available to him) he will use by some kind of maximization operation. This direct extension is somewhat precarious, but it does make sense to assume that a person might choose to live and garden on land having the highest positive cumulative weighting of factors.

DECISION: WHERE TO BUILD THE SETTLEMENT?

Decisions about the physical location of a hamlet (not considering land rights) cause settlement pattern variation along a "Stability-Mobility Axis." The problem is one of finding an ideal site for a village, and (seen over time) a decision of when to move to a new site. Analytically, these decisions are made after the context of what land rights are claimed has been established. Economic factors are important, one being the availability of garden land. Land is plentiful but ideal land is limited, and customarily people cultivate a given plot for only a year or two. Thus the best land in the immediate vicinity is soon used up and, other things being equal, a person prefers a shorter walk to his garden rather than a longer one. On the other hand, gardens should be far enough from the hamlet to discourage raiding by voracious domestic pigs. Water supply is important, for settlements must be near a spring or brook with adequate water for drinking, bathing, and washing foods. Ownership of tree crops is a conservative factor, since people plant coconuts and areca palms around their homes. They do not trust one another where these are concerned, and they like to watch their trees to prevent pilferage. If they move, they often put a taboo on their trees to protect them magically. Thus people do not in general readily abondon the trees they own. Settlement sites have both practical and aesthetic characteristics, and people weigh such things as shelter, natural beauty, and view in selecting a site, or in comparing the relative merits of different sites. People also consider the economic costs of building houses. Either repair of an old house or the building of a new one requires time and effort, although usually new construction entails more than repair. Sago leaf thatch, bamboo, and wood must be available and accessible.

Social or kinship factors do not seem critical at this level, for the decision has already been made to live in a particular neighborhood or district, and (conceptually, at least) the problem is one of site selection, not one of with whom to live. It is assumed that the whole hamlet is settling or moving together.

Personal or psychological factors do count, however. The familiar has certain advantages. People know the resources and hazards of an older site; in a new one, they will have to learn them. Personal preferences, aesthetic satisfaction, and sentiments affect evaluations of site desirability.

Supernatural factors influence decisions about particular sites as they do for districts or neighborhoods. Ancestral spirits are probably less important for site selection, since they influence the affairs of whole districts around their sacred groves. On the other hand, wild ghosts (*akalo kwasi*) have particular local territories, but they are not part of a lineage's living-dead social corporation. Thus a new site may have unfamiliar and potentially dangerous ghosts. An important supernatural factor is that long residence in a single site increases supernatural danger. Taboo violations over time build up a residue of ill will among the spirits, the accumulation of detritus increases the risk of *arua* sorcery, and (although they may not realize it) pollution of the soil and water supply may make diseases associated with unsanitary conditions more likely.

Again, the model (Figure 34) for this kind of decision is a simple one. There is an either-or question: the group either stays put or moves to a new site. Since people always live somewhere, the first step is always deciding whether or not to move. The obvious model is again a cumulative, algebraic one. Positive factors favor staying on; negative ones favor abandonment of an old site. People decide to move when the disadvantages of an old site outweigh its advantages. Once the decision to move is made, people must consider the relative merits of potential sites. This presumably involves the maximization of economic, personal, and supernatural satisfactions. The supernatural element looms large, for people may select a new site on the basis of omens or divination, and they positively avoid known "bad luck" areas that they assume to be cursed or haunted. Although based on supernatural assumptions, their decisions are rational ones reached in logical steps.

DECISION: WITH WHOM TO LIVE?

Deciding with whom to live results in settlement pattern variations along the "Fusion-Fission Axis," and it is directly related to settlement size and concentration of population. Essentially the problem is one of choosing whether to live in a larger group, or to hive off and live in a smaller one. It is not made in a conceptually "pure" context, for it nearly always involves also the selection of a new site and construction of new houses.

In part economic considerations are those considered in any decision to move. One must find a new site, elect to abandon one's trees, and build a new home. But in this case, when leaving an old, larger group, there are social as well as physical, economic losses to consider. Trees

Figure 34. Factors Affecting Stability-Mobility Decisions

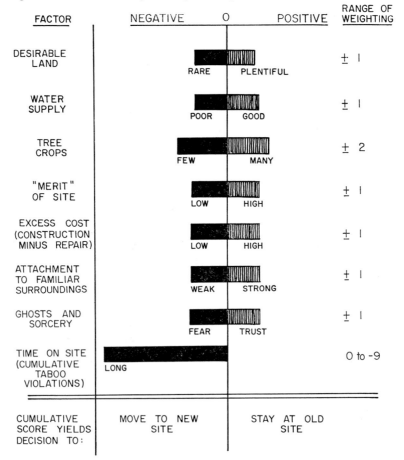

may be owned by groups of siblings, and in moving out of a larger hamlet the migrant subgroup leaves behind immediate rights to supervise and exploit those trees. More important, a man's house (*beu*) contains invaluable sacred relics and artifacts of the ancestors. In leaving these, the colonists give up an irreplaceable sacred resource.

Social factors are immensely important. Agnatic solidarity among fathers, sons, brothers, and cousins is easy to maintain in a large hamlet. It attenuates once people move away. Other kin obligations are less strong but should be considered. The larger group offers real advantages in terms of defense, communal work, and division of labor. Patron/client relationships involving Big Men can satisfy both sides of the relationships, and the hamlets of truly important men are noticeably larger. All these things emigrants to new hamlets must forfeit.

Personal or psychological factors can work either way. Affection between friends and relatives holds people together, but personal rivalries, quarrels, and love of privacy make a move to establish one's own separate hamlet seem more desirable.

Supernatural factors are also complex and contradictory. Known friends and relatives are presumably safe; strangers and new neighbors (who may be sorcerers) may not be. On the other hand, the greater population (particularly of ignorant women and children) in a larger village increases the danger of supernatural disaster. More people mean more chances for taboo infractions and hence greater risk of angering the spirits.

This decision-making process requires a somewhat more sophisticated descriptive model. One could describe it by means of a cumulative algebraic model, but it needs a series of regression curves for each factor showing the change of utility or desirability with increasing population size in a given settlement.

To begin with a single economic factor, and considering one hamlet and its population, average walking distance to garden increases with population size (Figure 35), since there is only a finite amount of desirable land adjacent to the hamlet. Presumably, then, the desirability (as a function of easy access to garden) of staying decreases with larger population size (see Curve 2 of Figure 35).

Other economic factors (jointly owned trees, sacred relics) are a constant plus factor influencing people to stay with the old group. So are the personal desire to maintain old friendships and the supernatural factors inherent in a preference for known friends and relatives (see Curve 3 of Figure 37).

For some social factors, larger populations are advantageous. Agnatic solidarity, mutual assistance, and the political advantages of Big

Figure 35. Relationship of Population, Available Garden Land, and Hamlet Stability

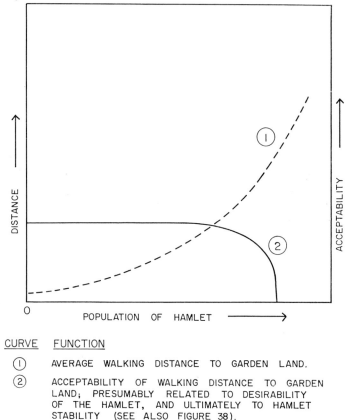

CURVE   FUNCTION

①   AVERAGE WALKING DISTANCE TO GARDEN LAND.

②   ACCEPTABILITY OF WALKING DISTANCE TO GARDEN LAND; PRESUMABLY RELATED TO DESIRABILITY OF THE HAMLET, AND ULTIMATELY TO HAMLET STABILITY   (SEE ALSO FIGURE 38).

Men/follower relationships are enhanced by increasing numbers of people. For these purposes, and since men are innately social animals, there is a minimum feasible population (three in the Baegu sample), with increasing positive value (indicating an influence toward staying with the group) as population size increases (see Curve 4 of Figure 36). This increases with diminishing marginal utility (slope of the curve) and reaches a plateau positive value where decreasing need for cooperation no longer improves social efficiency in larger groups (above twenty-two in traditional Baegu society). On the other hand, such personal or psychological factors as frequency of quarreling and love of privacy make larger groups less desirable. In like manner, more people increase the supernatural danger. A curve describing these factors would begin (Curve 5 of Figure 36) with a high positive value (influence to

Figure 36. Relative Utility of Smaller or Larger Hamlets

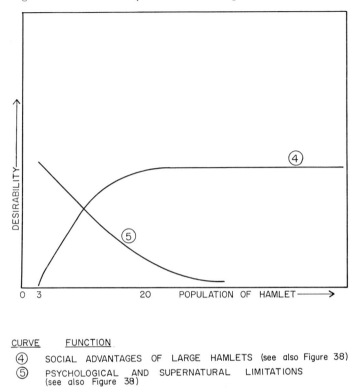

CURVE   FUNCTION

④   SOCIAL ADVANTAGES OF LARGE HAMLETS (see also Figure 38)

⑤   PSYCHOLOGICAL AND SUPERNATURAL LIMITATIONS
        (see also Figure 38)

stay with the group) and decline regularly with increasing population, approaching asymptotically the zero ordinate of no tendency at all to remain with the increasingly larger group.

The cumulative sum of algebraically adding these values for the continuously varying population abscissa (or of integrating all the curves) would be a measure of the relative desirability (as he sees it) of a person's staying with his older, larger group, or of splitting off to start a new hamlet with a smaller population (Figure 37). One unusual feature of this model is that all resultant values are positive. In accordance with the nomenclature and signification being used, this should mean an inevitable decision to stay with the larger group. This is clearly incorrect, but in its own way it is not far wrong. In Baegu ideology people *ought* to live and work together; thus the constantly positive result expresses the Baegu *normative* preference for cooperation and coresidence. This is the thinking that made possible the large but ephemeral "towns" of Marching Rule days. Yet in empirical reality

Figure 37. Fusion-Fission Decisions

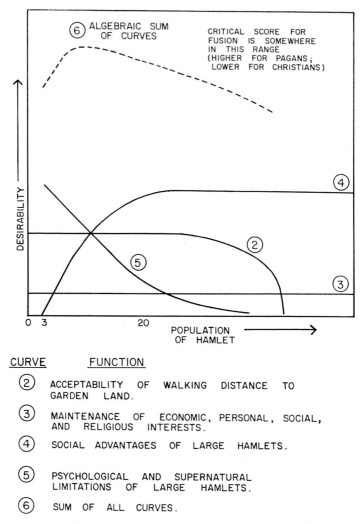

CURVE   FUNCTION

② ACCEPTABILITY OF WALKING DISTANCE TO GARDEN LAND.

③ MAINTENANCE OF ECONOMIC, PERSONAL, SOCIAL, AND RELIGIOUS INTERESTS.

④ SOCIAL ADVANTAGES OF LARGE HAMLETS.

⑤ PSYCHOLOGICAL AND SUPERNATURAL LIMITATIONS OF LARGE HAMLETS.

⑥ SUM OF ALL CURVES.

such large settlements are rare, and when they appear they do not persist. There is a strain toward fragmentation with a minimum positive score critical for fusion or maintenance of settlement integrity (Curve 6 of Figure 38). While cumulative value remains above that threshold, settlements stay intact. When cumulative value falls below the critical score, fission occurs and a small group splits off to establish an independent hamlet. Incidentally, comparison of this curve with a graph of actual settlement population distribution reveals only a very rough fit, but nonetheless a suggestive one, supporting the idea of an "optimum" hamlet population range (Figure 38).

Figure 38. Optimum Population Range

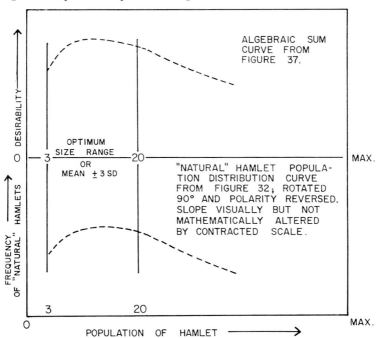

RESIDENTIAL DECISIONS AND THE INDIVIDUAL

Residential decisions must be made at critical points in a person's life history. The examples above are impersonal ones, illustrating the values or criteria culturally valid for the decision-making process. To see what decisions mean in terms of human life, one needs a different device. One useful scheme for this purpose is the flow chart based on the logical sequence involved in decision-making. Flow charts, a by-product of the computer revolution and particularly of computer languages, are useful in that they identify discrete steps in the process of making a decision, indicate at what points in the process a decision or subdecision must be made, adumbrate the criteria to be considered at that point, and indicate the way a particular result will close or open future options. Lacking a real standard, I have borrowed the style and conventions (slightly modified) used by Geoghegan (1970) and Keesing (1970a) for the description of ethnographic situations. Figure 39

Figure 39. Elementary Logical Flow Chart Illustrating Typical Symbols

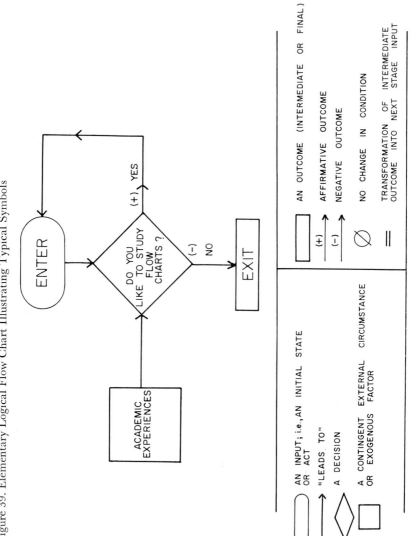

ENTER

ACADEMIC
EXPERIENCES

DO YOU
LIKE TO STUDY
FLOW
CHARTS ?

(+) YES

(-)
NO

EXIT

⬭ AN INPUT; i.e., AN INITIAL STATE
    OR ACT

↑ "LEADS TO"

◇ A DECISION

▢ A CONTINGENT EXTERNAL CIRCUMSTANCE
    OR EXOGENOUS FACTOR

▭ AN OUTCOME (INTERMEDIATE OR FINAL)

(+)↑ AFFIRMATIVE OUTCOME

(-)↑ NEGATIVE OUTCOME

⊘ NO CHANGE IN CONDITION

= TRANSFORMATION OF INTERMEDIATE
   OUTCOME INTO NEXT STAGE INPUT

defines common symbols and presents a whimsical flow chart (suggested at various times by James Baltaxe and Richard Lowenthal of the Department of Anthropology at Illinois) demonstrating how they work.

In reality Baegu men make numerous decisions at different times, but abstractly they fall into three broad groupings corresponding roughly to the three residential problems already described: what rights and property to claim, where to build the hamlet, and with whom to live. Figure 40 is a hypothetical flow chart for residential decisions encountered during the life of a typical Baegu male.

Logically first and usually temporally first in the course of growing to adulthood is the problem of deciding what rights and property to claim. Decisions in this Group One category (Figure 40) imply that an individual commits himself to future interaction with a particular array of people. That is, he will commit himself to reside and garden in a particular neighborhood or district by deciding to claim rights to use land in that area. He exercises one or more of his residential options (resulting from his cognatic kin relationships) by sacrificing to the ancestors, erecting a house, and planting a garden. His other potential options lapse temporarily, but they are in abeyance, not voided or forgotten.

Decisions of this nature (Group One) normally occur as a young man reaches adulthood, becomes economically self-sufficient, begins to participate fully in the ritual community, and considers marriage seriously. Assuming that our typical young man has grown up among his lineage mates (*'ae bara*) living on their own land (patrilocal residence), he must elect whether to continue living with the same people or to accept another alternative. Seen in terms of residence at the neighborhood or district level, he is in effect choosing virilocal, avunculocal, or uxorilocal residence. For decisions in this group there are two critical nodes in the development of the ultimate decision. First, there is the question of the adequacy of "Rights and Property" factors: one's relationships (personal, political, and social) with agnatic kinsmen living and dead (supernatural), and the availability of adequate natural and cultural resources. Second is the nature of courtship and the marriage the boy eventually contracts. Typically with good agnatic relationships, adequate resources, and an approved marriage, the young man will live virilocally in a neighborhood or district "owned" by his own clan or lineage. In atypical cases, where agnatic relationships are strained or resources are perceived as inadequate, he may elect to live and work among some of his other kinsmen, usually in a neighborhood or district "owned" by his mother's kin (avunculocal residence). Finally, if romantic love or his gonads tempt him into a disapproved marriage, he

Plate 18. Saulifoia and Kafeta, wife and sister of a Langane priest, posing self-consciously in ceremonial regalia en route to a feast.

might prefer to seek refuge among his matrilateral kinsmen or to live with his bride's people. On the neighborhood or district level, this is avunculocal or uxorilocal residence.

Second in normal sequence (logically and ontogenetically) comes the decision of with whom to live, Decision Group Two of the flow chart (Figure 41). (In describing the criteria or factors in decision-making earlier in this chapter, I presented this one last, since it is more complex and harder to describe.) Analyzed now at the hamlet level rather than at the neighborhood or district level, the virilocal norm for postmarital residence means that there is an initial strain for residence as part of a preexisting larger village, with the bride coming to live with and work for the groom's parents. But this situation does not persist indefinitely, for the young couple must eventually build a dwelling house (*luma*) of their own and decide where to construct it. Critical junctures in making this decision include the relative status or prestige of the two kindreds joined in the marriage alliance and the quality of the affinal relationship — in this case, how the bride gets along with her in-laws. Typically virilocal residence will continue with the young couple living within the same or in an adjacent clearing. But if the girl's family is demonstrably superior, or if she and her in-laws simply cannot tolerate one another, uxorilocal residence (at the hamlet level) may result. Finally, there is the question of optimum hamlet size (if such a thing exists), a conceptual catch-all taking account of a range of economic, social, personal, and supernatural factors. Other things being equal, if hamlet population is within the preferred size range, virilocal residence will continue; if it is too big, a nuclear family and perhaps some friends or relatives will break away and live neolocally in a different hamlet.

There is also, subsumed within Decision Group Three on the flow chart (Figure 40), the recurring problem of continuing in the old site or moving the settlement. This is in some ways the easiest to describe, for the factors are straightforward, and such moves are usually precipitated by an obvious crisis. When the disadvantages of an old site reach the critical point where they cumulatively outweigh the advantages, people move to a new site. Otherwise they stay where they are.

Obviously a flow chart such as Figure 40 is grossly oversimplified. A chart is based on a logical sequence, yet in real life things may occur in almost any order. A sequence or loop can begin or repeat at almost any point, similar later patterns can develop in initially avunculocal or uxorilocal situations, and charts (based on what usually happens) cannot account for all events or permutations. After all, the function of a flow chart is to clarify, to help us understand complex processes.

A chart that did not simplify, that tried to consider everything, would look like a plate of spaghetti and meatballs and would utterly fail to accomplish its only purpose.

THE RESIDENTIAL PROBLEM FOR WOMEN

Although the Baegu see residential decisions as a male affair, women do have something to say about marriage, housebuilding, and family activities. The logical sequence for a woman is considerably different, as Figure 41 shows. In general, her decisions depend on her relationship to her husband.

For women, Decision Group One (Figure 41) involves the establishment of initial residence for a newly married couple. Although technically a girl's father has jural authority over her marriage, truly forced marriages are rare to the point of nonexistence and in practice a girl says "yes" or "no" for herself. Spinsterhood, whether voluntary or by default, results in continued patrilocal residence for the girl as an affiliated spinster with her natal relatives or neighbors. Assuming her marriage is generally approved, a girl will live virilocally with her husband. In disapproved marriages, the couple avoids adverse public opinion by seeking shelter with the groom's more distant (usually uterine) kin.

Decision Group Two of the flow chart (Figure 41) pertains to residential decisions once the marriage becomes routine. In the normal virilocal pattern, the question is one of remaining part of a larger settlement or moving out to form an independent residential group. One consideration is the relative social status of bride's and groom's kin. Another factor is obviously the young woman's relationship to her in-laws. If her affinal relationships are good, she and her husband simply stay with the group, subject of course to his or their joint option to move out if conditions change or if population size exceeds an intuitive optimum. If affinal relationships are poor, they are apt to assert a measure of independence by living in a partially separated clearing, still associated with the settlement as a whole. Terrible affinal relationships will probably cause the young couple to abandon the scene and live neolocally. In all of these situations, the wife is not independent. Her attitudes certainly affect her husband's judgment, but the decision is his.

Decision Group Three on the chart (Figure 41) depends on whether or not the marriage persists. If the marriage continues, particularly if it is a fruitful one, a woman stays with her husband and her life pattern conforms to his. Marriages end by divorce or death. A widowed woman has the option of continuing to live with her dead husband's kin or of returning to her own natal lineage. Her decision depends upon her children, her age, and her own status versus that of her husband's family. A childless widow usually returns home, where she is again available in the marriage market, albeit at the reduced price appropriate for used goods and subject to the payment of compensation to her dead husband's kindred. Nursing infants naturally must remain with their mothers. A strong-willed woman of high status might succeed in taking her older children back home with her, but most cannot. If the widow returns home, she should leave her children to be fostered by her affines, who are of course her children's lineage. Most women prefer to keep their young and continue to live as widows with their former husband's group (Table 23).

The disposition of children in cases of marital dissolution by divorce depends upon who was the guilty party. When the woman's laziness or infidelity caused the divorce, she forfeits her rights to her children and returns home in shame. When the man is the offender, he still theoretically retains his rights to their children, but in two instances (of separation, not full divorce) which I knew personally, the angry wife took the children home to her father with her, subject only to some grumbling by her affines.

ECOLOGICAL IMPLICATIONS

Ecological and social organization are certainly not unique to the human condition. Ecological adaptation is a problem facing all organisms. Animal populations make these adaptations biologically, behaviorally, or socially. Man does so in addition by means of technology, belief systems (religion and social structure), and reason (thinking the problem through and invention). Social organization in itself is not uniquely human. All multi-cellular organisms involve organization, the mere existence of two sexes requires some obvious social cooperation, colonial and herd animals are commonplace, and elaborate insect societies and nonhuman primate groups exist. There is real value in a social science that, while avoiding simple-minded reductionism, is firmly based in the natural sciences. By keeping things in this perspective we avoid species conceit — the unwarranted assumption that mankind is a thing apart.

There is a long history of respectable attempts to keep anthropology in the natural world. The cultural and social evolutionists, from Forde (1934) and Childe (1936) through White (1949) and Steward (1955) to Sahlins (1958) and Service (1962), have been an influential minority insisting upon the vital relevance of natural environment to human

Plate 19. Lokaufa, a young girl of the Langane clan, with facial tattoos to enhance her beauty (photograph by Kathryn P. Ross).

activity. Vayda (1956), Shimkin (1964), Harris (1964), and Rappaport (1967) do so without a distracting reliance upon *a priori* evolutionary schema. Frake (1962) even relates ecology to the *avant garde* practice of ethnosemantics within the "new ethnography." Given this perspective one can draw a few tentative conclusions about residence rules, residential customs, land ownership, and settlement patterns. First, there is the strong presumption that they must have some ecologically adaptive value. Second, since they serve to localize and regularize habitation, it would seem logical to assume that they fall within a general class of biological or ethological phenomena called spacing mechanisms.

Spacing mechanisms are behavioral patterns that cause a population (of a single animal species) to distribute itself more or less evenly over its range. The importance of this is that by preventing the accumulation of too many individuals of the same species in one area it prevents unduly fierce intraspecific competition. Hall (1966:21-29) describes the "sink behavior" that results from overcrowding: aggression rises, cooperation declines, normal mating and nurturance patterns break down, and eventually there is a catastrophic population decline. Durkheim (1897) coined the name "anomie" for what is essentially the same condition for human groups, the alienation of individuals from the social system. There are therefore grounds for believing that population pressure can have unfortunate results for either animal or human populations.

Human beings have a proven ability to exist happily in a wide range of demographic settings. Perhaps the small hunter-gatherer band is the "natural" human social organization, but we have also lived successfully in large Neolithic villages and (although we seem now to have lost the knack) in urban civilizations. Overcrowding is not an abstract condition; it exists only in relationship to the resources available and exploitable at any given technological level.

Seen within this scientific framework, the most important effect of spacing mechanisms for human populations is not simply that they prevent overcrowding and competition, but that they relate the population meaningfully to the available resources. Spacing mechanisms promote an effective and equitable use of goods. This entails, first, easy access by all of the population. Second, it prevents over-exploitation of local stands of a particular resource. Third, and far less concretely, it enables individuals to develop a sentimental attachment to and to learn the assets and hazards of a particular home territory or home range, giving the individual security and letting him operate more efficiently by concentrating on truly important happenings while ignoring familiar routine stimuli of low communicative content. One should remember that spacing mechanisms are not synonymous with territoriality, the defense of a specific area by an individual or group of animals. Territoriality is but one possible spacing mechanism.

SPACING MECHANISMS IN MALAITA

In some ways, talk of overcrowding and a need for spacing mechanisms in Malaita sounds superfluous. Population in the bush is relatively sparse, and the rain forest regenerates quickly, restoring used garden land to adequate fertility. With little population pressure so far, land is virtually a free good. Given these conditions, it might be feasible for the population to agglomerate into large villages, abandoning the interior and other areas between settlements.

Nevertheless, there are perceivable advantages to a dispersed settlement pattern. For one thing, relative isolation inhibits the spread of communicable diseases. Vital statistics, birth and death records, are nonexistent, so it is not possible to speak precisely about causes of death. But Baegu parents worry more about infant diarrhea than about any other medical problem affecting their children. Children do die of dysentery or other diseases exhibiting symptomatic diarrhea and presumably caused by inadequate sanitation. Epidemiologically, the danger of death due to such diseases of poor hygiene should be less in smaller settlements where there is less likelihood of water and soil pollution, less chance of contamination by garbage and fecal matter, and plentiful water supplies for drinking, washing, and bathing. Scabies infestations are less common among Baegu children, who have easy access to fresh water for washing, than they are among children of the arid, offshore islands in the Lau Lagoon, where water must be laboriously hauled by canoes from the mainland. Albert Damon's (1969) 1968 medical survey found other evidence of differential disease incidence, presumably resulting from availability or scarcity of fresh water. Only 15 percent of the Baegu suffered from trachoma, whereas almost 100 percent of the Lau had the disease. Intestinal parasitism was only 75 percent for Baegu, yet again almost 100 percent for Lau. Tuberculosis, the Solomon Islands' current number two health problem after malaria, is known to be a disease of crowded conditions and close personal contact. Finally, epidemic respiratory diseases are greatly feared and a very real threat. In 1966 and 1970 death rates soared when pneumonia epidemics swept through the hill country. In prevailing cool, wet conditions, the Baegu people are highly susceptible to these diseases. A dispersed settlement pattern with less close personal contact retards the spread of such killer plagues.

Going beyond the disease field, Goodenough (1956a:174-75) suggests that secondary forest is considerably easier to clear for garden land than is primary rain forest. A bush fallowing agricultural economy could continue gardening in secondary growth areas by using an area intensively and for longer periods at a time, ignoring the unused primary forest. However, a population can give itself more flexibility by using a single plot for short periods of time, thus keeping more land spread over a wider area within the garden–secondary growth–garden regenerative cycle. The initial clearance investment is great, but future options are easily maintained this way when population is widely distributed. The advantages of having garden land spread over a wide area rather than concentrated in one spot are the classic ones accruing from not having all of one's eggs in a single basket. Hurricanes and the heavy rains accompanying them can, by flooding and land slumping, destroy gardens in a given area. But with planting done in a number of places, a population will probably always have some of its food supply spared in times of natural disaster. Taro blights or insect plagues can spread rapidly, destroying crops in areas they affect. Dispersed gardens, like dispersed settlements, may retard the spread of such plagues, and if gardens are planted in widely scattered sites, some fields will probably survive to provide emergency rations and future planting stock. The practice of gardening in scattered spots over a wide total area, and of keeping a seemingly excessive amount of land in the secondary growth stage of potential use, may be seen as a form of insurance or spreading the risk. It costs a bit more initially, but it creates flexibility and makes total loss less likely.

Customary marriage practices are also cultural things that have ecological significance in the sense that they, too, may serve to distribute or space a population suitably in respect to the resources available. Jean Peterson of the University of Hawaii studied the Agta people, sometimes called the Dumagat, of Luzon, Philippine Islands, intensively from 1968 to 1970. Curiously enough, some traits of these hunter-gatherers (such as their concepts of land title and their exogamous marital system) are uncannily like those of the horticultural Baegu, lending some credence to the speculations of Keesing and Keesing (1971:110), Heider (1967), and Watson (1965) concerning the subsistence basis of the early settlers of Melanesia. Part of Peterson's (1972) explanation of Agta marriage is that territorial exogamy gives children hunting rights in at least two land areas associated with at least two sets of kinsmen, paternal and maternal, whereas endogamous marriage would not accomplish this. Carried out for several generations, probably even more than two land areas would be involved. One can easily adapt her ideas to apply to the Baegu situation, where descent lines are customarily associated with territorial districts. The Baegu keep land title and land use rights conceptually and practically separate. Residual title to land "belongs" to the descent group associated with a plot or district, but a Baegu person has customary rights to forage on or to farm land associated with any of his kinsmen, agnatic or uterine (see Chapter 8). That is, if he or she is cognatically related to the land-owning corporation, he may use the land; put another way, land use rights are inherited bilineally. Exogamy means that (after a few generations) a person is cognatically related to at least two and possibly more descent groups and that he is apt to have remembered ancestors in several different clans, associated with several different districts of land. Endogamy would conversely limit a person's land use rights, since he would not have so many relatives or ancestors outside his own descent group. The Baegu view of land use rights (cognatically or bilineally defined) and their historic tendency toward patrilateral cross-cousin marriage and clan exogamy (see Table 15 in Chapter 7) mean that people will have options to use land in several areas, not just the area associated with their own descent groups. From the perspective of cultural ecology, therefore, exogamous marriage has selective or adaptive value, because it gives people the right to use the resources of other areas if their "own" area is unsuitable for either natural or cultural reasons. It enhances the whole population's chances of survival.

Then, too, there are intellectual and emotional reasons having a supernatural basis. Fertility of the soil, in Malaitan cosmology, depends on the will of the ancestral spirits. This good will is invoked by the living (by means of sacrifices and elaborate ceremonies) from ancestors buried in sacred groves, where the spirits reside, scattered over the entire hill country. Ancestral spirits are especially concerned with the areas in the vicinity of their own sacred grove. Living people worship and sacrifice to the ancestors of the sacred grove near where they live and work. As the Baegu see it, when settlements are widely dispersed, all the groves are attended and all the important spirits remembered, insuring complete supernatural coverage. If people were to abandon an area, concentrating in other spots, some ancestral spirits might be forgotten. These would become wild ghosts (*akalo kwasi*), unremembered, malevolent, and uninterested in the well-being of the land and the people. Hence for the Baegu it is wise for people to share the ritual burden and to keep as many shrines in an active status as they can. They do this by living and gardening in a dispersed pattern.

There is finally a questionable, somewhat negative argument. Although horticultural people may not need vast areas of land, there is

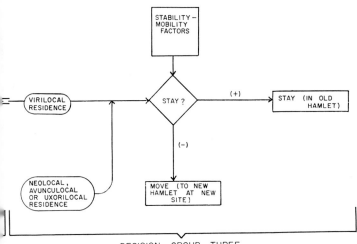

STABILITY—
MOBILITY
FACTORS

STAY ?

(+)

STAY (IN OLD
HAMLET)

(−)

VIRILOCAL
RESIDENCE

NEOLOCAL,
AVUNCULOCAL
OR UXORILOCAL
RESIDENCE

MOVE (TO NEW
HAMLET AT NEW
SITE)

DECISION GROUP THREE
(STABILITY — MOBILITY AXIS)

Figure 41. Residential Decisions (Baegu Females)

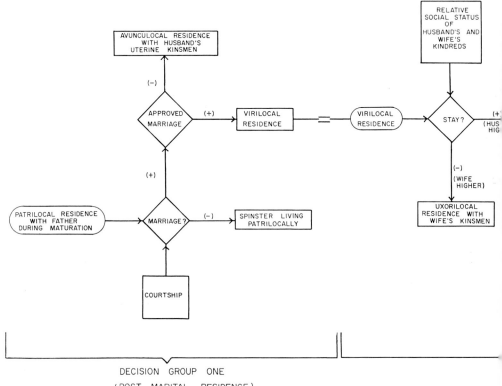

AVUNCULOCAL RESIDENCE
WITH HUSBAND'S
UTERINE KINSMEN

RELATIVE
SOCIAL STATUS
OF
HUSBAND'S AND
WIFE'S
KINDREDS

(−)

APPROVED
MARRIAGE

(+)

VIRILOCAL
RESIDENCE

VIRILOCAL
RESIDENCE

STAY ?

(+
(HUS
HIG

(+)

(−)
(WIFE
HIGHER)

PATRILOCAL RESIDENCE
WITH FATHER
DURING MATURATION

MARRIAGE ?

(−)

SPINSTER LIVING
PATRILOCALLY

UXORILOCAL
RESIDENCE WITH
WIFE'S KINSMEN

COURTSHIP

DECISION GROUP ONE
(POST − MARITAL RESIDENCE)

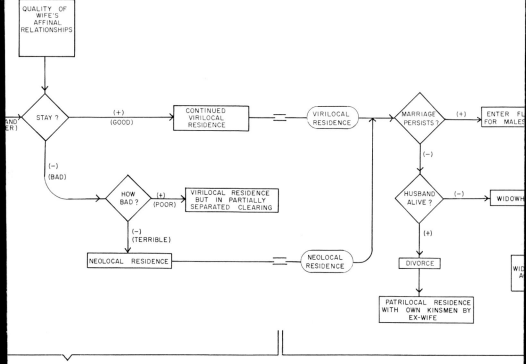

DECISION GROUP TWO

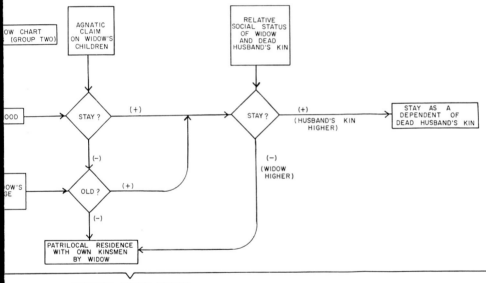

DECISION GROUP THREE

at the same time no reason for them to concentrate in larger settlements (smaller areas) just because they are farmers. But a hunting or
gathering people may actually need larger areas. A dispersed settlement
pattern, such as that found in the Baegu hills, may be a way of maintaining foraging rights over larger areas for use in times of hardship,
or it may be a conservative remnant of conditions from an era when
hunting and gathering were of more importance than they are today.
Wild pigs, birds, small game, and wild plant foods can be important
auxiliary food sources. Bulmer and Bulmer's (1964:73) archaeological
work in the New Guinea Highlands suggests that Melanesia may have
been settled before agriculture was the dominant economic pattern.
Watson (1965) and Heider (1967) have suggested that some unusual
features of Highland social structure may reflect a greater importance
of hunting and gathering in the not-too-distant past. Thus, because it
perhaps once had functional value, because of its possible present or
future contingency use, and because there is no pressing reason to
change, a dispersed settlement pattern in interior Melanesian areas
may be seen as having some adaptive value for other than agricultural
activities.

In summary, there is good reason to assume that Melanesian groups
living in interior, mountainous areas would benefit from a dispersed
settlement pattern. Therefore, they need spacing mechanisms that
create and maintain this dispersion.

SPACING MECHANISMS AND CULTURE

But even given this need for spacing mechanisms, human ecology,
social organization, and territorial behavior differ significantly from
what they are among other animal species. Men, for example, cannot
space themselves and defend their territories by urinating along its
borders or erecting a feather crest; they do not do so by singing, building nests, or attacking all visitors. The obvious answer is that human
beings distribute themselves in ways they see as proper, and maintain
this spacing, by cultural means. Human spacing mechanisms are part
of our cultural belief and value systems.

There are several noteworthy unique characteristics of human behavior in this domain of socio-territorial or spacing behavior. Human
social and territorial boundaries are relatively permeable. Unlike ba-
boons, human beings can leave an old group and join another with
relative ease, or migrate from one geographic area to another. Tour-
ism, trade, and conquest are to some extent pan-human traits. Perhaps
more important, we can fiddle with our own systems. We can define

territorial or social boundaries to suit ourselves. We can modify or negotiate as we see fit, and we can invent.

If modern anthropology is right in either a logical or a practical sense, "culture" is categories and rules for behavior of a very general nature, and the profoundly significant character of these cultural rules is that as a system they are generative. Having learned the system, a person can in any situation generate culturally appropriate behavior, just as in language a speaker can in any situation generate novel yet correct sentences. Cultural rules, like language, while not innate in any specific form, are species-specific human behavior in that we all have an inborn capacity to create, learn, and use them; that no other known species can do so; and that in the course of normal development all human beings do in fact do so. They are not innate in the sense of being specific responses that we are programmed to produce, elicited by given releasing stimuli; and for that matter they are, as Chomsky (1959:54-58) argues for language (other than specific vocabulary or grammatical paradigms), very unlikely to be learned by conditioning. The beauty of this sort of structure for behavior is that it is flexible; we can create new arrangements, permutations, or transformations if there is need to do so. As a corollary to this, specific rules or rule systems can, like languages, exist in almost infinite variety.

SPACING MECHANISMS FOR HUMAN POPULATIONS

If human spacing mechanisms are in large part cultural rather than morphological, physiological, or simply behavioral, then they must share some of the characteristics of other cultural systems such as language. Although not innate in any given form, they should be of a form species-specific to man. They should, as Chomsky (1957:49-60) argues linguistically, be ultimately reducible to rules that can be applicable to novel situations, according the structurally proper transformations or manipulations. They should, as Levi-Strauss or Chomsky might argue, concord in a general way with the ultimate structural realities of the culture, and they should perhaps in specific instances, as Hymes (1961) argues for specific languages, have some adaptive value.

Anthropologists have always been aware that human residence was in large measure a culturally determined fact, that it was not random, and that residence rules both had some value in distributing or assigning people and in turn could be affected by social or ecological realities. But anthropologists have by and large looked at such problems only in bits and pieces. Social anthropologists write down residence rules, demographers look for significant trends in population arrangement, and archaeologists write about settlement patterns. With this much interest in the subject already extant, it seems that a logical approach would be to attack all of these problems as a single system, which in fact they are.

Since residence rules are part of the sphere of influence of social anthropologists, it may be logical to begin with them. The antique approach was, unfortunately, to reduce the whole problem to the terse statement that a society was patrilocal or matrilocal. This was concrete enough to warm the cockles of any compulsive's heart, but such terminology was nonproductive and proved to be inadequate to account for complex, real situations. Murdock (1949:16-21) provided a much expanded vocabulary for describing residence but remained within the older tradition. British social anthropologists, having spent more time with the classics as school boys than Americans do, gave us "virilocal" and "uxorilocal," more satisfactory in many ways but still not radically new. Critical reexamination of anthropological residence rules began seriously in the 1950's. Working with the U.S. Navy administration in the newly established Trust Territory of the Pacific (Micronesia), Fischer (1958:508-17) stressed the inadequacy of traditional residence rules. He pointed out, first, that they were meaningless unless one specified precisely the person and context intended. Who, for example, is living with whose father in "patrilocal" residence? While a man may be in fact living patrilocally, his wife is living not with her father (she did that before marriage), but virilocally with her husband. Even finessing this problem and granting that someone somewhere is at home with father, context or level of analysis remains important. Does "patrilocal" residence mean in the same house, the same village, neighborhood, or district? What may appear to be neolocal residence at the village level may be patrilocal residence on a district level of analysis. Fischer further explained that the rule for residence changed during a person's life span, children living with their parents, spouses with each other, and aged parents with their offspring. During the same time period, Goodenough (1956b:30-34) argued from his experiences in Truk that residence rules were more complex than simple statements of where people live. He felt that they should be phrased as rules about where a person ought to live. Arguing from Gilbertese data, he decided that descriptions of residential patterns must take into account multiple factors. As he demonstrated, residence rules were far from firm and were intimately bound up with land tenure, population density, descent-group prestige, and inheritance of traditional rights (Goodenough 1955: 77-83). Frake's (1962) milestone paper resulting from his work in Mindanao showed that residence rules properly ought not be stated

Plate 20. A serious small boy in the crowd at a Masu clan mortuary feast (*maoma*).

simply in terms of where a person should live. Using an ethnoscientific approach to see things as the Subanun see them, Frake (1962:57-58) showed that actual residence resulted from a formal set of postulates that served as guides to making decisions maximizing certain ecological and cultural values.

Following Frake's basic ideas, residence in Northern Malaita is a result of choice based on multiple factors: economic, social, personal, and supernatural. Real people consider these inputs when making their own decisions about where they should live. From studying and analyzing these decisions, made by many people in many situations at many times, an ethnographer can formulate residence rules. These rules may or may not be explictly stated or recognized by the people themselves. The Baegu, for example, are as bad about residence as social anthropologists have been. They simply ignore exceptions and complexities and say, "We live with our fathers and brothers."

If the folk themselves err on the side of oversimplification, we can easily err in the other direction. After a year and a half in the field and two years spent wrestling with the problem, my minimum of seven formal rules for Baegu residence cannot begin to approach Frake's three rules in elegance and parsimony. These seven rules express explicit Baegu norms and values, account for most of the observable characteristics of Baegu residence, and include the implicit economic, social, personal, and supernatural factors described above. They are:

1. Remember the ancestors;
2. Avoid contamination by women;
3. Use the land properly;
4. Maintain the distinction between nature and culture;
5. Maintain agnatic solidarity, yet recognize cognatic rights;
6. Provide for cooperation and hospitality; and
7. At the same time, provide for the individual's right to privacy, diminish the scope of quarreling and conflict, and avoid the supernatural dangers of too much social contact.

Using this system of rules as a guide, Baegu people make residential decisions: what rights or property to claim by gardening and housebuilding, where to build a settlement and when to move it, and with whom to live. The settlement pattern (how people live relative to one another and relative to the land itself) that an ethnographer sees results from the sum of individual decisions made according to these cultural residence rules. For the Baegu, this means:

1. In named districts, titularly owned by a semi-localized patrilineal descent group, utilized by an agnatic core of that descent group plus affiliated cognatic or affinal kinsmen, and focused about

shrines where the ancestors are buried and where their living descendants worship (rules 1, 2, 3, and 5) ;

2. In widely scattered hamlets of an "optimum" size (sometimes grouped in vague neighborhoods), large enough for cooperation and solidarity but not so big as to be annoying or dangerous, and spaced so as to provide easy access to resources (rules 3, 6, and 7) ;
3. In hamlets that are occasionally moved, peopled by a core of agnatic kinsmen having a semisacred men's house (rules 1, 5, and 6) ;
4. In hamlets with a distinct physical and cognitive separation between the sexes (rules 1, 2, and 7) ; and
5. In sharply defined, well-cleared hamlets with equally well-cared-for gardens (rules 1, 3, and 4).

In summary, settlement patterns and residence rules are the spatial dimension of social organization. Settlement patterns, the empirical reality that the ethnographer sees, result from individual decisions. These decisions, placing people on the landscape in rational and predictable patterns, are made in accordance with explicit or implicit residence rules. Rules may normatively specify a particular type of residence, but more likely they express values or guidelines for choices. They take into account (in simplified or codified form) economic, social, personal, and supernatural factors important in the specific cultural-ecological situation. The whole system (culturally important factors, residence rules, residential decisions, and settlement pattern) is cybernetic or goal-seeking in nature and is in effect a human spacing mechanism. Spacing mechanisms in human populations, as for all natural populations, have adaptive ecological value. But human spacing mechanisms are complex cultural systems rather than physiological, morphological, or behavioral ones. As cultural systems they, like language, are structured, generative or productive, and almost infinitely variable.

13. Summary and Conclusions

A concluding summary is inherently redundant. If the message is not clear after several hundred pages, there is little hope of communicating much by tacking a few more pages on at the end. Its function is perhaps more aesthetic than informative. A concluding summary, like a musical coda, recapitulates and closes the argument. It goes back to the introduction, runs over the recurrent themes again, hits the conclusions to stress them, and crashes into a finale.

The introduction anticipated both specific and general conclusions. For the specific Malaitan case, one should have expected a description of spatial and residential behavior among the Baegu in the mountains of northern Malaita, an analysis of how such behavior develops and how observable patterns come to be, and an explanation of why such patterns are functional or utilitarian. In the more general case, the problems to be manipulated were the nature of residence rules and settlement patterns, how human beings can create and maintain satisfactory population distribution, and the efficacy of a single-dimensional (the spatial) approach to ethnographic description and analysis, particularly for sorting out complex situations where social relations involve multiple ideologies.

Five comprehensive statements summarize Baegu settlement patterns, the overt manifestations of residential behavior. The Baegu hill country is divided into named districts, titularly owned by semi-localized patrilineal descent groups, utilized by an agnatic core of that descent group plus affiliated cognatic or affinal kinsmen, and focused about shrines where the ancestors are buried and where their living descendants worship. The hill people live in scattered small hamlets with a mean size of eight to sixteen people (that are sometimes vaguely grouped into neighborhoods), large enough for cooperation and solidarity but not so big as to be annoying or supernaturally dangerous, and spread so as to avoid overcrowding and to provide all with easy access to available resources. Hamlets, which are occasionally moved, usually contain a core of agnatically related males and have a semi-sacred men's house. Bush people observe a distinct physical and metaphysical separation between the sexes. Hamlets and gardens are sharply defined from the surrounding forest and are generally well cared for and neatly maintained.

Baegu residential behavior, and the resultant settlement patterns, are complex but rational cultural processes. In making residential decisions and carrying them out, they explicitly or implicity consider several factors or inputs. Economic factors include presence and accessibility of resources and desirable settlement site characteristics. Social factors include kinship obligations, cooperation, hospitality, and patron-client relationships. Personal or psychological factors include personal ambition, competition and rivalry, love of privacy, aesthetic standards, and the likelihood of quarrels. Supernatural factors involve beliefs about ancestral spirits, ritual obligations, the taboo system, fear of male-female interaction, and a nature-culture dichotomy.

On the basis of such multiple considerations, Baegu people make residential decisions. In electing what land rights to claim (choosing what spirits to honor), they connect themselves to a ritual-residential community in a particular district or neighborhood. At various times in their lives, they must decide where to locate a settlement and when to move a hamlet to a new site. They also face the problems of deciding whether they should remain with a given residential group, or alternatively if they should split off to found a new, smaller hamlet elsewhere.

Although no one really knows what goes on in the mind of an individual when he makes a decision, it is possible to describe abstractly typical residential decisions by means of utility curves and to put these together in logical flow charts. The simple decision models represent the various factors or criteria as multiple inputs with a single output (the decision) resulting from cumulative, algebraic manipulation of the various utilities used in the model. The logical flow charts sequentially describe how the various decisions go together and result in varying residential behavior during a typical Baegu individual's life span.

Baegu people do not behave according to a single residential rule that specifies where they should live. Instead, they observe several rules that relate to residential behavior. These "residence rules" contain a sort of folk wisdom expressing Baegu norms or values concerning economic, social, personal, and supernatural factors relating to residence. As a set these rules are a practical guide to the making of residential decisions maximizing the values inherent in the system. Baegu rules (which they either verbalize or agree with) are: remember the ancestors, avoid contamination by women, use the land properly, maintain the distinction between nature and culture, maintain agnatic solidarity and cognatic rights, provide for cooperation and hospitality, and at the same time avoid the social and supernatural hazards of overcrowding while providing for individual rights to privacy. The end result of these processes, distributing the population over the landscape, is the characteristic Baegu settlement pattern.

The whole array of norms and values, specific cultural interpretations of the various factors, decision-making processes, residence rules, land tenure, and settlement patterns is best seen as a single system that is in effect a human spacing mechanism. For the Baegu, as for all people, residential behavior and settlement patterns are traditional adaptations to local ecological conditions. The people live on and use their land in ways that are most satisfying and most efficient.

In the Baegu case, this involves equitable distribution over the whole range of their communal territory, assuring relatively easy access (roughly half an hour's walk) for all to the most desirable garden land and reducing competition for good hamlet and house sites. Perhaps even more important to the Baegu, on a theological level it ensures that all the ancestors (who first settled the land and whose spirits are responsible for its continuing fertility and productivity) will be remembered, honored, and pacified. Widespread settlement coupled with a short period of use for each plot maintains soil fertility and assures that there will be plenty of easily cleared secondary growth in many areas potentially available for new gardens. Having many small gardens in many places increases flexibility and minimizes the chances of loss from natural catastrophes such as floods, landslides, or blights. Exogamic marriage and cognatic definition of land use rights maximize alternative options and flexibility in land exploitation.

The size range for Baegu hamlets (eight to sixteen people) balances several ecological advantages. Being above minimum size, they provide for common defense, mutual cooperation, adequate division of labor, and the satisfaction of kinship and political obligations. Being below maximum size, they offer easy access to available resources, reduce the danger of disease caused by poor sanitation, inhibit the spread of highly communicable respiratory disease, reduce the threat of ritual pollution, reduce social tensions, and provide opportunities for individual privacy.

The construction of typical hamlets, by separating males and females, reduces the supernatural dangers of inadvertent male-female contact. "Proper" construction plus good maintenance insures that human culture (things *fera*) is adequately defined and distinguished from wild, uncultured nature (things *kwasi*).

There is also utilitarian value in moving to a new site from time to time. In this way the Baegu avoid actual pollution from garbage, fecal matter, flies, and disease organisms. Increasing ritual pollution and taboo violation make an old site supernaturally dangerous, requiring expensive sacrifices. Increasing depreciation of houses may make repairs unduly expensive. Eventually it becomes more economical simply to abandon the old and move to a new location.

Leaving the specific Baegu of Malaita case and turning now to general conclusions about human nature, we should ask what general interest implications one can find in the Malaitan information.

First, one could conclude that it is most realistic to interpret the whole range of norms and values relevant to land, space, and residence, customary land tenure, residential decision-making processes, much of spatial behavior, residence rules, and settlement patterns not as discrete pieces of behavior but as a single system of residential behavior. Settlement patterns, essentially empirical or statistical phenomena, are the observable distribution of people over the landscape relative to natural, social, and supernatural resources that the ethnographer or prehistorian can see and verify. Residence rules are largely a social scientific construct. They rarely exist as explicit statements of where people ought to live; if they do, they are too abstract or too simplistic (ignoring valid exceptions and acceptable deviance) to be useful. Frake's model is probably correct in that ethographically valid residence rules are multiple, the multiple rules form a coherent subsystem, and they rarely apply directly to a single specific decision about where to live. Such rules contain culturally accepted norms, values, and folk beliefs about conditions relevant to the problem of where people ought to live. Operationally, people use these rules in making decisions about where to live, with whom to live, and when to move. If residence rules are explicit or manifest, they contain a succinct distillation of locally accepted knowledge, and people may use them overtly as guides to decision-making. If residence rules are implicit or latent, they reflect certain evaluations about economic, ecological, social, personal, and supernatural factors. People still act on the basis of these cultural beliefs, but the ethnographer has to infer and state the rule. In making residential decisions, people act to maximize the multiple (sometimes contradictory) values inherent in the set of rules with a single "best" decision. Many decisions made many times by many individuals are typical residential behavior and generate settlement patterns.

A second justifiable conclusion is that the whole system of residential behavior functions as a human spacing mechanism, having much the same adaptive value for human populations as spacing mechanisms do for other species. Their value in human ecology is that in various places in various ways they distribute a population over its range relative to the available resources in such a way as to limit intrapopulation competition to acceptable levels and to assure adequate access by individuals to the resource base. If they do not, the system will fail because of external pressures or internal revolution. This gives the population ecological flexibility and permits satisfactory development of behavioral, social, and cultural patterns. For human populations, optimum size and distribution is defined both by given natural conditions and by cultural interpretations of those conditions.

A further conclusion is that human spacing mechanisms are not direct ecological responses but processes acting through cultural media. If perceived natural and social conditions are exogenous factors, norms, values, and beliefs are cultural and endogenous inputs to the decision-making process. In this sense cultural factors are at once input, process, and output. The whole system of residential behavior operates in many ways, as do so many systems of human behavior, in a quasi-linguistic manner, perhaps a species-specific characteristic we all share. Fitting residential behavior to a procrustean linguistic model, residence rules are a "grammar" for using a "morphophonemics" composed of architectural elements and forms. Specific values, norms, beliefs, and cultural assumptions pertaining to residential and spatial problems are analogically the contextual constraints of this "language" of residential behavior. Individual decisions are in metaphor the utterances in this grammar; collectively they form settlement patterns, the corpus of data. In making residential decisions, people use an architectural vocabulary and a grammar of residence rules (affected by context) that make their decisions and behavior both predictable and generative. That is, they will behave in acceptable, understandable ways even in novel situations. The resulting settlement patterns (synchronic view), or ongoing residential and spatial behavior (diachronic view), are then the end products of the language itself.

This "language" of residential behavior communicates to the people themselves. It communicates "correct" behavior, predictable in the sense that it is within a culturally defined range of acceptable or normal (as opposed to eccentric) behavior, and "correct" furthermore because it establishes a satisfactory relationship between society and its environment and spatially among the members of the society. It communicates to the ethnographer, enabling him to understand within one small domain the rules of the culture and the transformational gram-

Plate 21. Baegu children along a forest trail leaving Langane Mountain.

mar by means of which native "speakers" of the "language" use them in regular, productive ways. And in a sense it also communicates on an impersonal level within the ecosystem itself. Human ecosystems (population, culture, and total environment) are at least in part cybernetic mechanisms, for they are goal oriented, partially self-aware, and in a pinch can be redirected to achieve these goals. Adjustments can be made in the system by redefining the goal, by tinkering with the perceptions of self-awareness of the system (its own acuity in comparing present with desired state), or by modifying the means for attaining goals. Residential behavior, being concerned simultaneously with goals, perceptions, and means, is therefore crucial to the internal flow of communication and to the operation of the entire system.

A final bit of information that settlement patterns, residential behavior, and spatial behavior communicate to the ethnographer is the parameters of the spatial dimension of social organization or, if you prefer, social structure. One way of grappling with the beast is to attack it one dimension at a time; in this case, the spatial dimension. Social interaction and the whole pattern of social relations have a spatial dimension. Communities are anchored in space by their land tenure, their settlement patterns, their residential behavior, and the geographical aspects of their cosmology. Constrained by physical reality, people assume spatial relationships with one another when they interact.

Theoretically it might be possible to come to understand the whole social system in terms of one dimension. There are many dimensions or aspects to social organization; emotions, economic transactions, and terminology (to name a few) are other equally valid and in some ways more relevant dimensions. But there is a satisfying (albeit perhaps illusory) solidity to the idea of concentrating on physical space and spatial relations that reassures by its familiar and commonsense three-dimensional guise. This empirical bias comes out in anthropology by appeals to concentrate on understanding the behavior of people "on the ground." It should be apparent that this can be overly simplistic, for one can be too concrete. It is patently impossible to describe adequately the trees of so complex a thing as social organization without invoking the abstract forest of structure. The underlying idea is that if we can understand the pattern on the ground, we can by approaching along one dimension sneak up and grab at least a piece of social structure before it eludes us. (The so-called cognitive approach to culture and language in modern anthropology and linguistics seems to preclude the ultimate success of discovery techniques and total empiricism, however.)

This assay at ethnography has therefore marshaled its evidence in terms of the spatial dimension: ecology, folk geography, and cosmology;

land tenure, spatial behavior, settlement patterns, residential behavior, and, where social behavior was concerned, its spatial aspects. If this kind of approach has scientific merit, it should provide some illuminating insights into Baegu social organization. It should, within the limitation of its admittedly parochial approach, offer a reasonable way to approach structure and think about confusing systems where both classical unilineal and nonunilineal (or cognatic) ideologies really do seem to matter.

In ethnographic summary a few salient points emerge. Seen from a conventional social anthropological point of view that makes a frontal assault on social organization, the Baegu are structurally biased toward patrilineality with their emphasis on titular ownership of land by patrilineal descent groups and by their emphasis on agnatic solidarity in social interaction. This is also true statistically, for most residential units do indeed have as their core a group of agnatically related persons who numerically outnumber their other coresidents. Yet a close look at the ramifications of land tenure and use and at social and ritual patterns as related to settlements reveals that, both jurally and ideologically, cognatic relatives have very real rights and are full members by right (not tolerance) of the community. They use land and sacrifice to the ancestral spirits with full rights to do so.

It would be misleading to say that the Baegu are agnatic, because this would obscure the obvious rights of cognates in the community. Agnate "owners" have no power to deny use of land by non-agnatic relatives; agnatic "ownership" is titular. It would be equally wrong to say they are a cognatic society, because this would ignore their very obvious and real agnatic bias. People or whole societies are neither unilineal nor cognatic. As it seems to work out, in some contexts (titular land ownership and automatic ritual community membership) rights and obligations based on agnatic descent or relationships are paramount. In other contexts (rights to use the land for residence or gardening) cognatic relationships and thinking are more important.

Perhaps this answer would have appeared in any case eventually, but in this instance a single-dimensional (spatial) approach proved highly useful. For a farming people land is obviously important. By examining spatial problems (land tenure and residence) intensively, it became clear that whereas titular ownership was through the ancestral spirit cult intimately bound up with patrilineal descent, within the context of use of the land for residence and gardening cognatic descent was the relevant consideration, for no one can effectively prevent a cognatic relative from exercising his rights.

A one-dimensional ethnographic description is a long way from being an adequate portrayal of a way of life. That will take a much fuller ethnography ("complete" ethnographies do not exist), and that is still a long time in the future. After all, the Baegu spend a lifetime learning Baegu culture. In a way this has been an exploratory essay to see if an analysis focusing on one dimension can, by simplifying and reducing things, help clarify anthropological problems. On the one hand, a pedestrian approach to behavior "on the ground" keeps one's feet firmly there — but, on the other, it is frightfully easy to bog down in the mud that ground offers. The ultimate criterion for judging anthropological worth would obviously be a test in the field: to generate "proper" Baegu behavior based on principles stated in the ethnography that would be accepted as such by the world's most qualified experts, the Baegu people themselves. This can be and has been done for specific hypotheses, but even the most generous patron balks at spending for large-scale practical testing. The only feasible criteria remain those always available to learned men: does the ethnographic description (within its own limited realm) make sense, and does it give promise by its insights and results of being a fruitful way to approach future anthropological problems?

Appendix A: Baegu Phonology

Since the standard typewriter keyboard and printers' typefaces were not designed for linguists, it has been necessary to modify International Phonetic Alphabet notation for use in this monograph. Unless a modifying clause indicates otherwise, typewritten symbols correspond to the phonetic characteristics indicated in the following table.

While speech patterns tend to be fairly rapid, most people's pronunciation is precise, with syllables being clearly enunciated and easily separable. With a very few exceptions, the penultimate syllable is lightly accented.

Typewritten symbol	Phonetic symbol
a	a
e	ɛ
i	i
o	o
u	u
aa	a; elongation with phonemic value
ee	ɛ; elongation with phonemic value
ii	i; elongation with phonemic value
oo	o; elongation with phonemic value
uu	u; elongation with phonemic value
b	b; pre-nasalized $_m$b
d	d; pre-nasalized $_n$d
f	f; sometimes /v/ in free variation in other than initial position
g	g; pre-nasalized $_n$g
gw	g; highly labialized g^w
k	k
kw	k; highly labialized k^w
l	l; clear apico-dental form
m	m
n	n
ng	ŋ
r	r; apical trill
s	s
t	t
w	w; pre-nasalized as ŋw by many persons
'	ʔ; glottal stop

Appendix B: Baegu Census Data

The sample area where I did my intensive census work and where I knew nearly all of the residents at least slightly includes the population inhabiting the Sasafa River drainage basin and the central massif or ridge overlooking the Sasafa Valley from the center of the island (Map B-1).

Although I have tried my best to be careful, there may be a few cases where figures given in the text or in Table B-1 do not correspond exactly with those recorded in the hamlet-by-hamlet headcounts. These are probably

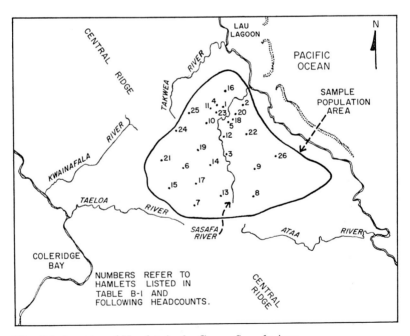

Map B-1. Location of Hamlets in the Census Sample Area

errors of omission, where I have revised (because of additional knowledge acquired later) classifications made on the scene and often on the spur of the moment, and which I forgot to note in revised form. I doubt that any such inconsistencies will be of sufficient magnitude to be statistically significant.

I came to know the people here gradually over my two-year period in the field (1966-68), learning their biological, social, and residential relationships to one another. I accomplished the actual census (physical enumeration) of the people during a one-week period in June, 1968.

Table B-1 summarizes census data for the sample area. Tables B-2 and B-3 are organized according to religious affiliation and altitude of hamlets there. Headcounts of hamlet residents (as of June, 1968) conclude Appendix B.

TABLE B-1. SUMMARY TABLE OF CENSUS DATA

	Approximate altitude in feet	Approximate miles from the sea	Religion	Households	Population
1. Abuisaia	1,000	2	SSEC	5	26
2. Adomose	500	1	SSEC	3	10
3. Ai'aofia	1,000	3	PAGAN	6	21
4. Ailali	500	2	MM	21	93
5. Anoketo	1,000	2	MM	12	49
6. Ao'ana	3,000	6	PAGAN	4	13
7. Borumalakwa	2,500	5	PAGAN	7	22
8. Faakwao'abu	2,000	3	PAGAN	6	20
9. Fatakalie	2,000	3	PAGAN	10	28
10. Fauboso	1,500	3	PAGAN	3	17
11. Faukwakwaoa	1,000	2	SDA	9	30
12. Fera'inomae	1,000	3	PAGAN	2	10
13. Gwaikabarai	2,000	4	PAGAN	4	13
14. Gwaikiri	2,000	4	PAGAN	8	28
15. Gwasumoko	3,000	6	PAGAN	2	6
16. Kafo'ote'ote	500	2	SSEC	3	7
17. Kilie	3,000	6	PAGAN	1	8
18. Liufania	500	3	MM	1	3
19. Maelanafe	2,500	5	PAGAN	3	12
20. Matakwadolo	500	3	MM	2	6
21. Ngali'abu	3,000	6	PAGAN	2	9
22. Ngaliana'ago	2,000	2	PAGAN	2	9
23. Ngalianarufo	1,000	2	SSEC	7	32
24. Ngalifulibeu	2,500	5	PAGAN	5	22
25. Ngalikwao	1,500	3	PAGAN	5	20
26. Rue	2,500	2	PAGAN	3	9
Totals				136	523

TABLE B-2. BREAKDOWN OF POPULATION BY RELIGION

	Population	
Religious affiliation	Subtotals	Totals
Christians.		256
MM — Melanesian Mission (Anglican).	151	
SSEC — South Seas Evangelical Church (Fundamentalist Protestants).	75	
SDA — Seventh Day Adventists.	30	
Pagans.		267
		523

TABLE B-3. BREAKDOWN OF POPULATION BY HAMLET ALTITUDE

Approximate altitude	Pagans	Christians	Total population
3,000 ft.	36	0	36
2,500 ft.	65	0	65
2,000 ft.	98	0	98
1,500 ft.	37	0	37
1,000 ft.	31	137	168
500 ft.	0	119	119
Totals.	267	256	523

TABLE B-4. HEADCOUNTS OF HAMLET RESIDENTS IN JUNE, 1968

Hamlet numbers are the same as in Map B-1 and Table B-1. Households are those who share a cooking hearth. Hamlet headmen (an informal status) are marked by an asterisk (*). Heads of households are listed first.

1. ABUISAIA HAMLET

Household	Name	Sex	Estimated age	Comments
a.	Lebekona	M	34	
	Tafiela	F	31	
	Aralifu	F	8	
	Mamuela	M	5	
	Gesuna	F	2	
b.	*Wasi	M	48	Plantation laborer in Guadalcanal.
	Saloe	F	44	
	Jackie	M	18	At school in Honiara.
	Siana	F	16	
	Anisi	M	15	
	Diki	M	10	
	Ofata	M	6	

Household	Name	Sex	Estimated age	Comments
c.	Bulasimanu	M	42	
	Sarai	F	38	
	Lida	M	13	
	Orofaia	F	11	
	Wasi	M	7	
	Lifuta	M	11 mos.	
d.	Kwaona	M	47	Wife is dead.
	Fiu	M	18	At school in Honiara.
	Leta	F	15	
	Lina	F	10	
e.	Reboi	M	49	
	Oolo	F	41	
	Salome	F	6	
	Meke	M	2	

2. ADOMOSE HAMLET

a.	*Mae'otoa	M	42	
	Melita	F	40	
	Sasae	F	10	
b.	Diake	M	36	
	Lifuta	F	30	
	Rafisi	F	5	
	Oeta	M	4 mos.	
c.	Alaia	F	72	Husband is dead.
	Lamaua	F	67	Husband is dead.
	Mugonasau	F	58	Husband is dead.

3. AI'AOFIA HAMLET

a.	Erekona	M	28	
	Rosina	F	25	
	Eteli	F	2	
b.	Ege	M	33	Wife is dead.
	Siuana	F	8	
c.	Raralasa	M	36	
	Gaeli	F	34	
	Beni	M	9	
	Ngasi	F	6	
	Igi	M	2	
d.	*Beni	M	60	Wife is dead.
	Otaofia	M	16	
	Rakoegau	F	7	
e.	Gwaena	F	26	Husband is dead.
	Furikona	M	10	
	Ramokalia	M	6	
	Dioi	F	2	

Household	Name	Sex	Estimated age	Comments
f.	Sauka	F	38	Husband is dead.
	Faiga	M	12	
	Ngangale	F	4	
	Afuna	F	14 mos.	

4. AILALI VILLAGE

Household	Name	Sex	Estimated age	Comments
a.	Sedea	M	75	First wife is dead.
	Kwaliola	F	65	Baelelea woman.
	Lisa	F	4	Adopted child; daughter of Maeuria of Ngalifulibeu by her first husband.
b.	Bulasimanu	M	65	
	Toosimaoma	F	64	
	Fito	M	26	Plantation laborer in Guadalcanal.
	Alanaua	F	24	
c.	Lebefiu	M	55	
	Tolelangi	F	45	
	Singiala	M	20	
	Samson	M	17	Plantation laborer in New Georgia.
	Sure'au	M	14	
	Iluela	M	10	
	Dautoa	F	2	
	Laugau	F	80	Husband is dead; mother of Tolelangi.
	Soeti	M	19	Orphan.
d.	Bauro	M	45	
e.	*Dongofoa	M	50	
	Kikimae	F	45	
	Teteau	M	19	
	Feralao	M	8	
	Lemenari	F	4	
f.	Meke	M	28	
	Minarii	F	25	
	Taefalu	M	11 mos.	
	Maomara	F	48	Husband is dead; mother of Meke.
	Fulaga	M	19	Orphan.
g.	Kwaomata	M	55	
	Dautoa	F	38	
	Maasiala	F	18	
	Lauga	M	12	At school in Auki.
	Delite	F	6	
	Sedea	M	4	
	Roboniu	M	1	

Household	Name	Sex	Estimated age	Comments
h.	Ausolo	M	48	
	Barafarii	F	41	
	Isiga	M	20	
	Siusau	F	17	
	Fereti Tu'u	F	11	
	Ami	M	8	
	Aumo'oe	F	1 mo.	
i.	Matakwa	M	26	
	Saulifoia	F	26	
	Hilda Mary	F	3	
j.	Alasia	M	43	Wife is dead.
	Renegau	F	14	
	Maomagwao	F	10	
	Benjamin	M	6	
	Veronica	F	4	
k.	Basia	M	48	First wife is dead.
	Sasoke	F	39	First husband is dead.
	Robert	M	19	Laborer in Honiara.
	Mamunia	F	10–11	
	Sauisita	F	9	
	Niuga	M	6	
l.	Oiakalo	M	31	
	Lisi	F	28	
	Kwangainau	M	2	
	Dingariko	F	2 wks.	
m.	Kwanafia	M	58	
	Borosau	F	54	
	Robert	M	28	Laborer in Auki.
	Fereti	F	16	
n.	Faukona	M	47	
	Takadau	F	45	
	Alasia	M	20	Plantation laborer in Guadalcanal.
	Aumo'oe	F	18	
	Takasa	F	3	
o.	Kwaga	M	44	
	Dingariko	F	37	Toabaita woman.
	Ofena	F	14	
	Taloe	M	12	
	Otaiwai	M	7	
	Niuga Tu'u	M	4	

Household	Name	Sex	Estimated age	Comments
p.	Fiusi	M	42	In hospital at Uru.
	U'uga	F	37	
	Sangota	F	14	
	Faukona	M	12	At school in Auki.
	Kwanafia	M	8	
	Sarania	M	4	
	Basi	M	18 mos.	
q.	Otaiwai	M	28	
	Roda	F	25	
	Singiala	M	2 mos.	
r.	Waniga	M	34	
	Suta	F	29	
s.	Lofe'au	F	57	Husband is dead.
	Kalefaka	F	18	
t.	Afuga	M	62	Plantation laborer in New Georgia.
	Angisibeu	F	59	
	Saunaua	F	21	

5. ANOKETO VILLAGE

Household	Name	Sex	Estimated age	Comments
a.	Furikona	M	55	
	Saungara	F	53	
	Sauala	F	27	
	Oruaramo	F	25	
b.	*Joe Sulaofia	M	65	
	Naome	F	44	
c.	Sakobaea	M	45	
	Ranasau	F	55	
	Boramo	M	17	
d.	Ramo	M	29	
	Tadatii	F	24	
	Salome	F	3	
	Isiga	M	2	
e.	Fau	M	45	
	Oodo	F	43	
	Kwaingoru	F	11	
	Naome	F	4	
f.	Misikwi	M	44	
	Burabo	F	40	
	Dalielo	M	11	
	Niumalefo	M	9	
	Barafa	F	7	
	Laugau	F	4	
	Batisoni	M	1	
	Gesuna	F	78	Husband is dead; mother of Misikwi.

Household	Name	Sex	Estimated age	Comments
g.	Sukuania	M	65	
	Tolilangi	F	65	
h.	Aliki	M	43	
	Koi	F	31	
i.	Labuga	M	38	
	Eta	F	34	First wife.
	Aratabu	F	35	Second wife; a widow.
	Ramo'alafa	M	16	
	Kwadi	M	15	
	Foukonai	M	12	
	Lalitoa	F	3	
j.	Tosilifu	M	42	
	Barafa	F	34	
	Beni	M	6	
	Lediomea	M	3	
	Furikona	M	1	
k.	Aniga	F	38	Husband is dead.
	Maata	F	10–11	Twin.
	Orofitoa	F	10–11	Twin.
	Beti	F	7	
	Dioni	M	3	
l.	Toasi	F	58	Husband is dead.
	Ngangasi	F	53	Husband is dead.
	Birina'ai	F	11	Orphan.

6. AO'ANA HAMLET

Household	Name	Sex	Estimated age	Comments
a.	*Wane'au	M	54	
	Ngalearii	F	53	
	Liuomea	M	17	
	O'oruomea	F	15	
	Kwanafia	M	9	
b.	Rikomalefo	F	52	Husband is dead.
	Maanatafi	F	33	Spinster.
c.	Mongarii	F	40	Spinster.
	Ranasau	F	34	Spinster.
d.	Naga	M	46	
	Siuana	F	45	
	Dioi	F	10	
	Dioni	M	8	

7. BORUMALAKWA HAMLET

Household	Name	Sex	Estimated age	Comments
a.	*Ramoegau	M	55	
	Rokonasau	F	45	
	Rimalefo	M	22	
	Deferii	M	19	
	Fauga	M	13	
	Lulumori	M	11	
b.	Naolana	M	51	Wife is dead.
	Amua	F	17	
	Makosu	M	25	Bachelor.
c.	Alaikona	M	32	Bachelor.
	Filikwai	M	29	Bachelor.
d.	Alasao	F	49	Spinster.
	Alifoa	F	17	
e.	Kwanga'inau	M	28	Bachelor.
	Orui	F	33	Spinster.
	Dingangala	F	15	
f.	Ulufi	M	33	
	Siuna	F	42	
	Dioseleni	F	12	
g.	Liuga	M	43	Wife is dead.
	Bongi	M	8	
	Kekeu	M	34	Bachelor.

8. FAAKWAO' ABU HAMLET

Household	Name	Sex	Estimated age	Comments
a.	*Ramoga	M	52	
	Alide	F	41	
	Rafe	M	15	
	Beli'ofa	M	12	
b.	Talokwaimae	M	39	Wife is dead.
	Aiwake	M	25	Bachelor.
c.	U'uga	F	44	Husband is dead.
	Odolee	M	21	
	Barafarii	F	16	
	Angianarii	F	12	
d.	Sango	F	48	Husband recently dead.
	Otae	M	25	
	Ngangale	F	19	
	Eda	F	13	
e.	Gere	M	48	Bachelor.
	Inakeri	M	19	Orphan.

Household	Name	Sex	Estimated age	Comments
f.	Toofolea	M	53	
	Talofila	F	52	
	Kafa	M	17	
	Foangasi	M	14	

9. FATAKALIE HAMLET

a.	*Beliga	M	75	
	Siosana	F	65	
	Sasae	F	35	Spinster daughter.
b.	Keso	M	29	
	Mamunia	F	22	
c.	Aro	M	33	Wife is dead.
	Totoi	M	9	
d.	Aba	M	70	Wife is dead.
	Felega	M	10	
	Ara	M	28	Bachelor.
e.	Konafia	M	48	
	Tafili	F	41	
	Ete	M	11	
	Mouna	M	9	
f.	Aluna	M	41	Wife is dead.
	Alamia	M	11	
g.	Tagini	M	37	Bachelor.
	Rodoalasa	F	11	
	Bolai	M	9	
h.	Maona	M	52	
	Aumata	F	50	
	Saloana	F	21	
	Tagini	M	13	
i.	Fale'orea	M	58	
	Orumalao	F	50	
	Rakona	F	10	
j.	Aro	M	32	
	Bebe	F	22	

10. FAUBOSO HAMLET

Household	Name	Sex	Estimated age	Comments
a.	*Gugumae	M	85	Wife is dead.
b.	Felega	M	44	
	Orufia	F	29	Second wife.
	Misinare	M	20	Plantation laborer in Guadalcanal.
	Mosena	F	14	
	Christina	F	10	
	Tafinari	F	8	
	Angiadarii	F	5	
	Afuga	M	2	
	Misiringi	F	15	Orphan.
c.	Loboi	M	38	
	Gale	F	36	
	Rinauta	F	14	
	Sango	F	11	
	Amai	F	9	
	Saunari	F	7	
	Ede'au	M	4	

11. FAUKWAKWAOA HAMLET

Household	Name	Sex	Estimated age	Comments
a.	*Buaga	M	53	
	Toliomea	F	43	
	Buaga Tu'u	M	11	Adopted child.
b.	Rimanu	M	58	
	Lauma	F	51	
	Steven	M	18	
c.	Kwanga	M	23	
	Sarati	F	25	
d.	Tome	M	47	
	Alamoa	F	44	In SDA Hospital for childbirth.
	Uguni	M	21	
	Luke	M	18	
	Keti	F	9	
	Joanne	F	7	At school in Kwailabesi.
	Semu	M	2	
	Harold	M	. .	Born August 2, 1968. (Not included in census conducted June, 1968.)
e.	Taua	F	27	Spinster.
	Nanae	F	13	
f.	Aulelea	M	34	
	Mumusu	F	31	
	Tagana	F	6	
	Desi	F	4	
	Kofisau	F	18	

Household	Name	Sex	Estimated age	Comments
g.	Duku	F	57	Husband is dead.
	Sangolifoia	F	23	Spinster.
h.	Au	M	38	Plantation laborer in Guadalcanal.
	Afunakwa	F	33	
	Osikona	M	11	
	Dinge	F	3	
i.	Tagini	M	45	Wife is dead.
	Kwaiabe	M	9	

12. FERA'INOMAE HAMLET

a.	*Otairii	M	44	Wife is dead.
	Timifiru	M	16	
	Oitabu	F	13	
b.	Uguni	M	44	In hospital at Uru.
	Ana	F	38	
	Samo	M	14	
	Dionasi	M	12	
	Felega	M	8	
	Orodiena	M	7	
	Tomalina	M	3	

13. GWAIKABIRAI HAMLET

a.	Ologa	M	45	
	Siuona	F	40	
	Beringi	F	4	
b.	Abiga	M	38	
	Roko	F	36	
	Fou	M	14	
	Fanakera	M	8–9	
c.	*Udu'ota	M	75	
	Dongata	M	35	Wife is dead.
	Tolea	M	28	
	Kwadi	M	25	
d.	Kwai'eroi	M	39	Wife is dead.
	Ologa Tu'u	M	7	

14. GWAIKIRI HAMLET

a.	*Rimanu	M	60	
	Burifoa	F	60	
	Fauga	M	26	
b.	Ruru'ota	M	75	
	Angina	F	65	

Household	Name	Sex	Estimated age	Comments
c.	Sulumae	M	29	Wife is dead.
	Kauta	M	7	
	Eda	F	3–4	
d.	Kabola	M	50	
	Kwaina'uru	F	36	
	Nauga	M	13	
	O'odo	F	11	
	Gwaro	M	8	
	Bita	M	6	
	Ngalana	F	6 mos.	
e.	Meliga	M	35	Wife is dead.
	Gwali	M	9	
	Toata	M	5	Twin.
	Ailiki	M	5	Twin.
f.	Sedi	M	70	
	Maugwo	F	57	
g.	Faragi	M	47	
	Ofeala	F	40	
	Dongomalefo	M	11	
	Lafea	M	6	
	Oote	F	3–4	
h.	Oiga	M	51	
	Kofai	F	48	

15. GWASUMOKO HAMLET

a.	*Otairobo	M	41	
	Faneala	F	33	
	Rebi	F	12	
	Rokoigau	F	2	
b.	Wane'au	M	22	Bachelor.
	Nokesi	M	19	

16. KAFO'OTE'OTE HAMLET

a.	Nunukwai	M	34	
	Oruna	F	31	
b.	*Meke	M	39	Plantation laborer in New Georgia.
	Saoni	F	26	
	Ago	M	1	
c.	Birinasau	F	35	Spinster.
	Ema	F	29	Spinster.

17. KILIE HAMLET

Household	Name	Sex	Estimated age	Comments
a.	*Sufui	M	44	
	Araitafi	F	38	
	Loboi	M	19	
	Orialasi	F	17	
	Kisumalefo	M	11	
	Angina	F	7	
	Sikwa'ae	M	4	
	Alanala	F	2	

18. LIUFANIA HAMLET

a.	*Ofataloa	M	50	
	Tosimaoma	F	42	
	Saafi	F	10	

19. MAELANAFE HAMLET

a.	Ugulaua	M	45	
	Kwaimamu	F	39	
	Sanga	M	12	
	Lifuala	M	9	
	Kafeta	F	6	
	Lolenala	F	3	
	Eda	F	6 mos.	
b.	Makuiniu	M	37	
	Wiki	F	28	
	Rafisi	F	1	
c.	*Erefiu	M	65	Wife is dead.
	Dasau	F	28	Spinster daughter.

20. MATAKWADOLO HAMLET

a.	*Kurae	M	52	
	Arofai	F	48	
	Barafarii	F	16	
b.	Lauga	M	24	
	Maafuliu	F	24	
	Sukuania	M	20 mos.	

21. NGALI'ABU HAMLET

a.	*Mamuela	M	35	
	Rauna'ala	F	29	
	Tafiala	F	7	
	Tale'au	M	5	
	Afuna	F	2	

Household	Name	Sex	Estimated age	Comments
b.	Naai	F	26	Spinster.
	Firinau	M	15	
	Tanai	F	13	
	Laugao	F	11	

22. NGALIANA'AGO HAMLET

a.	*Maefasia	M	32	
	Mei	F	30	
	Bulaikwai	M	9	
	Saugweri	F	6	
	Kabu	F	2	
b.	Manusau	M	85	Wife is dead.
	Subuomea	M	49	Bachelor.
	Aba	M	18	
	Takasia	M	16	

23. NGALIANARUFO HAMLET

a.	Otainau	M	35	
	Margaret	F	35	
	Angisibeu	F	12	
	Konai	M	10	
	Ofala	F	4	
	Bubuna	F	3 mos.	
b.	Waniga	M	43	
	Siufi	F	36	
	Lalona	F	12	
	Kwaimani	M	8	
	Tolaga	M	5	
	Fininga	F	3	
	Ngangaifoa	M	4 mos.	
c.	Lebeta	M	37	
	Takona	F	28	
	Soeti	M	2	
d.	*Tolaga	M	48	
	Afuna	F	47	
	Fingina	F	27	Housekeeper at SDA Mission, Kwailabesi.
	Tafinari	F	14	
	Lonole	F	8	
	Riri	M	18 mos.	
e.	Feralao	M	38	
	Taua	F	28	
	Ruti	F	2	

Household	Name	Sex	Estimated age	Comments
f.	Makuna	F	36	Husband is dead.
	Keta	M	12	
	Dongata	M	10	
	Malefo	M	3	
g.	Orufaia	F	48	Husband is dead.
	O'oruga	F	24	Spinster.
	Takadau	F	4	Foster child.

24. NGALIFULIBEU HAMLET

a.	Wede	M	42	
	Misifali	F	34	
	Filibi	M	8	
	Alisi	F	13 mos.	Foster child.
	Sedai	M	27	Orphan and bachelor.
b.	*Gwaraga	M	44	Wife is dead.
	Initoa	M	17	
	Kwaga	M	14	
	Marega	F	11	
	Saloe	F	9	
	Fito	M	7	
	Tafasi	F	26	Spinster.
c.	Ramaloo	M	28	First wife is dead.
	Maeuria	F	28	Second wife; also a widow.
	Liukali	M	3	
d.	Manuirii	M	52	
	Maomara	F	45	
	Uiki	M	18	
	Renegao	F	11	
	Ofakwasi	M	9	
e.	Kala'uma	M	47	Wife is dead.
	Tome	M	9	

25. NGALIKWAO HAMLET

a.	Eliza Kao	M	80	
	Fakalifu	F	80	
b.	*Osikona	M	45	
	Ngangale	F	41	
	Rosina	F	12	
	Arati	F	8	
	Meu	M	5	
	Minarii	F	11 mos.	

Household	Name	Sex	Estimated age	Comments
c.	Laugwaro	M	44	
	Olina	F	41	
	Afuga	M	13	
	Aliki	M	7	
d.	Kafa	M	47	
	Tafina	F	36	
	Oola	F	10	
	Maomara	F	7	
	Saulifoia	F	6	
	Saranaioia	M	6 mos.	
e.	Osifera	M	22	Orphan.
	Alani	M	11	Orphan.
f.	Aliki	M	42	Widower; remarried in June, 1968.
	Kafa	M	18	Son of Aliki.

(Aliki and Kafa not counted in census, because they moved temporarily to a Fataleka village in June, 1968.)

26. RUE HAMLET

Household	Name	Sex	Estimated age	Comments
a.	Tome	M	35	Wife is dead.
	Kafu	M	11	
b.	Kafeta	F	45	Husband is dead.
	Laukaufa	F	13	
	Auga	M	10	
	Saulifoia	F	13	
c.	*Au'agara	M	50	
	Fauga	M	28	
	Lusimoni	M	19	

Appendix C: Glossary of Baegu Words and Idiomatic Phrases

Since technically the glottal stop is a consonant, alphabetically arranged glossaries should have a category for words beginning with a glottal stop. But the native speaker of English tends to overlook (not to hear) glottal stops, so I have followed nonscholarly practice and have alphabetized this glossary according to standard English orthography to make references easier for nonlinguists. Glosses of Baegu terms are meant to be used as guides to meaning in a practical sense, not as formal or rigorous definitions.

aabu	sacred, forbidden
abagwaro	upper arm band made of shell beads
abala	unit of length equal to a man's arm span (approximately one fathom)
'ae	one (of a thing);leg; stem; trunk (of a tree)
'ae bara	a patrilineal descent group; clan, lineage, or lineage segment
'ae ni mae	epic chant about the exploits of ancestral heroes
'ae oko	midwife or maternity nurse (who does not assist in the actual birth)
'afe	wife
agae	formal sacred dance
agero	areca palm (and its nut), used as a mild narcotic
'ai	stick; tree
'ai ni gao	a hard, dark wood resembling ebony
akalo	ancestral spirit, god, demon
akalo kwasi	wild ghosts not associated with a particular descent group or shrine
aku	me (indirect object), mine

akwakwa	mudskipper fish
'ala'ala	croton shrub
alafolo	combination war club and walking stick
alakwa	bachelor; adolescent male
alite	Indian almond, Pacific chestnut (*Terminalia* sp.)
alo	taro (*Colocasia* sp.)
anakwe	tern or gull
ano	personal animistic soul, spiritual double
ara	southeasterly tradewind
arai	husband; master; chief or ruler; important man
arua	sorcery or black magic based on contagion
asi	sea, saltwater
babala	lean-to, crude shelter
babala kai	yam storehouse
babatana	hysterical symptoms said to result from love magic
bae	to speak, to talk; altar for sacrifices
baekwa	dangerous organism; shark at sea, or Woodford's viper on land
baita	big; important
bali	side; half; segment of a unit
bali ni keni	bridal party at a wedding
bali ni wane	groom's party at a wedding
bara	group; family
baraa	affine of one's own generation
bebi	butterfly, moth
beu	men's house
bau aabu	shrine; burial place; sacred grove
beu akalo	house dedicated to ancestral spirits
beu tio	men's sleeping quarters
bibie	seat of sacred natural power (said to cause men to speak the truth, and used as a site for ordeals and oaths)
bii	leaf and stone oven
bii sa akalo	god's oven, dedicated to the ancestral spirits and used as part of a shrine for sacrifices
bina	hornbill bird
biru	necklace of porpoise teeth; by metaphor, a loose wooden palisade
bisi	menstrual isolation hut; women's latrine
bisi ni lafi	secluded place for giving birth
bobola	similar, the same as, sharing certain attributes
bobora	black, dark brown
bole	Pacific pigeon

boso	pig
bou	banana
bulu	blue, bluish-black
bubulu	star; firefly
dala	forehead ornament made of giant clam shell with a tortoise shell filigree centerpiece
darai	youth, unmarried young man
dee	edible hibiscus (*Hibiscus manihot*)
dengi	freshwater prawn
diena	good
dii	cross-cousin
diki	yellow-breasted sunbird
doo	thing
e doo	something; "so-and-so"
edu	a wild or bush taro (*Alocasia* sp.)
'ere	fire
esu	belt or girdle of shell beads worn by married women
faa	to cause, to make (a bound morpheme)
faa'afe	final phase of the marriage ceremony
faafia	to mark; to put on; to engage to be married; to betrothe
faakeni	to make effeminate; to emasculate
faangali	year (nutting season)
faaramoelae	to strengthen, to make vigorous
fai	and; four
falea	to give
falenga	gift
fanoi	heavens; space
fata	to speak
fau	stone, rock
fau boso	a black rock, probably basalt
fau 'ere	iron pyrites
fau 'oko	a soft black stone assumed to have magical properties that is used as a cosmetic for blackening teeth
fera	hamlet, village; place on land; tame or domesticated
fikua	working group, a section of men engaged in a specific purpose
fikua ome	war party
filu	tropical flower used as a badge of office for the highly prestigious *wane taloa*
finisi	bounty for a revenge killing
firi	tobacco
foa	prayers, to pray

fu	for, to, toward
fuaku	to me, for me
fuku	the Barringtonia tree (used for fish poison)
fungo	affine of senior or junior generation
furingale	the giant rat *Mus rex*
fusi	cat (obviously an English loan word)
futa	to be born, birth
futalanae	consanguineal kinship
futo	cuscus opossum
gaa	mother; maternal aunt
galu	necklace or chestpiece of shell beads
geo	megapode bird, bush turkey
gosile	malevolent forest ghost said to be the soul of an unborn child
gu	some (of a thing)
gule	relatedness, relationships
gwau	head
gwau ni foa	head or chief priest
gwou	empty
i	in; of
ie	fish (Baegu prefer the word *sakwari*)
ie tikwa	dugong or manatee
inikori	a soft, pulpy fruit from a deciduous tree (*Spondias dulcis*)
initoo	central or senior position; important status
kabarai	Malay apple (*Eugenia malaccensis*)
kafo	water; stream, river
kai	yam
kai rogi	sweet potato
kakama	swamp taro (*Cyrtosperma* sp.)
karai	chicken or jungle fowl
karu	crab
kate	pudding of taro and canarium almonds
kaufe	pandanus mat or umbrella
kaule	frigate bird
keni	female; woman, girl
kerua	they, them, theirs (dual)
ki	plural indicator (a bound morpheme)
kiki	wood rat in Baegu dialect; giant clam in Lau
kiriau	porpoise, dolphin
koa	mangrove
koburu	northwesterly monsoon; or any wind not a tradewind
kokoo	grandparent, grandchild, mother's brother, sister's son

korokoro	migratory New Zealand cuckoo
kula	side or section of a house
kula i langi	uphill (masculine) side of a house
kula ni keni	women's part of a house
kula ni wane	men's part of a house
kwae	tree fern, cycad
kwaimani	friend; trading partner (a formal exchange relationship)
kwasa	crocodile
kwasi	wild, untrained, uncontrolled
kwasilangae	elopement, escape into the forest
kwata	digging stick, dibble
labata	clearing in the forest for a hamlet
labu	spear; fence; fort
lafi	to give birth
lafua	to take off, to pull off or out
lafua masa	irrevocable act of divorce wherein a woman removes her pubic apron
lakeno	sacred pudding of coconut and taro, served at religious festivals
lakwa	a giant, net-weaving forest spider
lalo	women's sleeping quarters
langi	upper or superior ("no" in Lau dialect)
lau	more (of a quantity); again
lea	to go
lifona	tooth
loi	a fat, brown, ground-living carpet snake
lolofaa	district
losi	an edible cane or grass (*Saccharum edulis*)
lului wela	gift made to a man's parents-in-law at onset of a bride's first pregnancy
luma	dwelling house, family house, woman's house
luma nare	kitchen, cooking house
luma tio	sleeping house for a family group
lumaa	collectively, all of a wife's consanguineal kin
maa	eye, face, visage; front, aspect; father, paternal uncle
maa na	in front of
mae	dead, death, desiccated
madami	moon, lunar month
mai	here, toward
malinge	coconut
mamanaa	blessings, power, sucess, truth, efficacy, legitimacy
mango	vital principle; the breath

maoma	mortuary ceremony and sacrifice
masa	married woman's pubic apron
mole	suitable or ready for use
mou	to fear; afraid
na	action completed (indicates past tense); third person possessive marker
nagi	chert
nao	no; sexually experienced; proud or overconfident
nare	to cook
nau	I, me, my, mine
ngali	canarium almond (*Canarium* sp.)
ni	where, particle signifying location; preface to a feminine name
nia	he, him, his; she, her, hers; it, its
niu	coconut
no aabu	eagle
o	you; an exclamation
obi	cane (rattan)
'oe	you
oewania	common, stupid, vulgar, mentally deficient, insane
ofu	sugarcane
oko	bound, tied, lashed; string, belt
oko obi	red cane belt, the badge of an unmarried adolescent girl
ole	garden
ome	war, battle
oo	mythical pre-men; woodland ghosts
'o'o	slit-gong drum
ramo	warrior
rarangana	fat, grease
rau'ai	breadfruit
reba	carved wooden dance paddle
refoa	assistant to a priest
rogi	morning glory
ruana	second, the other
ruu	second, other
sa	preface to masculine names
saitamana	to understand; to know right from wrong
sakale	log fence or barricade
sakale boso	pigpen
sakwalo	flying fox, a giant fruit-eating bat
sakwari	fish

sango	the sacred cordyline plant
sao	sago or ivory-nut palm; thatch made from its leaves
sarea	to feed
saula	spouse of spouse's consanguineal kin
saungia	to dominate; to rule; to kill
sua	ritually impure
suru	neonatal isolation hut on the outskirts of a hamlet
ta'a	bad
tafo	arboreal snake, the Pacific tree boa
tafu	trash, garbage, rubbish; trash dump
tafuli'ae	strings of shell beads used as money; worth about $10.00 Australian
tale	trail, road; latrine
tale keni	women's latrine
tale wane	men's latrine
talisibara	oral genealogy, lineal pedigree
taloa	prestige, renown
tarawedi	bat
tare	a variety of *Pandanus* plant with thorns
tatale	hibiscus
tikwa	long
tio	to sleep
toa	people
toa ki	common people (plural form)
tolo	hill, mountain; connotes inferiority in the Lau dialect
too	to live, to reside, to stay
toto	wild orange raspberry-like plant
totole	rock slide
tu'u	little
ura	langouste, the Pacific crayfish, spiny lobster
usia	marketplace; to sell or trade
waaro	old, senile
wane	male; man; figuratively, a person or people
wane anifoa	assistant to a priest
wane asi	coastal or saltwater people
wane baita	Big Man, important man
wane darai	bachelor, adolescent male
wane initoo	man of high status, hereditary landowner (holds residual title)
wane ramo	war leader, exceedingly brave warrior
wane saungia	traditional district leader (no longer exist, if in fact they ever did)

wane taloa	man of great prestige (a ceremonial office)
wane tolo	hill or bush people living in the interior
wela	child
wela aabu	neonate
wela sarea	foster or adopted child
wela saungia	foster or adopted child
wela tu'u	infant

Bibliography

Allan, Colin H.
   1957. *Customary Land Tenure in the British Solomon Islands Protectorate: Report of the Special Lands Commission.* Western Pacific High Commission, Honiara, Guadalcanal, British Solomon Islands Protectorate.

Barnes, J. A.
   1962. "African Models in the New Guinea Highlands." *Man* 62:5-9. London.

Barrau, Jacques
   1959. "The 'Bush Fallowing' System of Cultivation in the Continental Islands of Melanesia." *Proceedings of the Ninth Pacific Science Congress* 7:53-55. Honolulu, Hawaii.
   1965. "L'Humide et le sec." *Journal of the Polynesian Society* 74:329-46. Wellington, New Zealand.

Barton, Roy F.
   1949. *The Kalingas.* University of Chicago Press. Chicago.

Beaglehole, J. C.
   1966. *The Exploration of the Pacific.* Stanford University Press. Stanford, California.

Birdwhistell, Ray
   1964. Remarks at Primate Communications Symposium, annual meeting of the American Association for the Advancement of Science (Section H), Montreal, Quebec, Canada.

Bohannan, Paul
   1966. *Social Anthropology.* Holt, Rinehart, and Winston. New York.

British Solomon Islands Protectorate, Department of Lands and Surveys.
   1962. Aerial photographs of northern Malaita, Series VI 543A/RAF/350 of July 26 and Series V 543A/RAF/354 of July 27.

Bruner, Edward M.
   1968. "Some Observations on Cultural Change and Psychological Stress: Indonesia." Paper read at Eighth International Congress of Anthropological and Ethnological Sciences, Tokyo and Kyoto, Japan.

Buchler, Ira R., and Selby, Henry A.
1968. *Kinship and Social Organization.* Macmillan. New York.

Bulmer, Ralph
1968. "The Strategies of Hunting in New Guinea." *Oceania* 38: 302-18. Sydney, Australia.

Bulmer, Susan, and Bulmer, Ralph
1964. "The Prehistory of the Australian New Guinea Highlands." *American Anthropologist* 66 (no. 4, pt. 2):39-76. Menasha, Wisccnsin.

Capell, A.
1954. *A Linguistic Survey of the South-Western Pacific.* South Pacific Commission, Noumea, New Caledonia.

Carneiro, Robert L.
1960. "Slash-and-Burn Agriculture: A Closer Look at Its Implications for Settlement Patterns." *Selected Papers of the Fifth International Congress of Anthropological and Ethnological Sciences* (ed. A. F. C. Wallace), pp. 229-34. University of Pennsylvania Press. Philadelphia.

Childe, V. Gordcn
1936. *Man Makes Himself.* Reissued in 1951 by Mentor, New American Library. New York.

Chomsky, Noam
1957. *Syntactic Structures.* Mouton and Company. s'Gravenhague, Netherlands.
1959. "Review of *Verbal Behavior* by B. F. Skinner." *Language* 35:26-58. New York.

Cochrane, D. G.
1969. "Choice of Residence in the Solomons and a Focal Land Model." *Journal of the Polynesian Society* 78:330-43. Wellington, New Zealand.

Colonial Office
1946. *Among Those Present.* His Majesty's Government Stationery Office. London.

Conklin, Harold C.
1955. "Hanunoo Color Categories." *Southwestern Journal of Anthropology* 11:339-44. Albuquerque, New Mexico.

Coon, Carleton S.
1962. *The Origin of Races.* Alfred A. Knopf. New York.

Crocombe, R. G.
1964. *Land Tenure in the Cook Islands.* Oxford University Press and the Australian National University. Melbourne, Australia.

Crocombe, R. G., and Hogbin, G. R.
1963. *Land, Work, and Productivity at Inonda.* New Guinea Research Unit and the Australian National University. Canberra, Australia.

Damon, Albert
1969. Personal correspondence concerning statistical treatment of Malaitan census data.

Davenport, William
1959. "Nonunilinear Descent and Descent Groups." *American Anthropologist* 61:557-72. Menasha, Wisconsin.

Doxiadis, C. A.
   1968. "Man's Movement and His City." *Science* 162:326-33. Washington, D.C.

Durkheim, Emile
   1897. *Suicide*. Reissued in 1951 by The Free Press. New York.

Dyen, Isidore
   1965. *A Lexicostatistical Classification of the Austronesian Languages*. IJAL Memoir 19. Bloomington, Indiana.

Evans-Pritchard, E. E.
   1940. *The Nuer*. Clarendon Press. Oxford.

Eyde, David
   1968. Remarks at annual meeting of the American Anthropological Association, Seattle, Washington.

Firth, Raymond
   1936. *We, the Tikopia*. Reissued in 1963 by the Beacon Press. Boston.
   1940. "The Analysis of Mana: An Empirical Approach." *Journal of the Polynesian Society* 49:483-509. Wellington, New Zealand.
   1957. "A Note on Descent Groups in Polynesia." *Man* 57:4-8. London.

Fischer, John L.
   1958. "The Classification of Residence in Censuses." *American Anthropologist* 60:508-17. Menasha, Wisconsin.

Forde, C. Daryll
   1934. *Habitat, Economy and Society*. Methuen and Company. London.

Fortes, Meyer
   1958. "Introduction." *The Developmental Cycle in Domestic Groups* (ed. Jack Goody), pp. 1-13. Cambridge Papers in Social Anthropology #1. Cambridge.
   1959. "Descent, Filiation and Affinity: A Rejoinder to Dr. Leach." *Man* 59:193-97 and 206-12. London.

Fox, C. E.
   1967. *The Story of the Solomons*. Diocese of Melanesia Press. Taroaniara, Nggela, British Solomon Islands Protectorate.

Fox, Robin
   1967. *Kinship and Marriage*. Penguin Books. Baltimore, Maryland.

Frake, Charles R.
   1956. "Malayo-Polynesian Land Tenure." *American Anthropologist* 58:170-73. Menasha, Wisconsin.
   1962. "Cultural Ecology and Ethnography." *American Anthropologist* 64:53-59. Menasha, Wisconsin.

Freeman, J. D.
   1955. *Iban Agriculture*. Her Majesty's Government Stationery Office. London.

Freeman, Otis W., ed.
   1951. *Geography of the Pacific*. John Wiley and Sons. New York.

Frost, Robert
   1949. "Mending Wall." *The Complete Poems of Robert Frost*. Henry Holt and Company. New York.

Garn, Stanley M.
1961. *Human Races.* C. C. Thomas. Springfield, Illinois.

Geoghegan, William
1970. "Cultural Code Rules in the Analysis of Lexical Systems." *Explorations in Mathematical Anthropology* (ed. Paul Kay). MIT Press. Cambridge, Massachusetts.

Goodenough, Ward H.
1951. *Property, Kin, and Community on Truk.* Yale University Press. New Haven, Connecticut.
1955. "A Problem in Malayo-Polynesian Social Organization." *American Anthropologist* 57:71-83. Menasha, Wisconsin.
1956a. "Reply (to Frake)." *American Anthropologist* 58:173-76. Menasha, Wisconsin.
1956b. "Residence Rules." *Southwestern Journal of Anthropology* 12:22-37. Albuquerque, New Mexico.
1967. "Componential Analysis." *Science* 156:1203-9. Washington, D.C.

Grace, George W.
1959. *The Position of the Polynesian Languages within the Austronesian (Malayo-Polynesian) Language Family.* IJAL Memoir 16. Bloomington, Indiana.

Hall, Edward T.
1966. *The Hidden Dimension.* Doubleday and Company. Garden City, New York.

Harris, Marvin
1964. *The Nature of Cultural Things.* Random House. New York.

Heider, Karl G.
1967. "Speculative Functionalism: Archaic Elements in New Guinea Dani Culture." *Anthropos* 62:833-40. Freiburg, Switzerland.

Hogbin, H. Ian
1939. *Experiments in Civilization.* George Routledge and Sons. London.
1944. "Native Councils and Courts." *Oceania* 14:257-83. Sydney, Australia.

Hymes, Dell H.
1961. "Functions of Speech: An Evolutionary Approach." *Anthropology and Education* (ed. Frederick G. Gruber), pp. 55-83. University of Pennsylvania Press. Philadelphia.

Ivens, Walter G.
1930. *The Island Builders of the Pacific.* Seeley, Service and Company. London.

Johnson, Osa Helen (Leighty)
1944. *Bride in the Solomons.* Houghton-Mifflin. Boston.

Keesing, Roger M.
1965. "Kwaio Marriage and Society." Ph.D. dissertation, Department of Social Relations, Harvard University. Cambridge, Massachusetts.
1967. "Christians and Pagans in Kwaio, Malaita." *Journal of the Polynesian Society* 76:82-100. Wellington, New Zealand.
1968. "Chiefs in a Chiefless Society." *Oceania* 38:276-80. Sydney, Australia.
1970a. "Kwaio Fosterage." *American Anthropologist* 72:991-1019. Washington, D.C.

1970b. "Toward a Model of Role Analysis." *A Handbook of Method in Cultural Anthropology* (ed. Raoul Naroll and Ronald Cohen). The Natural History Press. Garden City, New York.

Keesing, Roger M., and Fifi'i, Jonathan
1969. "Kwaio Word Tabooing in Its Cultural Context." *Journal of the Polynesian Society* 78:154-77. Wellington, New Zealand.

Keesing, Roger M., and Keesing, Felix M.
1971. *New Perspectives in Cultural Anthropology.* Holt, Rinehart, and Winston. New York.

Langness, L. L.
1964. "Some Problems in the Conceptualization of Highlands Social Structures." *American Anthropologist* 66 (no. 4, pt. 2):162-82. Menasha, Wisconsin.

Leach, E. R.
1961. *Rethinking Anthropology.* Athlone Press. London.

de Lepfervanche, Marie.
1968. "Descent, Residence and Leadership in the New Guinea Highlands." *Oceania* 38:161-89. Sydney, Australia.

Lessa, William A.
1964. "The Social Effects of Typhoon Ophelia (1960) on Ulithi." *Micronesica* 1:1-47. Agaña, Guam.

Levi-Strauss, Claude
1962a. *La Pensée Sauvage.* Librairie Plon. Paris.
1962b. *Le Totémisme Aujourd'hui.* Presses Universitaires de France. Paris.

London, Jack
1923. *The Cruise of the Snark.* Macmillan. New York.

Lynch, Kevin
1960. *The Image of the City.* MIT Press. Cambridge, Massachusetts.

Maranda, Pierre, and Maranda, Elli Köngäs
1970. "Le Crâne et l'utérus: deux théorèmes Nord-Malaitains." *Échanges et Communications* (eds. Jean Pouillon et Pierre Maranda), pp. 829-61. Mouton. s'Gravenhague, Netherlands.
n.d. Personal conversations during 1966-68.

Mason, Leonard
1968. "The Ethnology of Micronesia." *Peoples and Cultures of the Pacific* (ed. Andrew P. Vayda), pp. 275-98. Natural History Press, Doubleday and Company. Garden City, New York.

Massal, Emile, and Barrau, Jacques
1955a. "Pacific Subsistence Crops: Taros." *South Pacific Commission Quarterly Bulletin* 5 (no. 2):17-21. Sydney, Australia.
1955b. "Pacific Subsistence Crops: Sweet Potato." *South Pacific Commission Quarterly Bulletin* 5 (no. 3):10-13. Sydney, Australia.

Mauss, Marcel
1954. *The Gift.* Trans. I. Cunnison. The Free Press. Glencoe, Illinois.

Mayr, Ernst
1931. "The Birds of Malaita (British Solomon Islands)." *American Museum Novitates* 504:1-26. New York.

Meggitt, M. J.
1964. "Male-Female Relationships in the Highlands of Australian New Guinea." *American Anthropologist* 66 (no. 4, pt. 2):204-24. Menasha, Wisconsin.

Murdock, George Peter
1949. *Social Structure*. The Free Press. Glencoe, Illinois.
1964. "Genetic Classification of the Austronesian Languages: A Key to Oceanic Culture History." *Ethnology* 3:117-26. Pittsburgh, Pennsylvania.

Ogan, Eugene.
1966. "Nasioi Marriage: An Essay in Model-Building." *Southwestern Journal of Anthropology* 22:172-93. Albuquerque, New Mexico.

Oliver, Douglas L.
1955. *A Solomon Island Society*. Reissued in 1967 by Beacon Press. Boston.
1958. "An Ethnographer's Method for Formulating Descriptions of Social Structure." *American Anthropologist* 60:801-26. Menasha, Wisconsin.

Palmer, Bruce
1968. "Recent Results from the Sigatoka Archaeological Program." *Prehistoric Culture in Oceania* (eds. I. Yawata and I. H. Sinoto), pp. 19-27. Bishop Museum Press. Honolulu, Hawaii.

Peterson, Jean
1972. Personal conversations in Urbana, Illinois, and Honolulu, Hawaii.

Pike, Kenneth L.
1954. *Language in Relation to a Unified Theory of the Structure of Human Behavior*. Summer Institute of Linguistics, Glendale, California.

Pouwer, Jan
1964. "A Social System in the Star Mountains." *American Anthropologist* 66 (no. 4, pt. 2):133-61. Menasha, Wisconsin.

Rappaport, Roy A.
1967. *Pigs for the Ancestors*. Yale University Press. New Haven, Connecticut.

Russell, T.
1950. "The Fataleka of Malaita." *Oceania* 21:1-13. Sydney, Australia.

Sahlins, Marshall D.
1958. *Social Stratification in Polynesia*. University of Washington Press. Seattle.
1963. "Poor Man, Rich Man, Big Man, Chief: Political Types in Melanesia and Polynesia." *Comparative Studies in Society and History* 5:285-303. Ann Arbor, Michigan.

Sapir, Edward
1921. *Language*. Harcourt, Brace and World. New York.

Scheffler, Harold W.
1965. *Choiseul Island Social Structure*. University of California Press. Berkeley, California.

Service, Elman R.
1962. *Primitive Social Organization*. Random House. New York.

Shimkin, Demitri B.
1964. *Introduction to Human Ecology*. For the University Committee on Human Ecology, University of Illinois, Urbana, Illinois.

Steward, Julian
  1955. *Theory of Culture Change.* University of Illinois Press. Urbana, Illinois.
Sturtevant, William
  1964. "Studies in Ethnoscience." *American Anthropologist* 66 (no. 4, pt. 2):99-131. Menasha, Wisconsin.
Turpin, Richard
  n.d. Personal conversations in Auki, Malaita, 1966-68.
Vayda, Andrew P.
  1956. "Maori Conquests in Relation to the New Zealand Environment." *Journal of the Polynesian Society* 65:204-11. Wellington, New Zealand.
Wallace, Anthony F. C.
  1961. *Culture and Personality.* Random House. New York.
Watson, James B.
  1965. "From Hunting to Horticulture in the New Guinea Highlands." *Ethnology* 4:295-309. Pittsburgh, Pennsylvania.
White, Leslie
  1949. *The Science of Culture.* Grove Press. New York.
Whorf, Benjamin L.
  1956. *Language, Thought and Reality: Selected Writings of Benjamin Lee Whorf* (ed. J. B. Carroll). John Wiley and Sons. New York.

Index

Acculturation, 63-71, 222
Adornment, 68, 272 (photograph)
Adultery, 67, 121
Adult status, 213
Affinal relationships: terminology, 137, 152; in marriage, 145-52; obligations, 210, 213, 220; conflicts in, 270
Aging: attitudes toward, 216
Agnatic systems: for land use, 80, 231-32; descent groups, 137-41; in marriage, 214-16; importance, 224-25, 226-28, 241, 290; obligations, 256
Agricultural labor, 59, 66-67, 155, 213
Agriculture. *See* Gardening
Ailai (village), 13, 23
Americans: influence, 58-59, 110
Ancestor worship. *See* Spiritualism
Anglicans: interactions with pagans, 100-104, 147, 240; Melanesian Mission, 60, 157
Animals, 40-42
Anomie: definition, 273
'Are'Are people, 23, 49, 61

Baegu: territory, 4, 13, 23, 38, 39 (map), 98 (aerial map), 112-18, 119 (map), 199-202, 228-32; nature, 9, 53, 55-56; social organization, 10-11, 52-53; photographs of males, 16, 19, 21, 38, 82, 94, 105, 106, 199, 200, 280, 288; language, 20-22; effects of tropical storms on, 31-32; stereotypes, 53, 129; importance of swine to, 85; census, 96-102; mental universe, 104, 108-11, 125-27, 233-34, 237-38, 239-42; attitudes toward outsiders, 109-10, 202; classification, 114-15; settlements, 123-24; definition, 202
Bamboo: uses, 76-77
Barter. *See* Market
Bell (British District Officer): death, 107, 190-91, 207
"Big Man" leader: influence in community, 11, 53, 188-93, 224, 227; characteristics, 55, 199-202; children for, 214, 218; hamlets, 261